The Art of Freelancing

A Step-by-Step Guide on How to Become a Successful Freelancer

Humera Shazia

Table Of Content

Contents

FAQs

Question: What is Freelancing?

Answer:

A freelancer is a person who is not a permanent employee of a company.

Freelancers are self-employed and they find work from different sources. Freelancing is a unique way of working.

Freelancers aren't permanent employees of a company; instead, they're self-employed and get work from various places.

Clients hire freelancers to do specific tasks or projects. Once the job is done, freelancers aren't obligated to keep working for the same client.

Question: What are the benefits of freelancing?

Answer:

Freelancing has many benefits, like being your own boss and choosing when and where you work. Freelancers can take on a variety of projects, gaining different skills and experiences.

They enjoy flexibility and can work from anywhere with an internet connection.

This independence allows for a better work-life balance and the potential to earn more by working with multiple clients.

While freelancers need to manage their own affairs, the freedom and opportunities for personal and professional growth make freelancing an appealing option for many.

Question: Does freelancing pay you money or is it scam?

Answer:

Freelancing is a legitimate way to earn money, and many people around the world make a living through freelance work.

It involves offering your skills and services to clients on a project basis. However, it's important to be cautious and do your research when exploring freelance opportunities, especially on online platforms. While there are numerous legitimate freelancing opportunities, there are also scams where individuals may attempt to take advantage of freelancers.

To avoid scams, use reputable freelancing platforms, carefully vet potential clients, and be cautious of requests for upfront payments or suspicious job offers. Overall, freelancing is a genuine and viable way to earn income, but it requires diligence and awareness to navigate the online landscape effectively.

Question: Why should I learn freelancing?

Answer:

Learning freelancing can open doors to a world of flexibility, independence, and diverse opportunities. By acquiring freelancing skills, you gain the ability to choose your projects, set your schedule, and work from anywhere.

This independence is not only empowering but also allows you to explore different aspects of your field, building a versatile skill set.

Freelancing provides a platform for personal and professional growth, offering the chance to earn a varied income, develop a unique portfolio, and adapt to the changing demands of the job market. Whether you're looking for a side hustle, a full-time career, or a way to enhance your skills, learning freelancing can be a valuable investment in your future.

Question: What do I need to start freelancing?

Answer:

To start freelancing, first, figure out what skills you're good at or want to learn. Create a portfolio that showcases your best work and consider focusing on a specific area to stand out.

Set up an online presence with a website or social media profiles. Join freelancing platforms like Upwork or Fiverr to find clients. Decide on your pricing and create a basic contract template. Invest in tools you need for your work, and set up a reliable payment method. Lastly, promote yourself through networking and social media to attract clients. With these steps, you'll be ready to kickstart your freelancing journey!

Question: I do not know any skills; can I still do freelancing?

Answer:

Freelancing is a serious business; you do need to make up your mind before you get started. You may get started with basic skills and keep on improving as you move on. You can still explore freelancing even if you're not yet sure about specific skills. Start by identifying your interests and passions. Then, consider learning skills that align with those interests. There are various online platforms offering courses in a wide range of subjects, often at different skill levels.

Also, freelancing platforms have opportunities for beginners in areas like writing, graphic design, virtual assistance, and more. As you gain experience, you can gradually expand your skill set.

Freelancing can be a journey of continuous learning and skill development, so don't hesitate to begin, learn along the way, and discover what you enjoy and excel at.

Question: How to choose a skill?

Answer:

To choose a skill for freelancing, start by thinking about what you enjoy doing or are curious about. Consider your existing strengths, even if they seem unrelated. Check out freelancing platforms like Upwork to see what skills are in demand and align with your interests. Choose something that you can learn and try out, and don't be afraid to experiment with different skills to find what you enjoy and excel at. Keep in mind that your choice isn't permanent, and as you gain experience, you can adjust and refine your focus based on your evolving interests and market trends.

Question: Can I start earning after reading this book?

Answer:

While "The Art of Freelancing: A Step-by-Step Guide on How to Become a Successful Freelancer" can provide valuable insights and guidance on freelancing, earning immediately after reading the book depends on various factors. Your success in freelancing will be influenced by the time and effort you invest in applying the book's principles, building your skills, creating a portfolio, and actively seeking opportunities. Additionally, the freelancing market can be competitive, and success often comes with experience and perseverance. The book can be a valuable resource, but it's essential to combine the knowledge gained with practical action and a proactive approach to see tangible results in your freelancing journey.

In this book, you won't find instructions on acquiring a specific skill; instead, it focuses on sharing practical tips and tricks for freelancing in a straightforward and effective manner. You'll gain insights into the essential do's and don'ts crucial for freelancers. The book also introduces various freelance marketplaces, providing detailed discussions on platforms such as Fiverr, PeoplePerHour, and Freelancer. This information equips you to effectively navigate these platforms and maximize your earning potential.

Question: How to set a goal?

Answer:

To set effective goals in freelancing, start by clearly defining your objectives, whether they involve financial gains, skill development, or portfolio building.

Break down long-term aspirations into smaller, measurable targets, and establish specific timeframes for achievement.

Align goals with your ongoing skill development, emphasizing quality over quantity in your work. Regularly evaluate and adjust goals, considering financial milestones, network expansion, and celebrating achievements along the way. This personalized and adaptable approach will guide your freelancing efforts and contribute to long-term success.

Question: Is English communication necessary for freelancing?

Answer:

Effective English communication is often crucial for freelancing success. Since freelancers often work with clients from diverse backgrounds, clear communication is essential for understanding project requirements, discussing expectations, and delivering work that meets client needs. Good communication also helps build trust and maintain positive client relationships.

Furthermore, many freelancing platforms and clients prefer freelancers with strong English language skills, as it is a widely used medium for business communication. While the level of proficiency required may vary depending on the type of freelancing work, having good English communication skills can enhance your opportunities and overall success in the freelancing.

Question: How to improve communication skills?

Answer:

To enhance your communication skills, practice active listening, expand your vocabulary through regular reading, seek constructive feedback, and participate in conversational groups and public speaking opportunities.

Take communication courses online, observe effective communicators, and practice writing regularly to refine your written expression.

Utilize technology for varied communication formats, be mindful of non-verbal cues, and consistently work on improving pronunciation and intonation through activities like reading aloud. By incorporating these strategies, you can steadily strengthen your overall communication abilities, fostering success in freelancing and other professional pursuits.

Question: How much time is needed for freelancing?

Answer:

The amount of time needed for freelancing can vary widely and is largely dependent on factors such as the type of work, the number of clients, and your personal preferences.

Some freelancers work part-time while balancing other commitments, dedicating a few hours each week to freelancing.

Others may choose to freelance full-time, investing 30 to 40 hours or more per week. The flexible nature of freelancing allows you to tailor your schedule to your needs. It's essential to consider the demands of your specific projects, client expectations, and your desired income level when determining how much time to dedicate to freelancing. Finding the right balance is key to both productivity and maintaining a healthy work-life equilibrium.

Question: How much do I need to invest to start freelancing?

Answer:

The initial investment required to start freelancing varies depending on your specific field and existing resources.

Basic necessities include a computer and relevant software tools, and additional investments may include training or courses to enhance skills, fees associated with freelancing platforms, and potential expenses for creating a professional online presence.

While some freelancers start with minimal costs, budgeting for essential tools and considering future investments as your freelancing business grows can contribute to long-term success.

Question: How much can I earn from Freelancing?

Answer:

Earnings from freelancing can vary widely based on factors such as your skills, experience, the demand for your services, and the rates you set. Some freelancers earn a part-time income, while others generate a full-time or even substantial income. High-demand skills such as programming, graphic design, writing, and digital marketing often command higher rates. Freelancers with specialized expertise and a strong portfolio may attract clients willing to pay premium prices. It's common for freelancers to start with modest earnings and gradually increase their rates as they gain experience and build a client base. The potential for earnings in freelancing is significant, but success typically involves consistent effort, ongoing skill development, and effective marketing of your services.

Question: Is it necessary to display a picture on profile?

Answer:

While displaying a real picture on your freelancing profile is not strictly necessary, it can be beneficial for building trust and creating a more personal connection with potential clients. A genuine profile picture adds a human touch, making you appear approachable and professional. Clients often appreciate being able to put a face to the name, and it can contribute to a sense of transparency. However, if you have privacy concerns or personal preferences that lead you to use an alternative image or logo, make sure it still presents a professional and trustworthy image. Ultimately, the decision to use a real picture depends on your comfort level and the image you want to convey in your freelancing career.

Question: Is a bank account necessary for freelancing?

Answer:

While not mandatory, having a bank account is highly recommended for freelancing.

A dedicated business account adds professionalism, simplifies financial management, and allows for the separation of personal and business finances. It facilitates payment processing, expense tracking, and record-keeping, streamlining administrative tasks. Clients often prefer direct payments to a bank account, contributing to efficient transactions. Overall, a business bank account enhances your credibility, organizational structure, and financial transparency in your freelancing endeavors

Question: Is a Debit/Credit card necessary?

Answer:

While having a debit or credit card is not strictly necessary for freelancing, it can significantly enhance your financial flexibility and convenience.

Many freelancing platforms and clients prefer electronic payments, and having a card allows you to easily receive and make transactions.

It also simplifies online purchases, subscription payments, and other financial transactions related to your freelancing work. A card can serve as a backup payment method and is often required for verification purposes on various platforms. While alternative payment methods may be available, having a debit or credit card can streamline your freelancing experience and provide a convenient way to manage your finances.

Question: How can we transfer funds from freelance marketplaces?

Answer:

Freelancers can transfer funds from freelance marketplaces through various methods, including direct bank transfers, PayPal, alternative payment processors like Skrill or Payoneer, physical checks by mail.

Each platform typically offers multiple options, allowing freelancers to choose the method that best suits their preferences and location. It's essential to review the available payment methods, considering factors such as fees, processing times, and security measures, to ensure a seamless and secure transfer of funds from the freelance marketplace to the freelancer's chosen financial account.

Question: Can I use my parents bank account for freelancing?

Answer:

Using your parents' bank account for freelancing transactions can be complicated and is generally not recommended.

Most freelancing platforms and clients prefer payments to be made to the account associated with the freelancer's name and details for transparency, security, and legal reasons.

Mixing personal and business finances in this way can create challenges in tracking income and expenses for tax purposes.

It's advisable to have your own bank account for freelancing to maintain a clear separation between personal and business transactions. If you are underage or face limitations in opening a bank account, consider exploring options like opening a joint account with a parent or guardian or researching specific banking regulations in your region. Always prioritize legal and transparent financial practices to avoid potential issues in the future.

Question: What is a bid?

Answer:

In the context of freelancing and online job platforms, a bid refers to a proposal or an offer submitted by a freelancer in response to a posted job or project.

When a client posts a job on a freelancing website, freelancers interested in the project can submit their bids to express their interest in taking on the work.

A bid typically includes details such as the freelancer's proposed cost for the project, the time frame for completion, relevant experience, and any additional information that may help the client make a decision. Clients can review the bids received and choose the freelancer they believe is the best fit for their project based on factors like expertise, cost, and delivery time. The bidding process is a common way for freelancers to compete for and secure projects on online platforms.

Question: What is a gig?

Answer:

In the context of freelancing and online platforms, a "gig" refers to a specific job or task that a freelancer undertakes for a client.

It's a short-term, often one-time, project or assignment for which the freelancer is hired to provide a particular service or skill.

Gigs can vary widely in scope and nature, encompassing tasks such as graphic design, writing, programming, digital marketing, and more.

Freelancers often refer to each individual job or project they take on as a "gig." The term is commonly associated with platforms that facilitate short-term and project-based work, such as Fiverr or Upwork, where freelancers offer their services to clients seeking specific tasks to be completed.

Question: What is a milestone?

Answer:

In freelancing, a "milestone" refers to a specific, significant stage or point in a project that is identified and agreed upon by both the freelancer and the client.

It represents a key deliverable or achievement within the overall project timeline. Milestones are often used to break down larger projects into manageable phases, making it easier to track progress and ensure that both parties are on the same page.

When a milestone is reached, it may trigger a payment, serve as a checkpoint for client feedback, or mark the completion of a crucial aspect of the project. Freelancing platforms often provide tools for setting up and managing milestones to facilitate transparent communication and payment processes between freelancers and clients.

Question: Is laptop compulsory for Freelancing?

Answer:

While having a laptop is a common and convenient tool for freelancing, it's not necessarily compulsory.

The choice of device depends on the nature of your freelancing work and personal preferences.

Many freelancers use laptops due to their portability and versatility, allowing them to work from various locations.

However, if your work primarily involves tasks that can be accomplished on a desktop computer or if you prefer working in a fixed space, a desktop computer may be a suitable alternative.

Some freelancers even use tablets or smartphones for specific tasks, such as communication or project management. Ultimately, the key is to have a device that meets the requirements of your freelancing work and provides the necessary tools for effective communication, project management, and task completion.

Question: Are IT skills compulsory for freelancing?

Answer:

While having IT skills can be advantageous and open a wide range of freelancing opportunities, they are not necessarily compulsory for all types of freelancing.

The skills you need depend on the specific services you offer. For example, if you're a web developer, graphic designer, programmer, or digital marketer, strong IT skills are essential. However, freelancing encompasses a diverse array of fields, including writing, consulting, virtual assistance, marketing, and more, where technical IT skills may be less critical.

It's crucial to identify the skills required in your chosen freelancing niche and focus on developing expertise in those areas. Additionally, being tech-savvy and having basic computer literacy is generally beneficial for most freelancers, as it facilitates efficient communication, use of freelancing platforms, and collaboration with clients.

💻 Freelancing

Freelancing is a flexible and self-employed work arrangement where individuals, known as freelancers or independent contractors, offer their skills and services to clients on a project-by-project basis.

Unlike traditional employment, freelancers are not permanent employees of a company; instead, they operate as independent businesses. Freelancers have the freedom to

- choose their projects,

- set their rates, and

- work from any location,

often using online platforms to connect with clients. The scope of freelancing is vast and covers a multitude of industries, including writing, design, programming, marketing, and consulting. This dynamic work model allows individuals to pursue diverse projects, build a portfolio of work, and enjoy the autonomy of managing their own businesses.

Freelancing is a work arrangement where individuals, commonly referred to as freelancers or independent contractors, offer their skills and services to clients on a project-by-project basis. Unlike traditional employment, freelancers are not permanent employees of a company. Instead, they operate as independent businesses, providing services ranging from writing, graphic design, and programming to marketing, consulting, and more. Freelancers have the flexibility to choose the projects they take on, set their own rates, and determine their work schedules. This autonomy is one of the defining features of freelancing, allowing individuals to tailor their work to their preferences and lifestyle.

The rise of online freelancing platforms, such as Upwork, Fiverr, and Freelancer, has significantly facilitated the connection between freelancers and clients. These platforms serve as marketplaces where clients post projects, and freelancers submit proposals or bids to win the work. Communication, project management, and payments are often streamlined through these platforms, providing a secure and transparent environment for both parties.

One of the key advantages of freelancing is the diversity of opportunities it offers. Freelancers can work with clients from around the world, collaborate on projects spanning various industries, and build a diverse portfolio showcasing their skills and expertise. Additionally, freelancing provides a pathway to entrepreneurship, allowing individuals to establish their own businesses, set professional goals, and chart their career paths.

However, freelancing also comes with its own set of challenges. Income can be variable, and freelancers are responsible for managing their own taxes, health insurance, and retirement plans. The ability to navigate these challenges successfully often requires a combination of business acumen, self-discipline, and adaptability.

In short, freelancing represents a dynamic and evolving work model that has become increasingly popular in the modern workforce. It offers individuals the freedom to pursue a variety of projects, work with diverse clients, and shape their careers on their terms. The advent of online platforms has made freelancing more accessible, connecting talent with opportunities globally. While it presents unique challenges, many individuals find freelancing to be a rewarding and fulfilling way to work.

Chapter 1: Introduction to Freelancing

★Benefits of Freelancing

Learning freelancing can be advantageous for several reasons:

1. Independence:

Freelancers have the freedom to choose their projects, clients, and work schedules. This level of independence allows individuals to tailor their work to their preferences and lifestyle.

2. Diverse Opportunities:

Freelancing spans various industries and professions, offering a wide range of opportunities. Whether you're a writer, graphic designer, programmer, or consultant, there's a freelancing niche for almost every skill set.

3. Flexibility:

Freelancers often enjoy the flexibility of working from anywhere with an internet connection. This flexibility is particularly appealing for those who value a remote or nomadic work lifestyle.

4. Skill Development:

Freelancing provides a platform to continuously develop and refine your skills. As you take on diverse projects, you have the opportunity to expand your expertise and stay current in your field.

5. Building a Portfolio:

Freelancers can build a portfolio showcasing their best work. This portfolio becomes a powerful tool for attracting clients and establishing credibility in the freelancing marketplace.

6. Income Potential:

While income can be variable, successful freelancers often have the potential to earn a competitive income. As you gain experience and build a strong client base, your earning potential can increase.

7. Entrepreneurial Experience:

Freelancing offers a taste of entrepreneurship, allowing individuals to manage their own businesses. This experience can be valuable for those considering future entrepreneurial endeavors.

8. Global Reach:

Online freelancing platforms connect freelancers with clients from around the world. This global reach expands opportunities and exposes freelancers to diverse projects and perspectives.

9. Adaptability:

Freelancers learn to adapt to changing market demands, industry trends, and client preferences. This adaptability is a valuable skill in today's dynamic and evolving job market.

10. Work-Life Balance:

Freelancing can offer a better work-life balance for those who prioritize flexibility and autonomy. You have the ability to set your own hours and create a schedule that suits your lifestyle.

Learning freelancing provides individuals with a pathway to a more independent, flexible, and dynamic work life. It's a valuable option for those seeking diverse opportunities, skill development, and a way to shape their careers on their own terms.

⚲ Freelancing for Women

Although freelancing have benefits for all men and women but it holds particular importance for females for several reasons:

1. Flexible Work Arrangements:

Freelancing offers flexible work arrangements, allowing females to balance professional commitments with family responsibilities. This flexibility is especially beneficial for those who may be caregivers or want to create a work schedule that aligns with their lifestyle.

2. Equal Opportunities:

Freelancing provides equal opportunities for women to showcase their skills and expertise without encountering some of the gender biases that can exist in traditional workplaces. Online platforms often focus on merit, allowing females to compete based on their abilities rather than gender.

3. Work-Life Balance:

Freelancing allows women to better manage their work-life balance. The autonomy to set their own schedules and work remotely provides the flexibility needed to address personal commitments while pursuing a fulfilling career.

4. Career Re-entry:

Freelancing offers a viable option for women looking to reenter the workforce after a career break. It allows them to rebuild their professional portfolio, update their skills, and regain confidence at their own pace.

5. Reducing Gender Wage Gap:

Freelancing provides an avenue for women to set their own rates based on their skills and experience, potentially reducing the gender wage gap that can exist in traditional employment settings.

6. Global Opportunities:

Freelancing platforms connect women with clients from around the world, expanding their professional networks and providing access to a global marketplace. This exposure can lead to diverse opportunities and collaborations.

7. Entrepreneurial Empowerment:

Freelancing provides an entrepreneurial experience, allowing women to establish and manage their own businesses. This empowerment can foster a sense of independence and control over their professional destinies.

8. Skill Development:

Freelancing encourages ongoing skill development. Women can continuously enhance their skills, stay current in their fields, and explore new areas of interest, contributing to their professional growth.

9. Inclusivity:

Online freelancing platforms often prioritize inclusivity, creating a space where women from diverse backgrounds and regions can participate and thrive. This inclusivity fosters a supportive community for female freelancers.

10. Reducing Workplace Barriers:

Freelancing can help overcome some of the barriers that women may face in traditional workplaces, such as gender discrimination, office politics, or limited advancement opportunities.

Freelancing offers females the opportunity to pursue fulfilling careers on their own terms, providing flexibility, equal opportunities, and a platform for professional growth. It contributes to a more inclusive and empowering work environment for women across the globe.

Freelance Marketplaces

There are various freelance marketplaces that cater to different types of skills and services. Here are some prominent types of freelance marketplaces:

1. **General Freelance Platforms**

- Upwork
- Fiverr
- PeoplePerHour
- Freelancer
- Guru
- Toptal

- 99Designs
- Jooble
- Flexjobs
- SimplyHired
- Linkedin
- Behance
- Dribble
- ServiceScape
- DesignHill
- TaskRabbit

2. Creative Services

- Fiverr (known for creative and microservices)
- 99designs (specifically for graphic design)

3. Writing and Content Creation

- Textbroker
- Constant Content
- ClearVoice

4. Programming and Tech

1. Toptal (for top-tier software developers)
2. Stack Overflow Jobs
3. GitHub Jobs

5. Remote Work and Virtual Assistance

1. Remote OK
2. Virtual Assistant Jobs

6. Specialized Industries

- MediaBistro (for media professionals)
- Voices.com (for voice-over artists)
- Behance (for creative professionals)

7. Industry-Specific

- Topcoder (for software development and design challenges)
- 99designs (for graphic design contests)

8. Translation and Language Services

- ProZ
- Gengo

9. Video and Animation

- Mandy Network (for film and TV production)
- Animation Base

10. Photography

- Photography Jobs Online
- Shutterstock Custom
- Freepik

11. Consulting and Advisory

- Clarity.fm (for business advice)
- Catalant

12. Specialized Writing

- Contently (for content marketing)
- Skyword (content creation and marketing)

13. E-learning and Education

- Skillshare (for online courses)
- Udemy (for creating and selling courses)

14. Blockchain and Cryptocurrency

- Ethlance

- Crypto Jobs List

15.Local and On-Site Freelancing

- Craigslist (local job listings)

- TaskRabbit (for local tasks and errands)

These platforms cater to a wide range of skills and services, providing freelancers with diverse opportunities to connect with clients seeking their expertise. The choice of platform often depends on the nature of the work, industry specialization, and personal preferences.

☑ Advantages of Freelancing

Freelancing offers several advantages for individuals seeking a flexible and independent work arrangement. Here are some key benefits:

1. Flexibility:

Freelancers enjoy the freedom to set their own schedules, allowing for a better work-life balance. This flexibility is particularly valuable for those with personal commitments or varied lifestyle preferences.

2. Diverse Opportunities:

Freelancing spans a wide range of industries and skills, providing individuals with diverse opportunities to work on projects that align with their expertise and interests.

3. Autonomy:

Freelancers have the autonomy to choose their clients, projects, and rates. This level of control empowers individuals to shape their professional paths according to their preferences.

4. Global Reach:

Online freelancing platforms connect freelancers with clients from around the world, expanding their professional networks and providing access to a global marketplace.

5. Skill Development:

Freelancers continually enhance their skills as they take on different projects. This ongoing learning process contributes to professional growth and adaptability to changing industry trends.

6. Entrepreneurial Experience:

Freelancing offers an entrepreneurial experience, allowing individuals to manage their own businesses, set goals, and make strategic decisions to shape their careers.

7. Portfolio Building:

Freelancers can build a portfolio showcasing their best work. This portfolio becomes a powerful tool for attracting clients and establishing credibility in the freelancing marketplace.

8. Income Potential:

Successful freelancers often have the potential to earn competitive incomes. As freelancers gain experience and build a strong client base, their earning potential can increase.

9. Reduced Commuting Stress:

Freelancers can work from any location with an internet connection, eliminating the need for daily commutes. This not only saves time but also reduces stress associated with commuting.

10. Work Variety:

Freelancers have the flexibility to work on different projects and collaborate with diverse clients. This variety adds excitement and interest to the work, preventing monotony.

11. Reduced Overhead Costs:

Freelancers typically work from home or shared workspaces, reducing overhead costs associated with maintaining a physical office. This can lead to increased take-home earnings.

12. Work-Life Integration:

Freelancers often experience a more integrated approach to work and life, allowing them to seamlessly blend professional and personal responsibilities.

13. Accessibility:

Freelancing provides opportunities for individuals who may face barriers in traditional workplaces, such as individuals with disabilities or those in remote locations.

14. Easier Career Transitions:

Freelancing allows for smoother career transitions, enabling individuals to explore new industries or skills without the constraints of traditional employment.

15. Building a Personal Brand:

Freelancers can establish and promote their personal brand. This brand becomes a valuable asset in attracting clients and standing out in a competitive freelancing market.

In summary, freelancing offers a dynamic and adaptable work model that aligns with the evolving preferences and lifestyles of many professionals. The advantages include flexibility, autonomy, diverse opportunities, and the potential for both personal and professional growth.

☒ Disadvantages of Freelancing

Freelancing has its good parts, but there are also some tough things to deal with. People thinking about freelancing should know about these not-so-great parts.

First off, freelancers don't always get a steady income. Some days or weeks can be really busy, while others might be slow. Figuring out how to budget money and plan for the future can be tricky. Unlike regular jobs, freelancers don't have the security of a stable paycheck and work benefits, especially when things get tough economically. Freelancers have to do their own taxes, which can be confusing and need extra planning. They also don't usually get perks like health insurance, retirement help, or paid time off. Handling all of this on your own can be a bit challenging.

Working alone can get lonely, and freelancers miss out on the social side of working in an office. This can affect how they feel mentally. Also, if a big client stops working with them or there are fewer projects available, freelancers might face some tough times. Juggling lots of projects or dealing with sudden increases in work can be hard. Freelancers need to do extra stuff like sending invoices, talking about contracts, and managing projects. This takes up more time and skills, not just the main service they're offering.

Getting noticed in the freelancing world can be tough. Standing out and getting projects need good self-marketing and a good professional reputation. Climbing up the career ladder isn't as common for freelancers compared to regular jobs. Clients might change their minds, give unclear instructions, or delay payments. Handling relationships with clients becomes super important. Freelancers don't get the benefits that come with regular jobs, like retirement plans, health insurance, and chances for more learning.

Managing time can be hard because freelancers don't have a set work schedule. This can lead to working too much or struggling to meet deadlines. Taking a break means not getting paid, and taking long breaks might affect relationships with clients. Freelancers also have to handle legal stuff by themselves, making sure contracts are fair and they're protected in case of problems.

So, even though freelancing gives you flexibility and independence, it's important to think about and find ways to deal with these challenges for a successful freelancing career.

➲ Essentials of Freelancing

To thrive in the world of freelancing, several essentials can contribute to a successful and fulfilling career:

Skill Development: Continuously develop and enhance your skills to stay competitive in your chosen freelancing niche.

Market Research: Understand the demand for your skills in the freelancing marketplace and identify your target clients.

Create a Professional Profile: Build a compelling and professional profile on freelancing platforms, showcasing your skills, experience, and portfolio.

Clear Branding: Establish a clear personal brand that sets you apart from other freelancers. Clearly communicate what makes you unique and valuable to clients.

Effective Communication: Master effective communication skills to understand client needs, clarify expectations, and build strong working relationships.

Time Management: Develop strong time management skills to meet deadlines, balance multiple projects, and maintain a consistent work schedule.

Financial Management: Understand the financial aspects of freelancing, including setting rates, handling taxes, and budgeting for variable income.

Legal Understanding: Familiarize yourself with the legal aspects of freelancing, including contracts, intellectual property rights, and dispute resolution.

Networking: Actively network with other freelancers, industry professionals, and potential clients to expand your opportunities and professional connections.

Online Presence: Establish a strong online presence beyond freelancing platforms. This can include a professional website, social media profiles, and participation in relevant online communities.

Portfolio Development: Build a comprehensive portfolio showcasing your best work. Regularly update it to reflect your evolving skills and experience.

Client Relationship Management: Cultivate positive and professional relationships with clients. Understand their expectations and communicate effectively throughout the project.

Adaptability: Embrace adaptability to navigate changes in the freelancing landscape, industry trends, and client preferences.

Feedback Utilization: Learn from client feedback to improve your skills and enhance the quality of your services. Use feedback as a tool for continuous improvement.

Marketing Skills: Develop basic marketing skills to promote your services effectively. This includes crafting persuasive proposals, writing compelling pitches, and utilizing social media for self-promotion.

Client Diversification: Aim for a diversified client base to reduce dependency on a single client and mitigate risks associated with sudden changes in workload.

Self-Care: Prioritize self-care to maintain mental and physical well-being. Freelancing can be demanding, and taking care of yourself is crucial for sustained success.

By focusing on these essentials, freelancers can build a strong foundation for their careers, navigate challenges effectively, and position themselves for long-term success in the freelancing landscape. In next chapters we'll discuss all of these with more detail.

FREELANCING
VERSUS
JOB

	Freelancing	Job
EARNING		
01	Sky is the limit	Stable Earning
PAYCHECK		
02	Unsure Payouts	Define Payouts
LEARNING		
03	Diversified learning	Static learning
WORK TIME		
04	No Fix Time	Fix Time
TEAM WORK		
05	Individual & Teamwork	Teamwork
FLEXIBILITY		
06	Great Flexibility	No Flexibility

The Art of Freelancing

Chapter 2: Choose Your Skills

◎ Define Your Goals

Defining your goals is a crucial step in providing direction, motivation, and purpose to your endeavors. Goals serve as a roadmap, guiding your actions and decisions. Here are key steps to define your goals effectively:

1. Identify Your Values

Reflect on your core values and principles. Your goals should align with what matters most to you, ensuring a sense of fulfillment. For example, Increase client satisfaction by maintaining a high feedback rating.

2. Clarify Your Vision

Envision your ideal future. What does success look like for you? Having a clear vision provides a destination for your goals.

3. Categorize Your Goals

Divide your goals into categories such as career, personal development, health, relationships, and finance. This ensures a holistic approach to goal-setting.

For example

- Take a specific number of planned breaks during the workday.

- Attend a certain number of networking events or webinars within the year.

- Acquire certification or training in a new skill relevant to your freelancing niche.

4. Set SMART Goals

Make your goals Specific, Measurable, Achievable, Relevant, and Time-bound (SMART). This framework enhances clarity and feasibility.

Example 1: Financial Goal

Specific: Increase annual income by 20%.

Measurable: Track income through invoicing software and monthly financial reports.

Achievable: Evaluate current client workload and identify opportunities for upselling or securing higher-paying projects.

Relevant: Aligns with the freelancer's overall objective of achieving financial growth.

Time-bound: Achieve the 20% increase within the next 12 months.

Example 2: Skill Development Goal

Specific: Obtain certification in advanced graphic design techniques.

Measurable: Complete an online certification course and pass the final assessment.

Achievable: Allocate dedicated time each week for coursework and practice projects.

Relevant: Enhances expertise in the freelancer's niche and allows for more complex and higher-paying projects.

Time-bound: Complete the certification within the next three months.

These SMART goals provide clear and actionable steps, making it easier for the freelancer to track progress and achieve the desired outcomes.

5. Short-Term and Long-Term Goals

Distinguish between short-term goals (achievable in the near future) and long-term goals (ambitious objectives requiring more time).

6. Prioritize

Prioritize your goals based on their importance and impact. Focus on high-priority goals while keeping others in mind for future planning.

7. Break Down Complex Goals

If a goal seems overwhelming, break it down into smaller, more manageable tasks. This makes the goal-setting process less daunting.

8. Quantify Where Possible

Assign specific quantities or metrics to your goals. This makes it easier to measure progress and success.

9. Create an Action Plan

Outline the steps you need to take to achieve each goal. An action plan provides a roadmap for implementation.

10.Review and Revise

Regularly review your goals to ensure they remain relevant and aligned with your evolving priorities. Revise as needed.

11.Seek Feedback

Share your goals with trusted friends, mentors, or advisors. Their perspectives can offer valuable insights and suggestions.

12.Celebrate Milestones

Acknowledge and celebrate achievements along the way. Recognizing progress boosts motivation and reinforces positive behavior.

13.Stay Flexible

Be open to adjusting your goals if circumstances change. Flexibility allows you to adapt to unexpected challenges or opportunities.

14.Visualize Success

Picture yourself achieving your goals. Visualization can enhance motivation and reinforce your commitment to the desired outcomes.

15.Accountabilit

Hold yourself accountable for your goals. Share them with someone who can provide support, encouragement, and gentle accountability.

Remember, goals are not set in stone; they can evolve as you grow and gain new insights. Regularly reassessing and refining your goals ensures that they remain meaningful and aligned with your aspirations.

Example:

Meet Alex, a new freelancer eager to embark on a successful freelancing career. Here's how Alex might define his goals:

Alex values autonomy, creativity, and continuous learning. His goals should align with these core values to ensure job satisfaction. (Identifying Values)

Alex envisions a future where he has a steady stream of clients, a diverse portfolio showcasing his creative skills, and the flexibility to balance work with personal pursuits. (Clarifying Vision)

Alex categorizes his goals into career advancement (building a client base, expanding services), personal development (learning new design techniques), and financial stability. (Categorize Goals)

Within the next three months, Alex aims to secure his first three clients for graphic design projects, complete an online course to enhance his design skills, and generate a set monthly income from freelancing. (Set SMART Goals)

Short-term goals include landing initial projects and establishing a professional online presence. Long-term goals involve becoming a recognized expert in his niche and potentially starting his design agency. (Short-Term and Long-Term Goals)

Alex prioritizes securing his first clients, as this will kickstart his freelancing journey. Building a strong portfolio and expanding services come next in line. (Prioritize)

Breaking down the goal of building a client base involves tasks like creating a compelling portfolio, crafting personalized pitches, and networking on freelancing platforms. Alex sets a specific target: secure three clients in the first three months, complete at least one online course, and achieve a monthly income goal. (Quantifying Where Possible)

Alex outlines actionable steps, such as optimizing his freelancing profile, creating a portfolio website, sending out tailored proposals, and dedicating specific hours each day to freelancing activities. (Creating an Action Plan)

Alex commits to reviewing his goals monthly, adjusting strategies based on feedback, and refining his approach as he gains experience. (Reviewing and Revising)

Alex shares his goals with a mentor from a freelancing community, gaining insights on effective pitching and portfolio building. (Seeking Feedback)

Alex celebrates small wins, such as landing his first client or completing a challenging project, reinforcing his progress. (Celebrating Milestones)

Alex remains open to adjusting his goals based on the evolving freelancing landscape and his personal growth. (Staying Flexible)

Alex visualizes receiving positive client feedback, seeing his work showcased in his portfolio, and enjoying the flexibility that freelancing provides. (visualizing success)

Alex shares his goals with a friend who also freelances, creating a support system for mutual encouragement and accountability. (accountability)

Alex's well-defined goals provide him with a roadmap for success, guiding his efforts as he takes the initial steps into the freelancing world.

✪ Your Skills

When analyzing what skills you already have for freelancing, consider the following steps:

1. Self-Reflection:

Reflect on your past experiences, both professionally and personally. Identify tasks and responsibilities you enjoyed or excelled in.

2. Passions and Hobbies:

Consider your hobbies and passions. Skills developed in these areas, even if not directly related to your profession, could be transferrable to freelancing.

3. Professional Background:

Assess your professional background. Identify skills gained from your education, training, and previous jobs. This could include technical skills, communication abilities, project management, etc.

4. Soft Skills:

Recognize your soft skills such as communication, time management, problem-solving, and teamwork. These are valuable in freelancing as well.

5. Feedback from Others:

Seek feedback from colleagues, friends, or mentors. They might offer insights into skills you might not have realized you possess.

6. Online Skills Assessment:

Utilize online skills assessment tools to identify your strengths. Platforms like LinkedIn, Skillshare, or Coursera often offer skills assessments.

7. Review Job Descriptions:

Look at freelancing job descriptions. Identify the skills and qualifications required for the types of projects you find interesting. Compare these with your own skill set.

8. Networking:

Engage in professional networking, both online and offline. Discussions with peers can help you discover skills that are in demand within your industry.

9. Explore Freelancing Platforms:

Explore freelancing platforms like Upwork, Fiverr, or Freelancer. Review the skills in demand and assess if you possess any of these skills.

10. Identify Niche Expertise:

Identify any niche expertise you have. Specialized skills often have high demand in freelancing.

11. Continuous Learning:

Be open to continuous learning. Identify areas where you can enhance your skills to meet the evolving demands of the freelancing market.

12. Passive Income Skills:

Consider skills that can lead to passive income, such as writing, graphic design, or coding, which can be monetized even when you're not actively working on a project.

By thoroughly analyzing your skills through these steps, you'll gain a clearer understanding of your strengths and be better equipped to position yourself in the freelancing marketplace.

Your Favorite Skills

If you're exploring freelancing and considering what skill excites you, it's essential to tap into your passions and interests. Reflect on activities or tasks that genuinely engage and motivate you. Here's a response from a freelancing perspective:

"I find the most excitement in graphic design. The creative process of transforming ideas into visual representations is not just a job for me; it's a passion. From crafting compelling logos to designing eye-catching marketing materials, every project is an opportunity to blend artistry with communication. The prospect of freelancing in graphic design allows me to turn my creative fervor into a profession, working on diverse projects and collaborating with clients who value unique and impactful visuals."

Remember, the key is to align your freelancing pursuits with what genuinely excites and motivates you, as this enthusiasm often translates into dedication and success in your chosen freelancing path.

Learning a New Skill

Learning a new skill for freelancing involves a structured and strategic approach. Here's a step-by-step guide to help you acquire the skills necessary for freelancing:

1. Identify the Skill:

Clearly define the skill you want to learn for freelancing. Whether it's graphic design, writing, coding, or digital marketing, pinpoint the specific area.

2. Set Clear Goals:

Establish clear and realistic goals for learning the skill. Define what you want to achieve and set milestones to track your progress.

3. Research the Skill:

Conduct thorough research on the chosen skill. Understand the industry standards, current trends, and the demand for that skill in the freelancing market.

4. Select Learning Resources:

Choose reliable learning resources. This may include online courses, tutorials, books, workshops, or mentorship programs. Platforms like Udemy, Coursera, and Skillshare offer a variety of courses.

5. Create a Learning Schedule:

Develop a dedicated learning schedule. Allocate specific time slots each day or week for skill development. Consistency is key to mastering a new skill.

6. Hands-On Practice:

Apply theoretical knowledge through hands-on practice. Create projects or exercises that allow you to implement what you've learned. Practical experience is crucial for skill mastery.

7. Join Online Communities:

Engage with online communities related to the skill you're learning. Platforms like Stack Overflow, GitHub, or industry-specific forums offer opportunities for networking, learning from others, and seeking advice.

8. Seek Feedback:

Share your work with peers, mentors, or online communities. Constructive feedback is invaluable for improvement and gaining different perspectives on your skill development.

9. Build a Portfolio:

As you progress, start building a portfolio showcasing your projects and achievements. A strong portfolio is essential for attracting clients in the freelancing market.

10. Explore Freelancing Platforms:

Familiarize yourself with freelancing platforms relevant to your skill. Understand how these platforms operate and what clients look for in freelancers.

11. Set Up Professional Profiles:

Create professional profiles on freelancing platforms. Optimize your profiles by highlighting your skills, experience, and the value you can offer to clients.

12. Apply for Entry-Level Projects:

Initially, target entry-level projects on freelancing platforms to gain practical experience and build a positive reputation.

13. Stay Updated:

Continuously update your skills based on industry developments. Subscribe to newsletters, follow industry blogs, and participate in webinars to stay informed.

14. Network with Professionals:

Network with professionals in your field. Attend virtual events, join LinkedIn groups, and connect with experienced freelancers who can provide guidance and insights.

15. Evaluate and Iterate:

Regularly evaluate your progress, identify areas for improvement, and iterate your learning strategy. Learning is an ongoing process, and adaptability is key.

By following these steps, you can systematically acquire the skills needed for freelancing and position yourself for success in the competitive freelancing marketplace.

Chapter 3: Business Communication and Freelancing

☛ Key Components of Business Communication

Business communication refers to the exchange of information within an organization or between different entities to facilitate business activities and achieve common goals. It encompasses a wide range of verbal, non-verbal, and written interactions that occur in various business contexts. Effective business communication is crucial for the smooth functioning of an organization, promoting collaboration, and building strong relationships with stakeholders.

For freelancers, knowing how to communicate well is like having a superpower. Imagine you're a superhero, and your power is to talk with clients, understand what they want, and tell them about your amazing skills. That's what good communication is for freelancers! When you get a job, you need to talk with the person who hired you, right? Maybe it's through emails or messages. You want to make sure you understand what they need and let them know how you're going to do it.

But it's not just about typing words. You also need to listen – it's like using your superhero ears. Sometimes clients give feedback or ask for changes. If you can understand what they're saying and talk back in a friendly way, it's like using your superhero charm. Good communication helps you avoid problems, finish your work the way clients want, and even get more jobs in the future. So, for freelancers, being a communication superhero is a big part of being successful!

Key components of business communication include Following:

1. Internal Communication

2. External Communication

3. Formal Communication

4. Informal Communication

5. Verbal Communication

6. Non-Verbal Communication

7. Written Communication

8. Business Etiquette

9. Feedback and Listening

10. Conflict Resolution

11. Technology in Communication

12. Crisis Communication

13. Cross-Cultural Communication

14. Public Relations

1. Internal Communication

Communication within an organization, involving interactions among employees, departments, and management is internal. This can include team meetings, memos, emails, and internal messaging systems. Communication within an organization refers to the exchange of information and messages among employees, different departments, and management. It encompasses various forms of interaction, such as team meetings, memos, emails, and internal messaging systems. Effective communication within an organization is crucial for ensuring that everyone is on the same page, understanding their roles and responsibilities, and working towards common goals. It facilitates the flow of information, ideas, and updates, fostering collaboration and cohesion among team members and different parts of the organization. Clear and transparent communication contributes to a positive work environment and helps in achieving organizational objectives.

In the freelancing world, internal communication is like the secret sauce that keeps the whole operation running smoothly. It's how freelancers talk and share information within their "one-person organization." Just like in a big company, internal communication for freelancers involves things like team meetings (even if it's just a meeting with oneself!), sending memos (maybe notes or to-do lists), emails, and using internal messaging systems like project management tools.

So, imagine you're the CEO, the manager, and the employee all at once. Internal communication is how you make sure you're on top of your game. It's not just about sending messages; it's about making sure you understand your goals, tasks, and plans. When freelancers communicate effectively internally, it's like being the mastermind behind the scenes, making everything flow seamlessly. It's the key to staying organized, motivated, and successful in the freelancing world!

2. External Communication

Communication with external entities, such as customers, suppliers, investors, and the public is external communication. This involves conveying the organization's messages and maintaining positive relationships with external stakeholders.

Communication with external entities in the context of an organization refers to the interaction and exchange of information with parties outside the organization. This includes customers, suppliers, investors, and the public. The goal is to effectively convey the organization's messages and maintain positive relationships with these external stakeholders. This communication can take various forms, such as advertising, public relations, customer support, and interactions with suppliers and investors. Building and maintaining strong communication channels with external entities are essential for fostering trust, meeting customer needs, securing partnerships, and enhancing the organization's reputation in the broader community.

In freelancing, external communication is like being the friendly face that represents your one-person business to the world. It's how you talk and connect with clients, collaborators, and anyone outside your freelancing bubble. Imagine it as a superhero reaching out to clients, suppliers, and the public. External communication for freelancers involves sending messages, providing support to clients, showcasing your work through advertising or social media, and interacting with anyone who's not on your freelancing team.

Picture yourself as the ambassador of your freelancing brand. It's not just about talking; it's about making sure your messages are clear, friendly, and create a positive image. When freelancers excel at external communication, it's like being the superhero who wins the hearts of clients, builds trust, and makes a mark in the big, wide world of freelancing. It's the key to expanding your freelancing universe and creating a stellar reputation!

3. Formal Communication

Official, planned communication within an organization, often following established channels and protocols is known as formal communication. Examples include official reports, company policies, and structured meetings.

Official, planned communication within an organization is the intentional and organized exchange of information following established channels and protocols. This type of communication is structured and formal, involving methods such as official reports, company policies, and structured meetings. It adheres to predetermined guidelines and is often used to convey important information, share updates, or discuss matters that require a systematic approach. This form of communication is essential for maintaining consistency, ensuring that key messages are delivered accurately, and upholding the organization's standards and procedures.

In the freelancing world, formal communication is like the rulebook that keeps everything organized and official. It's how you intentionally share information in a structured and planned way. Imagine it as creating your own set of official freelancing documents. Formal communication for freelancers involves things like creating official reports for clients, establishing clear policies for your work, and holding structured meetings, even if it's just you sitting down to plan your next moves.

Think of it as being the professional architect of your freelancing structure. Formal communication is not just about talking; it's about creating a system that ensures everything runs smoothly. When freelancers nail formal communication, it's like having a solid foundation for their freelancing empire. It's the key to being organized, professional, and creating a freelancing journey that's built to last!

4. Informal Communication

Unofficial, spontaneous communication that occurs organically within an organization is Informal Communication. This can include watercooler conversations, casual emails, and discussions outside of formal settings. Unofficial, spontaneous communication within an organization is the natural and unplanned exchange of information that occurs organically. This type of communication is informal and can take various forms, such as watercooler conversations, casual emails, and discussions outside of formal settings. Unlike official communication, it is not structured and often happens on the spur of the moment. While unofficial communication may lack the formality of planned channels, it plays a crucial role in fostering a sense of camaraderie, building relationships, and sharing insights among colleagues in a more relaxed and spontaneous manner.

In freelancing, informal communication is like the friendly chat you have with a colleague at the watercooler, even if it's just you chatting with yourself! It's the natural and unplanned way you exchange information. Imagine it as the easy-going, laid-back side of freelancing. Informal communication for freelancers includes things like casual emails, impromptu discussions about your project, and any relaxed communication that happens outside of the more structured, formal settings.

Think of it as being your own laid-back boss. It's not just about sending messages; it's about creating a vibe that's friendly and open. When freelancers embrace informal communication, it's like having a virtual watercooler where ideas flow freely, and you feel a sense of camaraderie with yourself. It's the key to making freelancing not just a job but a relaxed and enjoyable journey!

5. Verbal Communication

Communication using spoken words is called verbal communication. This includes face-to-face conversations, telephone calls, video conferences, and presentations. This can occur through various mediums, including face-to-face conversations, telephone calls, video conferences, and presentations. In verbal communication, individuals express their thoughts, ideas, and information orally, allowing for real-time interaction and exchange of dialogue. It is a dynamic form of communication that relies on spoken language to convey meaning and facilitate understanding between communicators.

In freelancing, verbal communication is like having a conversation with your clients or teammates, whether face-to-face or through the digital world. It's the spoken words that bring your freelancing projects to life. Imagine it as being the voice behind your freelancing skills. Verbal communication for freelancers includes face-to-face discussions, client calls, video conferences, and any time you present your work or ideas.

Think of it as being the eloquent speaker of your freelancing story. It's not just about talking; it's about expressing yourself clearly and ensuring that everyone is on the same page. When freelancers master verbal communication, it's like having a superpower that makes your freelancing journey smooth and collaborative. It's the key to building strong client relationships and making sure your freelancing voice is heard loud and clear!

6. Non-Verbal Communication

Non-verbal cues such as body language, facial expressions, gestures, and visual elements play a significant role in conveying messages. Non-verbal communication is a mode of communication that doesn't involve the use of words. Instead, it relies on conveying messages through non-verbal cues such as body language, facial expressions, gestures, and visual elements.

These non-verbal signals can convey emotions, attitudes, and intentions, adding depth and nuance to the communication process. Non-verbal communication often complements verbal communication and plays a crucial role in understanding and interpreting messages in various social and professional contexts.

In freelancing, non-verbal communication is like the silent but powerful language that speaks volumes without saying a word. It's all about the unspoken cues that add an extra layer of meaning to your freelancing interactions. Imagine it as being the body language of your freelancing journey. Non-verbal communication for freelancers includes everything from the expressions on your face to the gestures you make during a video call. Think of it as being the subtle artist of your freelancing canvas. It's not just about what you say; it's about how you express yourself without uttering a word. When freelancers master non-verbal communication, it's like having a secret code that enhances understanding and collaboration. It's the key to making your freelancing interactions not just clear but also rich with unspoken nuances!

7. Written Communication

This includes emails, reports, memos, business letters, and documentation. Clear and effective written communication is essential for conveying information accurately. Written communication involves the exchange of information through written words. This encompasses various forms such as emails, reports, memos, business letters, and documentation. Clear and effective written communication is crucial for conveying information accurately and ensuring that messages are understood as intended. It provides a tangible record of communication, allowing for reference and documentation. Written communication is widely used in professional and personal settings to convey complex information, share details, and maintain a written record of correspondence.

In the realm of freelancing, where digital communication is paramount, mastering written communication is indispensable for several reasons. Firstly, freelancers frequently engage in documenting project details, requirements, and agreements. Clear and concise written communication ensures that all involved parties have a comprehensive understanding of the project scope, deadlines, and expectations, reducing the likelihood of misunderstandings.

Professionalism in correspondence is another critical aspect of freelancing. Emails, messages, and project proposals constitute primary channels for professional communication. A freelancer's ability to express themselves clearly and professionally in writing is instrumental in building trust and credibility with clients, which is foundational for successful freelancing relationships.

Client communication heavily relies on written exchanges. From initial project proposals to regular status updates and final deliverables, freelancers need to articulate their thoughts effectively in writing to meet and exceed client expectations. This proficiency contributes to positive client relationships and fosters client satisfaction.

Moreover, written communication minimizes the risk of misunderstandings. When details are documented clearly, it reduces the chances of misinterpretation, ensuring that freelancers and clients remain aligned on project specifics. Also, a freelancer's written communication style contributes significantly to their brand image. Consistent, articulate communication reflects positively on a freelancer's professionalism, potentially leading to repeat business and positive referrals. In essence, strong written communication skills are foundational for success in freelancing, facilitating effective collaboration, client satisfaction, and the establishment of a professional freelancing brand.

8. Business Etiquette

Adhering to professional and cultural norms when communicating in a business setting is business etiquette. Business etiquette refers to the set of conventional practices and polite behaviors observed in professional settings. It encompasses a range of social norms and expectations that govern how individuals interact with each other in a business environment. This includes using appropriate language, tone, and behavior in various business contexts. Adhering to business etiquette is crucial for creating a positive and respectful workplace culture. This also includes considerations such as professional communication, punctuality, dress code, meeting conduct, and the proper use of technology. Following business etiquette helps build trust, foster positive relationships, and contribute to a harmonious and professional work atmosphere.

In the context of freelancing, understanding and applying business etiquette is equally vital for building and maintaining successful professional relationships. Freelancers often interact with clients, collaborators, and other professionals in a virtual space, making the nuances of business etiquette even more critical. Effective communication is a cornerstone of business etiquette in freelancing. This involves using professional and respectful language in emails, messages, and other written exchanges. Timely responses, clarity in communication, and expressing gratitude are essential components of maintaining a positive and respectful tone.

Moreover, punctuality in meeting deadlines and delivering high-quality work is a manifestation of good business etiquette. This reliability contributes to a freelancer's reputation and fosters trust with clients and collaborators.

Additionally, being mindful of cultural differences is crucial, especially in a global freelancing landscape, to avoid unintentional misunderstandings or offenses. Professional conduct extends beyond communication to the use of technology and virtual tools. Being proficient in the platforms commonly used in freelancing, such as project management tools and communication apps, demonstrates a freelancer's commitment to effective collaboration.

In essence, embracing and embodying business etiquette in freelancing not only contributes to a positive work atmosphere but also enhances a freelancer's professionalism and reputation in the competitive freelancing market.

9. Feedback and Listening

Encouraging feedback and active listening is important in business communication. This ensures that messages are understood, and concerns or suggestions are addressed. Feedback and listening in business communication involve creating an environment that encourages open communication and attentive understanding. Actively seeking feedback ensures that messages are comprehended, and any concerns or suggestions are acknowledged and addressed. This two-way communication approach fosters mutual understanding, promotes a culture of continuous improvement, and strengthens relationships within the business. By valuing feedback and practicing active listening, organizations can enhance communication effectiveness and adapt to the evolving needs of their team members and stakeholders.

In the context of freelancing, prioritizing feedback and active listening is equally crucial for successful collaboration with clients and partners. Freelancers often work remotely, making clear communication and understanding paramount. Encouraging feedback allows freelancers to gain insights into client expectations, preferences, and any adjustments needed to align with project goals. It creates a collaborative atmosphere where both parties feel comfortable expressing their thoughts.

Active listening, a key component of effective communication, involves attentively understanding the client's requirements, concerns, and feedback. This skill enables freelancers to deliver work that aligns closely with the client's vision and expectations. It also contributes to building trust and rapport, essential for long-term freelance relationships. Incorporating feedback and active listening into freelancing practices promotes a dynamic and responsive approach to projects. It demonstrates a commitment to delivering high-quality work that meets the client's needs, ultimately enhancing the freelancer's professional reputation and fostering client satisfaction.

10. Conflict Resolution

Addressing conflicts or misunderstandings that may arise in the course of business communication is called conflict resolution. Effective communication skills are crucial for resolving issues and maintaining a positive work environment.

Conflict resolution in business communication involves addressing conflicts or misunderstandings that may arise during professional interactions. Effective communication skills play a crucial role in resolving issues and maintaining a positive work environment. This process includes identifying the source of conflicts, facilitating open dialogue, and working towards mutually acceptable solutions. Through clear and empathetic communication, individuals can navigate conflicts, promote understanding, and contribute to a harmonious workplace where diverse perspectives are respected, and issues are addressed constructively.

In the freelancing realm, conflict resolution through effective communication is vital for maintaining healthy client relationships and successful project outcomes. As freelancers often work independently, managing potential conflicts requires adept communication skills. When conflicts arise, freelancers need to identify the root cause, whether it's a misunderstanding, differing expectations, or other issues. Open and transparent dialogue becomes a key tool in addressing these challenges. Freelancers must navigate discussions with clients, understanding their concerns, and expressing their perspectives clearly.

By employing effective conflict resolution strategies, such as active listening, empathy, and proposing constructive solutions, freelancers can mitigate issues and ensure that projects progress smoothly. Proactive communication helps build trust with clients, demonstrating a commitment to professionalism and client satisfaction. This, in turn, contributes to a positive reputation and the potential for ongoing collaborations.

11.Technology in Communication

Technology in communication refers to the utilization of various tools and platforms to enhance and streamline the communication process in a business or organizational context. This includes the use of technologies such as email, instant messaging, video conferencing, and collaborative software. Leveraging these technological advancements enables efficient and real-time communication, irrespective of geographical distances. It facilitates quick information exchange, enhances collaboration among team members, and contributes to the overall effectiveness of business communication strategies.

For freelancers, integrating technology into communication practices is essential for staying competitive and efficient. Utilizing email, instant messaging, and video conferencing platforms allows freelancers to connect with clients, discuss project details, and provide updates in a timely manner. Collaborative software aids in project management and document sharing, promoting seamless cooperation.

Technology not only expedites communication but also expands freelancers' reach to a global client base. Freelancers can showcase their portfolios on websites and leverage social media to enhance visibility and engage with potential clients. Embracing technology in communication empowers freelancers to navigate the digital landscape successfully, ensuring effective and streamlined interactions with clients and collaborators.

12. Crisis Communication

It is communicating effectively during challenging situations or crises. This involves providing timely and accurate information to stakeholders to manage the impact of adverse events. Imagine you're the captain of a ship, and suddenly, there's a storm. Crisis communication is like steering the ship through rough waters. For freelancers, it means talking to clients, team members, or anyone involved when things get tough. Maybe there's a problem with a project, or the client is unhappy. Crisis communication is about telling everyone what's happening, being honest, and finding solutions together.

Think of it as being a superhero communicator during challenging times. You want to share the right information quickly and calmly, like a superhero calming a storm. It's not just about saying things; it's about making sure everyone knows what's going on and feels reassured. Freelancers who master crisis communication can navigate through challenges smoothly, keep everyone informed, and save the day like true communication superheroes!

13. Cross-Cultural Communication

Cross-cultural communication is like speaking the language of the world. Imagine you have friends from different parts of the globe, and you want to talk to each of them in a way they understand and feel comfortable. For freelancers, it's like being a language expert in the diverse world of clients. You need to understand that people from different cultures might have different ways of saying things, and it's crucial to get it right.

Think of it as a global adventure where you learn about customs, traditions, and the unique ways people express themselves. It's not just about words; it's about understanding the feelings behind them. Freelancers who are good at cross-cultural communication can work with clients from anywhere, making the world feel like a smaller, friendlier place. It's like having a passport to success in the international language of business!

14. Public Relations

Public relations is like being the storyteller-in-chief for a company. Imagine you're in charge of telling everyone about a cool new superhero – that's the company you work for. Public relations for freelancers means making sure everyone sees and hears about the amazing things you can do. It's about creating a positive image and reputation so that when people think about hiring someone for a job, they think of you!

Think of it as being a friendly guide who shares exciting stories. Public relations isn't just about talking to clients; it's also about talking to the whole world. You might write stories, share them on social media, or even talk to journalists. Freelancers who are good at public relations can make their skills known far and wide, attracting more opportunities and becoming the superheroes of their professional world!

Business communication is like the heartbeat of freelancing success. It's not just talking or writing; it's a lively, always-moving process that keeps everything running smoothly. Imagine it as the secret sauce that makes freelancers connect with clients, team members, and the whole wide world.

Picture it as a dynamic dance where everyone understands each other's moves. When freelancers communicate well, it's not just about getting the job done; it's about creating a vibe of understanding, working together, and building awesome relationships. Whether it's chatting with a client, sending emails, or sharing ideas in a meeting, business communication is the magic wand that makes freelancing journeys successful and full of high-fives!

🗣 Communication Skills for Freelancing

Communication skills are paramount for freelancers, as they directly impact client relationships, project success, and overall professional reputation.

Here's why communication skills are crucial in the context of freelancing:

a) Client Interaction:

Effective communication is essential when interacting with clients. Clear and concise communication helps in understanding client requirements, expectations, and feedback, leading to successful project outcomes.

b) Project Understanding:

Freelancers need to grasp the intricacies of each project. Strong communication skills enable freelancers to ask relevant questions, seek clarification when needed, and ensure they have a comprehensive understanding of the client's needs.

c) Setting Expectations:

Clearly articulating project timelines, deliverables, and terms sets realistic expectations. This helps avoid misunderstandings and ensures that both parties are on the same page from the outset.

d) Negotiation and Agreement:

Negotiating terms, rates, and project scope requires effective communication. Freelancers need to express their value proposition while being receptive to client expectations, fostering a mutually beneficial agreement.

e) Feedback Handling:

Receiving and providing feedback is a regular part of freelancing. Strong communication skills allow freelancers to receive constructive criticism positively and implement necessary changes, improving the quality of their work.

f) Time Management:

Communicating project timelines, deadlines, and potential delays is crucial for managing client expectations. Transparent communication about project progress helps build trust and credibility.

g) Conflict Resolution:

In the event of conflicts or misunderstandings, effective communication is key to resolving issues diplomatically. Freelancers who can navigate challenges with professionalism maintain positive client relationships.

h) Building Relationships:

Establishing a strong professional rapport with clients is foundational for repeat business and referrals. Good communication fosters trust, loyalty, and a positive working relationship.

i) Remote Collaboration:

Many freelancers work remotely, making communication skills even more critical. The ability to convey ideas, provide updates, and collaborate effectively through virtual channels ensures successful remote work arrangements.

j) Pitching and Proposals:

Crafting persuasive pitches and proposals requires strong communication skills. Freelancers need to communicate their expertise, showcase their value proposition, and convince clients of their capabilities.

k) Adaptability and Flexibility:

Freelancers often work with clients from diverse backgrounds. Adapting communication styles to suit different clients and being flexible in your approach enhances professional relationships.

l) Professionalism:

Professional communication reflects positively on a freelancer's image. This includes using proper language, responding promptly to messages, and maintaining a respectful tone in all interactions.

m) Client Education:

Clients may not always be familiar with the freelancer's field of expertise. Communicating complex concepts in an accessible manner helps clients understand the value of the freelancer's work.

Communication skills are integral to every stage of freelancing, from initial client interactions to project delivery and beyond. Freelancers who prioritize effective communication enhance their overall professionalism and increase the likelihood of success in the competitive freelancing landscape.

⇪ Improving Communication Skills

Improving communication skills is a valuable investment in personal and professional development. Here are practical steps to enhance your communication skills:

Active Listening:

Practice active listening by giving your full attention to the speaker, making eye contact, and avoiding interruptions. This ensures you understand the message accurately before responding.

Clear Articulation:

Speak clearly and concisely. Avoid using jargon or overly complex language, especially when communicating with individuals who may not be familiar with your field.

Non-Verbal Communication:

Pay attention to your body language, facial expressions, and gestures. Non-verbal cues can significantly impact how your message is received.

Receive and Act on Feedback:

Seek feedback from colleagues, friends, or mentors on your communication style. Use constructive criticism to identify areas for improvement.

Practice Empathy:

Develop empathy by putting yourself in others' shoes. Understand their perspective and emotions, which enhances your ability to communicate with sensitivity and understanding.

Expand Your Vocabulary:

Continuously expand your vocabulary to express ideas more precisely. Read diverse materials and pay attention to how words are used in different contexts.

Body Language Awareness:

Be aware of your own body language and how it might be perceived. Project confidence, openness, and engagement through your posture and gestures.

Mind Your Tone:

Pay attention to your tone of voice. A friendly and respectful tone can convey positivity, while an inappropriate tone may lead to misunderstandings.

Use Visual Aids:

When applicable, use visual aids such as charts, graphs, or slides to complement your verbal communication. Visuals can enhance understanding, especially for complex topics.

Join Public Speaking Groups:

Join public speaking or Toastmasters groups to practice speaking in front of an audience. This builds confidence and hones your ability to articulate ideas effectively.

Read Aloud:

Reading aloud can improve pronunciation, fluency, and overall vocal communication. It also helps you become more comfortable with expressing ideas verbally.

Clarify and Confirm:

When in doubt, clarify and confirm. Repeat key points, ask questions for clarification, and summarize discussions to ensure everyone is on the same page.

Mind Your Pace:

Be mindful of your speaking pace. Speak at a moderate pace, allowing others to absorb and comprehend your message without feeling rushed.

Cultural Sensitivity:

Consider cultural differences in communication styles. Be sensitive to diverse communication norms and adjust your approach accordingly.

Role Play:

Practice communication skills through role-playing scenarios. This helps you become more comfortable with different conversational situations.

Use Technology Wisely:

Leverage technology for communication improvement. Record and review your speeches or presentations to identify areas for enhancement.

Take Communication Courses:

Enroll in communication courses, either online or in-person. Many platforms offer courses on public speaking, effective writing, and interpersonal communication.

Read Widely:

Read a variety of materials, including books, articles, and blogs. Exposure to different writing styles and perspectives can improve your own communication skills.

Remember, improving communication is an ongoing process. Consistent practice and a willingness to learn from experiences contribute to continuous enhancement of your communication skills.

❋Examples of Communication with Clients

Communication with clients in freelancing is vital for project success and client satisfaction. Here are real-world scenarios and examples of effective communication with clients:

Setting Expectations:

Scenario: A client has hired you for graphic design. Before starting the project, it's crucial to set clear expectations.

Example: "Thank you for choosing me for your graphic design project. To ensure we're on the same page, let's discuss your vision, preferred style, and any specific elements you want to include. This will help me deliver a design that aligns with your expectations."

Project Updates:

Scenario: You're in the middle of a web development project, and the client is eager for updates.

Example: "I wanted to provide a quick update on the web development progress. The homepage is now complete, and we're moving on to the navigation structure. I'll share a preview shortly, and I welcome your feedback to ensure the final product meets your requirements."

Handling Changes in Scope:

Scenario: The client requests additional features not initially discussed.

Example: "I appreciate your desire to enhance the project with additional features. Before proceeding, let's discuss the impact on the timeline and budget. I want to ensure we align on the changes and make any necessary adjustments to our original agreement."

Addressing Delays:

Scenario: Unexpected delays occur due to unforeseen circumstances.

Example: "I wanted to inform you about a minor setback in the project timeline due to [specific reason]. I am actively working to minimize the impact, and I appreciate your understanding. If there are any concerns, please let me know, and we can discuss a revised timeline."

Handling Feedback:

Scenario: The client provides feedback on a delivered milestone.

Example: "Thank you for your detailed feedback on the first draft. I'll incorporate your suggestions to refine the project. If there are specific areas that need further adjustment, please let me know. I want to ensure the final result meets your expectations."

Project Completion:

Scenario: The project is complete, and it's time to deliver the final product.

Example: "I'm thrilled to share that your project is now complete. I've attached the final files, and I've included a summary of the work done. Please review and let me know if there are any final adjustments needed. I appreciate the opportunity to work on this project with you."

Asking for Testimonials:

Scenario: The project went well, and you want to request a testimonial for your portfolio.

Example: "I'm glad we could successfully complete the project. If you're satisfied with my work, I would appreciate it if you could provide a brief testimonial. Your feedback helps me grow as a freelancer, and it serves as a valuable reference for potential clients."

Follow-Up for Future Projects:

Scenario: The project has concluded, and you want to express interest in future collaboration.

Example: "It was a pleasure working on your project. If you have any future needs or projects, I'd be delighted to collaborate again. Let's keep the lines of communication open, and feel free to reach out whenever you're ready to discuss new opportunities."

In each scenario, the key is to maintain transparency, manage expectations, and foster a positive client relationship through effective and respectful communication.

Chapter 4: Ways of Freelancing

⇖⇑⇗ Ways of Freelancing

Freelancing encompasses a wide range of skills and industries, providing individuals with diverse opportunities to work independently and offer their services.

Here are different ways of freelancing across various domains:

1. Writing and Content Creation

Freelance writers play a crucial role in content creation, crafting engaging and informative material for various platforms. They contribute to blogs, websites, articles, and marketing materials, showcasing versatility in writing styles. Freelance writers often specialize in specific areas, such as copywriting, technical writing, creative writing, or content marketing. Their expertise allows businesses to communicate effectively with their target audience, whether it's through compelling website copy, informative blog posts, or strategic marketing content. The freelance writing landscape provides opportunities for writers to leverage their unique skills and contribute to the diverse and dynamic world of online and offline content.

2. Graphic Design

Graphic designers are creative professionals who provide services in crafting visual elements, encompassing tasks such as designing logos, creating branding materials, illustrating concepts, developing infographics, and contributing to website design. Operating on a project basis, graphic designers collaborate with clients to meet their visual communication needs, ensuring a visually appealing and cohesive representation of their brand or message. Their skills in visual storytelling and design play a vital role in enhancing the overall aesthetic and impact of various digital and print materials, contributing to the success of businesses and individuals seeking a strong visual presence.

3. Web Development and Design

Freelance web developers and designers specialize in the creation and maintenance of websites for clients, offering a range of services such as front-end development, back-end development, or providing full-stack development solutions. Their expertise lies in building and optimizing the functionality, design, and user experience of websites, tailoring their services to meet the specific needs and objectives of clients. By combining technical skills with a keen understanding of user interface and experience, freelance web developers and designers contribute to the development of visually appealing, responsive, and functional websites that effectively serve their clients' purposes in the digital landscape.

4. Programming and Software Development

Programmers and software developers in the freelance realm provide coding and programming services, specializing in languages such as Python, Java, JavaScript, or focusing on specific frameworks and technologies. Their expertise lies in translating conceptual ideas into functional and efficient software solutions. By leveraging their programming skills, these freelancers contribute to the development of applications, scripts, and software products that align with the unique requirements of their clients. Whether it's creating custom applications, optimizing existing code, or solving intricate technical challenges, freelance programmers and software developers play a crucial role in delivering tailored and effective solutions to meet the diverse needs of their clientele.

5. Digital Marketing

Freelancers specializing in digital marketing offer a range of services, including social media management, search engine optimization (SEO), email marketing, and online advertising. Their role is to assist businesses in improving their online presence, expanding their reach, and effectively engaging with their target audience. Whether it's devising strategic social media campaigns, optimizing website content for search engines, crafting compelling email marketing campaigns, or managing online advertising initiatives, these digital marketing freelancers contribute to enhancing a brand's visibility and driving online success for their clients.

6. Virtual Assistance

Virtual assistants play a crucial role in providing remote administrative support to clients. Their responsibilities encompass a wide range of tasks, including email management, scheduling, data entry, customer service, and various administrative duties. Working from a remote location, virtual assistants contribute to the smooth functioning of businesses by handling essential administrative functions, allowing clients to focus on their core activities. Whether it's organizing calendars, managing correspondence, or ensuring efficient data management, virtual assistants offer valuable support to clients seeking assistance with their day-to-day operations.

7. Social Media Management

Social media managers play a key role in overseeing and enhancing clients' social media presence. Their responsibilities include creating engaging content, scheduling posts, interacting with followers, and analyzing social media performance. By strategically managing social media accounts, these freelancers help businesses build and maintain a strong online presence, connect with their target audience, and achieve their marketing goals. With a focus on content strategy, engagement, and performance metrics, social media managers contribute to the effective utilization of social platforms for brand promotion and customer interaction.

8. Online Tutoring and Coaching

Freelancers in the education sector provide valuable tutoring or coaching services across a range of subjects or skills. Whether offering academic tutoring, language coaching, career guidance, or personal development coaching, these freelancers play a crucial role in helping individuals enhance their knowledge and skills. By tailoring their expertise to the specific needs of clients, education freelancers contribute to the learning and growth of others. Their services often extend beyond traditional academic support, encompassing various areas of personal and professional development. Through one-on-one sessions or specialized programs, education freelancers empower clients to achieve their learning goals and navigate challenges in their educational journey.

9. Photography and Videography

Freelance photographers and videographers offer their expertise in capturing compelling visual content for clients. Their services extend to various domains, including documenting events, creating promotional videos, and producing multimedia content to enhance marketing efforts. Through their artistic and technical skills, these freelancers contribute to the visual storytelling of brands, events, and individuals. Whether it's capturing memorable moments or producing engaging videos, freelance photographers and videographers play a vital role in helping clients communicate their messages effectively through visually appealing and impactful content.

10.Consulting and Advisory Services

Consultants serve as experts in specific industries or domains, offering valuable advice and solutions to clients. Their services encompass a wide range of areas, including business consulting, financial guidance, marketing strategy consulting, and more. Freelance consultants leverage their extensive knowledge and experience to provide insights and recommendations tailored to their clients' needs.

Whether assisting with business development, financial planning, or strategic marketing, these professionals play a crucial role in helping clients make informed decisions and achieve their goals through specialized expertise and consultancy services.

11.Translation and Language Services

Freelance translators and language experts specialize in providing translation services for written content, audio, or video. Their expertise covers a wide range of languages and industries, allowing them to bridge communication gaps and ensure accurate and culturally appropriate translations for their clients. Whether translating documents, websites, or multimedia content, these professionals play a crucial role in facilitating effective communication across diverse linguistic contexts.

Through their linguistic skills and cultural understanding, freelance translators contribute to breaking down language barriers and fostering global communication in various fields and industries.

12.E-commerce Services

Many freelancers in e-commerce specialize in providing services related to online selling platforms. They play a key role in helping businesses thrive in the digital marketplace by offering services such as product listing, market research, e-commerce website development, and digital marketing.

Whether it's optimizing product listings for better visibility, conducting market research to identify trends, designing and developing user-friendly e-commerce websites, or implementing digital marketing strategies to drive online sales, these freelancers contribute to the success of e-commerce ventures. Their expertise in navigating the complexities of online retail platforms and understanding consumer behavior online makes them valuable assets for businesses looking to establish and grow their presence in the e-commerce space.

13.Animation and Multimedia Services

Animators and multimedia artists are skilled professionals who specialize in creating captivating visual content, including animated videos and 3D models, for clients across various industries such as entertainment, advertising, and education. Their expertise lies in bringing ideas to life through the use of animation, visual effects, and multimedia elements. Whether it's crafting animated characters for entertainment purposes, developing engaging advertisements with dynamic visuals, or creating educational content with interactive multimedia components, these freelancers contribute to the visual appeal and storytelling aspects of diverse projects. Their creative talents and technical skills make them valuable collaborators in projects that require a dynamic and visually striking presentation.

14.Legal and Financial Services

Freelance legal and financial professionals, including lawyers, accountants, and financial advisors, provide specialized expertise on a project or advisory basis. These professionals bring their legal and financial knowledge to the table, offering valuable insights and services to clients seeking assistance in navigating legal complexities or managing financial matters. Whether it's providing legal counsel, handling accounting tasks, or offering financial planning advice, these freelancers play a crucial role in helping individuals and businesses make informed decisions within the legal and financial realms.

Their flexible and project-based approach allows clients to access specific expertise as needed, making them essential contributors to the success and compliance of various ventures.

15.Health and Wellness Services

Freelancers in the health and wellness industry offer a range of services aimed at promoting overall well-being. This includes fitness training, nutrition coaching, mental health counseling, and holistic wellness coaching. These freelancers help individuals achieve their health goals, whether it's improving physical fitness, adopting a healthier diet, managing stress, or addressing mental health concerns. Their expertise contributes to the holistic health of their clients, fostering positive lifestyle changes and promoting a balanced approach to well-being. With the flexibility to offer services remotely or in-person, freelancers in the health and wellness sector play a vital role in supporting individuals on their journey to a healthier and more fulfilling life.

These are just a few examples, and the freelance landscape is continually evolving with new opportunities emerging in response to market demands and technological advancements. Freelancers can choose the niche that aligns with their skills, interests, and expertise to create a successful and fulfilling freelance career.

🏆 Wining Your Client's Trust

Building trust with clients is crucial for a successful and enduring freelancing relationship. Maintain transparent and open communication from the start. Clearly articulate your services, processes, and expectations. Respond promptly to messages and inquiries, showing your commitment to the project.

Demonstrate professionalism in all interactions. Use proper language, adhere to deadlines, and present yourself as a reliable and dedicated freelancer. Consistency in your behavior builds a trustworthy image. Take the time to thoroughly understand your client's needs and expectations. Ask insightful questions to ensure you have a comprehensive understanding of the project requirements. Deliver high-quality work that exceeds expectations. Consistently providing value reinforces your expertise and dedication, fostering trust in your abilities.

Honor project deadlines. Timely delivery not only showcases your reliability but also instills confidence in your commitment to the client's project. Clearly outline your pricing structure and terms in the initial stages of discussion. Avoid hidden fees or unexpected charges. Transparency in financial matters builds trust. Keep your client informed about project progress with regular updates. This includes milestones achieved, any challenges encountered, and proactive communication about potential delays.

Everyone makes mistakes. If an error occurs, address it professionally. Acknowledge the mistake, propose solutions, and assure the client that you are committed to rectifying the situation. Show respect for your client's opinions and suggestions. Actively listen to their feedback, incorporate constructive input, and make them feel valued as a collaborator in the project.

Educate your client about your process, the industry, or any technical aspects related to the project. This demonstrates your expertise and helps build trust in your capabilities. Maintain a consistent brand image across your communication channels. This includes your freelancing platform profile, website, and email correspondence. A cohesive brand presentation enhances credibility. Showcase positive client testimonials and a strong portfolio. Evidence of past successful collaborations acts as social proof, instilling confidence in potential clients.

Assure clients of the security measures you have in place to protect their information. This is especially relevant for projects involving sensitive data. Be realistic about what you can deliver and when. Setting achievable expectations helps prevent disappointments and builds trust in your reliability. Surprise your clients by going above and beyond their expectations. This could be delivering ahead of schedule, providing additional resources, or offering a small bonus service. Such efforts leave a lasting positive impression. By consistently embodying these principles, you can establish a foundation of trust with your clients, leading to long-term relationships and potential referrals.

💰 Charging High Price to Freelance Clients.

Charging more for your freelance services involves a combination of

- showcasing your value,

- effective communication, and

- positioning yourself as an expert in your field.

Here are strategies to charge higher rates to your freelance clients:

1. Build a Strong Portfolio:

Showcase a diverse and impressive portfolio that highlights your best work. Include case studies, testimonials, and examples that demonstrate the value you've provided to past clients. A strong portfolio establishes your credibility and justifies higher rates.

2. Demonstrate Expertise:

Position yourself as an expert in your niche. Share your knowledge through blog posts, articles, or social media. When clients perceive you as an authority, they are more likely to pay a premium for your specialized skills.

3. Continuously Upgrade Your Skills:

Stay updated with industry trends and invest in ongoing education. The more skills you acquire, the more valuable you become. Clients are willing to pay more for freelancers who offer a comprehensive skill set.

4. Effective Communication:

Clearly communicate the unique value you bring to the table. Explain how your services can solve specific problems for the client or contribute to their business growth. Articulate your expertise and the benefits clients will gain by choosing you.

5. Establish a Professional Brand:

Develop a professional brand that reflects your expertise. This includes a polished website, a well-crafted bio, and consistent branding across all platforms. A professional image can justify higher rates.

6. Provide Exceptional Customer Service:

Deliver exceptional customer service at every touchpoint. Respond promptly to inquiries, go the extra mile to exceed expectations, and ensure a positive client experience. Satisfied clients are more likely to value your services and be willing to pay premium rates.

7. Offer Customized Solutions:

Tailor your services to meet the unique needs of each client. By providing customized solutions, clients see the added value in your work, justifying higher rates compared to generic offerings.

8. Highlight Results and Impact:

Emphasize the results and impact of your work rather than just listing skills. Clients are more willing to invest in freelancers who can demonstrate a positive impact on their projects or business outcomes.

9. Charge by Value, Not by Hour:

Instead of charging by the hour, consider charging based on the value you provide. If your work significantly contributes to a client's success or revenue, clients may be more open to paying a premium for that value.

10.Networking and Referrals:

Network with industry professionals and build strong relationships. Referrals from satisfied clients or colleagues can lead to higher-paying opportunities. A positive word-of-mouth reputation enhances your perceived value.

11.Offer Premium Packages:

Develop premium service packages with additional benefits. This could include expedited delivery, extended support, or exclusive access to certain resources. Premium packages give clients options and justify higher rates for added value.

12.Negotiate with Confidence:

Approach rate negotiations with confidence. Clearly articulate why your rates are justified based on your skills, experience, and the value you bring. Be firm but open to compromise when necessary.

13.Stay Updated on Market Rates:

Know the current market rates for your services. This knowledge allows you to position yourself competitively while justifying rates that align with your expertise.

14.Limit Availability:

Create a sense of exclusivity by limiting your availability. If clients perceive that your time is in demand, they may be more willing to pay a premium for your services.

Remember, charging higher rates is not just about the numbers; it's about communicating your value effectively and establishing a reputation that justifies premium pricing.

Chapter 5: Setting Yourself Apart in the Freelance Arena

In the competitive realm of freelancing, distinguishing yourself is not just a choice; it's a necessity.

Setting yourself apart in the freelance arena requires a unique blend of skills, a commitment to exceptional communication, and a personalized approach to every project.

It's not merely about delivering a service; it's about crafting an experience that clients remember.

Whether it's showcasing an unparalleled skill set, mastering the art of effective communication, or consistently delivering beyond expectations, freelancers who stand out understand that they are not just offering a service—they are building lasting relationships and earning trust.

In this chapter, we delve into the strategies and mindset that can elevate your freelancing journey from ordinary to extraordinary.

⌕ Level of Skill

As a freelancer, setting yourself apart often hinges on your level of skill and expertise.

Here are ways in which your skill level can distinguish you:

1) Specialized Expertise:

Possessing a high level of expertise in a specific niche or industry sets you apart. Clients are often drawn to freelancers who have a deep understanding of their particular needs and can provide specialized solutions.

2) Advanced Technical Skills:

Mastery of advanced technical skills in your field can be a significant differentiator. Whether it's advanced programming languages, design software, or cutting-edge technologies, a high skill level positions you as a valuable asset for complex projects.

3) Portfolio Quality:

The quality of your portfolio speaks volumes about your skill level. Showcase your best work, emphasizing the diversity and complexity of projects you've successfully completed. A strong portfolio builds credibility and attracts clients seeking top-tier talent.

4) Innovative Problem Solving:

Your ability to creatively and effectively solve problems is a key indicator of your skill level. Clients appreciate freelancers who bring innovative solutions to the table, especially when faced with challenging projects.

5) Continuous Learning:

Demonstrating a commitment to continuous learning and staying updated with industry trends showcases a proactive approach to skill development. This adaptability is attractive to clients seeking freelancers who can navigate evolving landscapes.

6) Efficiency and Productivity:

A high level of skill often translates into increased efficiency and productivity. Completing projects in a timely manner without compromising quality positions you as a reliable and skilled freelancer.

7) Industry Recognition:

Recognition within your industry, such as awards, certifications, or mentions in relevant publications, can elevate your profile. Industry recognition is a powerful testament to your expertise.

8) Client Testimonials:

Positive testimonials from satisfied clients highlight your skill in delivering exceptional results. These testimonials serve as social proof of your capabilities and can influence potential clients in their decision-making process.

9) Consistent High-Quality Work:

Consistency in delivering high-quality work across projects is a hallmark of a skilled freelancer. Clients value reliability and know they can trust you to consistently meet or exceed their expectations.

10) Effective Communication of Skills:

Clearly and confidently communicating your skills to potential clients is crucial. Clearly articulate your expertise, outlining how your skills align with the client's needs and how you can add value to their projects.

11) Problem Prevention:

A highly skilled freelancer not only solves problems but also anticipates and prevents them. Proactively addressing potential challenges demonstrates foresight and enhances your reputation as a dependable professional.

12) Leadership in Projects:

Taking a leadership role in projects, providing guidance, and offering strategic insights showcase not only your technical skills but also your ability to contribute to the overall success of a project.

In the competitive freelancing landscape, emphasizing and continuously improving your skill set is a fundamental strategy for standing out and attracting clients who value expertise and excellence.

💬 Communication Skills

Exceptional communication skills are a powerful asset that can set you apart as a freelancer. Here's how effective communication skills can distinguish you in the freelancing landscape:

1) Clear and Transparent Communication:

Articulating ideas and project details clearly helps in avoiding misunderstandings. Clients appreciate freelancers who communicate transparently, ensuring everyone is on the same page regarding project scope, timelines, and expectations.

2) Active Listening:

Being an active listener demonstrates your commitment to understanding client needs. By actively listening to client feedback and requirements, you can tailor your approach to better meet their expectations.

3) Client Relationship Building:

Strong communication fosters positive client relationships. Establishing a rapport through clear and friendly communication helps build trust and can lead to long-term partnerships and repeat business.

4) Effective Email and Written Communication:

Well-crafted emails and written communication contribute to a professional image. Attention to detail, proper grammar, and a respectful tone in written communication enhance your overall professionalism.

5) Timely Response:

Responding promptly to client messages and inquiries demonstrates your reliability and commitment to the project. Clients appreciate freelancers who are attentive and responsive, especially during critical project phases.

6) Adaptability in Communication Styles:

Tailoring your communication style to suit the preferences of different clients showcases adaptability. Some clients prefer detailed updates, while others may appreciate concise summaries. Being adaptable ensures effective communication across diverse personalities.

7) Conflict Resolution:

Addressing conflicts professionally and diplomatically is a key communication skill. Freelancers who can navigate challenges and resolve conflicts with clients demonstrate maturity and problem-solving capabilities.

8) Client Education:

Many clients may not be familiar with the freelancer's industry or process. Communicating complex concepts in an accessible manner demonstrates your expertise and helps clients understand the value of your work.

9) Presentation Skills:

If your work involves presenting ideas or project updates, strong presentation skills are valuable. A clear and engaging presentation style can leave a lasting positive impression on clients.

10) Negotiation Skills:

Effective negotiation is a subset of communication skills. Freelancers who can negotiate project terms, timelines, and rates professionally and persuasively are more likely to secure favorable agreements.

11) Crisis Communication:

In the event of unexpected challenges or setbacks, communicating effectively during times of crisis is crucial. Clients appreciate freelancers who can provide transparent updates and propose solutions when facing difficulties.

12) Clarity in Setting Expectations:

Clearly setting expectations at the beginning of a project contributes to its success. Communicate what clients can expect in terms of deliverables, timelines, and potential challenges to avoid surprises later on.

13) Language Fluency:

Proficiency in the language(s) of communication, especially if you work with international clients, is essential. Clear and fluent communication builds confidence in your ability to deliver quality work.

14) Empathy and Understanding:

Demonstrating empathy and understanding of clients' concerns or challenges fosters a positive working relationship. Clients appreciate freelancers who are not only skilled but also empathetic to their needs.

By consistently honing and leveraging your communication skills, you position yourself as a reliable, professional, and client-focused freelancer, which can contribute significantly to your success in the freelance marketplace.

✈ Speed of Response

The speed of your response as a freelancer is a critical factor that can set you apart from others. Here's how a swift response time can distinguish you in the freelancing arena:

1) Client Impressions:

Responding promptly to client inquiries creates a positive first impression. Clients appreciate freelancers who are attentive and demonstrate a sense of urgency in addressing their needs.

2) Project Timeliness:

Quick response times often translate to efficient project management. Clients value freelancers who can communicate and make decisions promptly, leading to smoother project timelines and faster delivery.

3) Competitive Edge:

In a competitive freelancing market, being the first to respond to a job posting or client inquiry gives you a competitive edge. It signals your enthusiasm and commitment to the opportunity.

4) Client Confidence:

Rapid responses build client confidence. Clients feel reassured when they know they can reach you quickly for updates, clarifications, or in case of any issues. This confidence contributes to a positive client-freelancer relationship.

5) Communication Efficiency:

Efficient communication is a hallmark of a professional freelancer. Quick responses streamline communication channels, making it easier for clients to convey their requirements and for you to gather the necessary information.

6) Problem Resolution:

Swift response times are crucial in addressing problems or challenges that may arise during a project. Proactively addressing issues demonstrates your commitment to finding solutions and maintaining project momentum.

7) Availability and Accessibility:

A fast response indicates your availability and accessibility. Clients often prefer freelancers who are responsive, as it gives them assurance that you are actively engaged in their project and can be reached when needed.

8) Increased Opportunities:

Quick responses increase your chances of securing opportunities. Whether it's replying to job postings, client inquiries, or collaboration invitations, being prompt can make the difference between being considered or overlooked.

9) Positive Client Experience:

A swift response contributes to an overall positive client experience. Clients remember freelancers who are easy to communicate with and responsive, leading to potential repeat business or referrals.

10) Building Trust:

Trust is foundational in freelancing relationships. Rapid responses build trust by demonstrating reliability and professionalism. Clients are more likely to trust a freelancer who is prompt in communication.

11) Differentiation from Competitors:

Many freelancers may possess similar skills, but a quick response time can differentiate you from competitors. It highlights your commitment to client satisfaction and efficient collaboration.

12) Adaptability:

Rapid responses showcase your adaptability in a fast-paced environment. Whether it's adapting to changing project requirements or addressing client queries, being quick on your feet is a valuable trait.

The speed of your response is a tangible and impactful aspect of your freelancing approach. By prioritizing swift and efficient communication, you position yourself as a proactive, reliable, and client-focused freelancer in a competitive market.

✦Professional Behavior

Maintaining professional behavior is a key aspect that can set you apart as a freelancer. Here's how your professionalism can distinguish you in the freelancing landscape:

1) Reliability:

Consistently meeting deadlines and delivering high-quality work demonstrates reliability. Clients value freelancers who can be depended on to complete projects on time and with excellence.

2) Clear Communication:

Professional behavior includes clear and transparent communication. Articulating ideas, project updates, and expectations in a professional manner fosters a positive working relationship with clients.

3) Adherence to Guidelines:

Following project guidelines and client instructions meticulously showcases your professionalism. Clients appreciate freelancers who pay attention to detail and align their work with the agreed-upon specifications.

4) Ethical Standards:

Upholding ethical standards in your work and interactions builds trust with clients. Professional freelancers maintain integrity, avoid plagiarism, and prioritize honesty in all aspects of their freelance work.

5) Client-Centric Approach:

A professional freelancer places the client's needs at the forefront. Taking a client-centric approach involves understanding their requirements, addressing concerns promptly, and tailoring your services to meet their goals.

6) Politeness and Respect:

Professionalism extends to how you interact with clients and colleagues. Using polite and respectful language, even in challenging situations, contributes to a positive professional image.

7) Confidentiality:

Respecting client confidentiality is a crucial aspect of professionalism. Freelancers who prioritize the security and privacy of client information demonstrate trustworthiness.

8) Continuous Improvement:

A commitment to continuous learning and improvement showcases your dedication to staying current in your field. Professional freelancers actively seek opportunities for skill development and stay updated on industry trends.

9) Problem-Solving Skills:

Professional behavior involves approaching challenges with a problem-solving mindset. Instead of dwelling on issues, professional freelancers actively seek solutions, demonstrating resilience and adaptability.

10) Setting and Managing Expectations:

Professional freelancers excel in setting realistic expectations and managing them effectively. Clearly communicating project timelines, potential challenges, and deliverables contributes to a smooth client experience.

11) Punctuality:

Meeting deadlines and adhering to schedules is a hallmark of professional behavior. Punctuality reflects your commitment to respecting the client's time and project milestones.

12) Accountability:

Taking ownership of your work and being accountable for both successes and challenges contributes to a professional demeanor. Clients appreciate freelancers who are transparent about their contributions to the project.

13) Positive Attitude:

Maintaining a positive attitude, even in the face of challenges, is a professional attribute. Positivity fosters a healthy working relationship and contributes to a collaborative and constructive project environment.

14) Client Education:

Professional freelancers educate clients about their processes, methodologies, and industry best practices. Providing insights helps clients better understand the value of your work and enhances the overall professional experience.

15) Cultural Sensitivity:

Acknowledging and respecting cultural differences is an important aspect of professionalism, especially when working with clients from diverse backgrounds. Cultural sensitivity contributes to effective communication and collaboration.

By embodying these professional behaviors, you position yourself as a freelancer who is not only skilled in your field but also dedicated to providing a positive and reliable client experience. Professionalism is a powerful differentiator in the competitive freelancing market.

⧉ Presenting Your Work

Effectively presenting your work is a crucial skill that can set you apart as a freelancer. Here's how your presentation style can distinguish you in the freelancing landscape:

1) Visual Appeal:

Create visually appealing presentations that showcase your work in a professional manner. Use high-quality graphics, clear images, and well-designed layouts to make a positive first impression.

2) Storytelling:

Craft a compelling narrative around your work. Storytelling helps clients understand the context, challenges, and solutions involved in your projects, making your work more relatable and engaging.

3) Clarity of Purpose:

Clearly articulate the purpose of your work. Define the problem you addressed, the solution you provided, and the impact it had. Clients appreciate freelancers who can communicate the value of their work concisely.

4) Demonstration of Results:

Highlight the tangible results of your work. Whether it's increased website traffic, improved conversion rates, or any measurable outcome, providing evidence of your impact reinforces the value you bring to clients.

5) Case Studies:

Develop case studies that delve into the details of specific projects. Case studies allow you to showcase your process, challenges faced, and the successful outcomes, providing clients with a deeper understanding of your capabilities.

6) Interactive Presentations:

Consider using interactive elements in your presentations. This could include clickable prototypes, live demonstrations, or engaging multimedia components. Interactive presentations captivate the audience and enhance understanding.

7) Client Testimonials:

Incorporate client testimonials within your presentation. Positive feedback from previous clients adds credibility to your work and reinforces the satisfaction of those you've collaborated with.

8) Highlighting Unique Approaches:

Showcase any unique or innovative approaches you took in your projects. Clients are drawn to freelancers who bring creative and distinctive solutions to the table.

9) Adaptability in Presentation Styles:

Tailor your presentation style to match the preferences of different clients. Some may prefer formal, detailed presentations, while others may appreciate a more casual and conversational approach. Being adaptable showcases your awareness of client needs.

10) Addressing Challenges:

Be transparent about any challenges you encountered during the project and how you overcame them. Clients appreciate freelancers who can navigate obstacles and find effective solutions.

11) Visual Before-and-After:

Incorporate visual before-and-after comparisons to demonstrate the transformation your work achieved. This can be particularly effective in design, marketing, and other visual-based projects.

12) Conciseness and Focus:

Keep your presentations concise and focused. Avoid unnecessary details that may dilute the main message. Clients value freelancers who can communicate efficiently without overwhelming them with information.

13) Client-Centric Approach:

Present your work in a way that resonates with the client's goals and objectives. Emphasize how your work aligns with their vision and contributes to the overall success of their business or project.

14) Accessibility:

Ensure your presentations are accessible and easily shareable. Clients may want to review your work with their team or stakeholders, so providing user-friendly formats contributes to a positive experience.

15) Continuous Improvement:

Demonstrate a commitment to continuous improvement in your presentation skills. Solicit feedback from clients, analyze the effectiveness of your presentations, and make adjustments for future projects.

By mastering the art of presenting your work, you position yourself as a freelancer who not only produces excellent results but can also effectively communicate and showcase the value of your contributions.

💾 Defining Project Deliverables

The ability to effectively define project deliverables is a key competency that can set you apart as a freelancer. Here's how your proficiency in this area can distinguish you in the freelancing landscape:

1. **Clear and Detailed Scope:**

Provide a clear and detailed scope of work, outlining the specific tasks and objectives of the project. Clients appreciate freelancers who can articulate project parameters comprehensively.

2. SMART Goals:

Define project deliverables using SMART criteria (Specific, Measurable, Achievable, Relevant, Time-bound). This ensures that both you and the client have a clear understanding of what success looks like and how progress will be measured.

3. Client Collaboration:

Collaborate with the client in defining project deliverables. Solicit their input and ensure alignment between your understanding of the project scope and their expectations. This collaborative approach builds trust and reduces the likelihood of misunderstandings.

4. Prioritization of Deliverables:

Clearly prioritize project deliverables based on their importance and impact. This helps in managing client expectations and ensures that essential tasks are given the attention they deserve.

5. Detailed Timelines:

Establish detailed timelines for each deliverable, including milestones and deadlines. A well-structured timeline allows both you and the client to track progress and ensures that the project stays on schedule.

6. Interactive Prototypes or Mockups:

Depending on the nature of the project, provide interactive prototypes or mockups to visually represent deliverables. This helps clients visualize the final outcome and provides an opportunity for feedback before the project progresses too far.

7. Regular Progress Updates:

Commit to providing regular progress updates on project deliverables. Clients value freelancers who keep them informed about the status of each task and any challenges that may arise.

8. Flexibility and Adaptability:

Demonstrate flexibility in adapting project deliverables based on client feedback or changing project requirements. Being responsive to client needs showcases your commitment to delivering outcomes that align with their goals.

9. Risk Management:

Anticipate potential risks related to project deliverables and outline strategies for mitigating them. Proactive risk management demonstrates foresight and a commitment to ensuring the successful completion of the project.

10. Quality Assurance Standards:

Clearly define and adhere to quality assurance standards for each deliverable. Clients appreciate freelancers who prioritize the quality of work and take steps to ensure that deliverables meet or exceed expectations.

11. Client Involvement in Approval Process:

Involve the client in the approval process for each deliverable. This ensures that the client has the opportunity to provide feedback and sign off on completed tasks, fostering a collaborative working relationship.

12. Documentation of Deliverables:

Maintain thorough documentation for each deliverable. This includes specifications, user guides, or any relevant documentation that helps the client understand the functionality and use of the completed work.

13. Measurable Outcomes:

Clearly define how the success of each deliverable will be measured. Whether it's increased website traffic, enhanced user engagement, or other metrics, establishing measurable outcomes provides a basis for evaluating project success.

14. Post-Project Support:

Outline any post-project support or maintenance services related to deliverables. Offering ongoing support demonstrates a commitment to the client's satisfaction beyond the completion of the initial project.

15. Client Education:

Educate the client about the technical aspects of project deliverables, especially if they may not be familiar with certain processes or technologies. This helps in creating a shared understanding of the project's intricacies.

By excelling in the definition of project deliverables, you position yourself as a freelancer who is thorough, client-focused, and capable of delivering tangible results. This competence is integral to successful project management and client satisfaction.

Chapter 6: Mistakes and Problems in Freelancing

Embarking on a freelancing journey is an exhilarating adventure filled with opportunities for growth and success. However, like any pursuit, it comes with its share of challenges and pitfalls. In this chapter, we explore the common mistakes and problems that freelancers often encounter and, more importantly, how to navigate through them.

From the intricacies of project selection to the delicate balance of pricing oneself, freelancers face a myriad of decisions that can shape their careers.

By understanding these challenges and learning from the experiences of others, freelancers can transform setbacks into stepping stones toward a more resilient and rewarding freelancing career.

Join us as we delve into the nuanced landscape of freelancing, uncovering valuable insights that can turn stumbling blocks into building blocks for success.

☺ Which Project Should You Take?

The decision of which projects to take is a common challenge for freelancers.

Here are some mistakes and problems that freelancers often face when navigating this decision:

1. Overcommitting:

Mistake: Accepting too many projects simultaneously.

Problem: Overcommitting can lead to burnout, reduced quality of work, and missed deadlines.

2. Lack of Clarity:

Mistake: Accepting projects without a clear understanding of the client's expectations.

Problem: A lack of clarity can result in misalignment between the freelancer and client, leading to dissatisfaction and potential project disputes.

3. Ignoring Scope Creep:

Mistake: Failing to address scope creep (uncontrolled changes or additions to the project scope).

Problem: Scope creep can extend project timelines, increase workload, and strain client relationships.

4. Ignoring Red Flags:

Mistake: Ignoring warning signs or red flags during client interactions.

Problem: Ignoring red flags, such as difficult communication or unclear project requirements, can lead to problematic client relationships and project difficulties.

5. Underestimating Time and Effort:

Mistake: Underestimating the time and effort required for a project.

Problem: Underestimation can lead to rushed work, missed deadlines, and a negative impact on the freelancer's reputation.

6. Not Researching Clients:

Mistake: Accepting projects without researching the client's background or reputation.

Problem: Working with unreliable clients can result in payment issues, disputes, or a negative impact on the freelancer's portfolio.

7. Taking on Low-Paying Projects:

Mistake: Accepting projects with inadequate compensation.

Problem: Low-paying projects can undermine the freelancer's earning potential and may not justify the time and effort invested.

8. Ignoring Skill Misalignment:

Mistake: Taking on projects that are not aligned with the freelancer's skill set.

Problem: Working on projects outside of one's expertise can lead to subpar results and dissatisfaction for both the freelancer and the client.

9. Failure to Set Boundaries:

Mistake: Not establishing clear boundaries with clients regarding communication, revisions, and project scope.

Problem: Without boundaries, freelancers may face excessive client demands, frequent scope changes, and difficulties in managing expectations.

10. Ignoring Gut Feelings:

Mistake: Ignoring intuition or gut feelings about a potential project.

Problem: Gut feelings often indicate underlying issues, and ignoring them may lead to challenging client relationships or project complications.

11. Failure to Diversify Portfolio:

Mistake: Specializing too narrowly or not diversifying the types of projects accepted.

Problem: Lack of portfolio diversity may limit opportunities and make freelancers vulnerable to market fluctuations in specific industries.

12. Inadequate Contractual Agreements:

Mistake: Failing to establish clear contractual agreements with clients.

Problem: Without proper contracts, freelancers may face challenges related to payment, project scope, and dispute resolution.

To navigate these challenges, freelancers should prioritize effective communication with clients, conduct thorough project assessments, set clear boundaries, and continually evaluate the alignment between their skills and the projects they accept. Establishing a strategic approach to project selection is crucial for long-term success in freelancing.

🖚 Mistakes in Pricing Yourself

Determining the right pricing strategy is a common challenge for freelancers.

Here are some mistakes and problems freelancers often encounter when pricing themselves:

Underpricing:

Mistake: Setting prices too low to attract clients.

Problem: Underpricing undervalues the freelancer's skills, can lead to financial strain, and may attract clients who don't appreciate the true worth of the work.

Failure to Account for Expenses:

Mistake: Neglecting to factor in all business-related expenses when setting prices.

Problem: Failing to account for expenses can result in insufficient income to cover costs such as software subscriptions, equipment, and other overheads.

Ignoring Market Rates:

Mistake: Setting prices without researching industry or market rates.

Problem: Ignoring market rates can lead to prices that are too high, driving away potential clients, or too low, undercutting the freelancer's earning potential.

Inconsistent Pricing:

Mistake: Offering inconsistent pricing to different clients for similar services.

Problem: Inconsistent pricing can create confusion, erode client trust, and lead to disputes.

Not Valuing Experience:

Mistake: Failing to consider years of experience and expertise when determining prices.

Problem: Not valuing experience can result in undercharging for the value a seasoned freelancer brings to a project.

Discounting Too Quickly:

Mistake: Offering discounts without careful consideration.

Problem: Frequent or excessive discounts can devalue the freelancer's work and erode profit margins.

Ignoring Time Investment:

Mistake: Not factoring in the time invested in skill development and ongoing learning.

Problem: Ignoring the time investment can lead to pricing that doesn't reflect the freelancer's expertise and continuous improvement.

Overlooking Competitive Analysis:

Mistake: Failing to analyze competitors' pricing strategies.

Problem: Overlooking competitive analysis can result in setting prices that are out of sync with industry standards and client expectations.

Overestimating Value Perception:

Mistake: Assuming clients will automatically perceive the value of services at a higher price point.

Problem: Overestimating value perception may result in losing potential clients to competitors with more competitive pricing.

Not Communicating Value Clearly:

Mistake: Failing to effectively communicate the value of services to clients.

Problem: If clients don't understand the value they receive, they may perceive prices as too high, leading to negotiation challenges.

Ignoring Project Complexity:

Mistake: Charging a flat rate without considering the complexity of the project.

Problem: Ignoring project complexity can lead to underestimating the time and effort required for certain tasks, impacting profitability.

Lack of Flexibility:

Mistake: Adopting a rigid pricing structure without considering client budgets or project scopes.

Problem: Lack of flexibility may deter potential clients with specific budget constraints, leading to missed opportunities.

Navigating these pricing challenges requires freelancers to conduct thorough market research, consider their experience and expertise, communicate value effectively, and develop a pricing strategy that aligns with their business goals and the market dynamics. Regularly reassessing and adjusting pricing strategies based on industry trends and client feedback is essential for long-term success.

🕐 Mistakes and Problems in Calculating Hours

Calculating hours is a crucial aspect of freelancing, and freelancers often encounter challenges in this process. Here are some common mistakes and problems freelancers may face when calculating hours:

Underestimating Time:

Mistake: Underestimating the amount of time, a project or task will take.

Problem: Underestimation can lead to overcommitment, missed deadlines, and a negative impact on the freelancer's schedule.

Failure to Track Time Accurately:

Mistake: Not tracking time accurately or consistently.

Problem: Inaccurate time tracking can result in billing discrepancies, disputes with clients, and challenges in assessing project profitability.

Multitasking Challenges:

Mistake: Attempting to multitask without accurately allocating time to each task.

Problem: Multitasking can lead to time inefficiencies, reduced focus, and difficulty in accurately tracking the time spent on individual tasks.

Excluding Non-Billable Time:

Mistake: Neglecting to account for non-billable time, such as administrative tasks, client communication, or professional development.

Problem: Excluding non-billable time can result in an inaccurate representation of the freelancer's overall workload and may impact pricing strategies.

Ignoring Breaks and Rest:

Mistake: Neglecting to include breaks and rest periods in the calculation of billable hours.

Problem: Ignoring breaks can lead to burnout, decreased productivity, and an overall negative impact on the freelancer's well-being.

Inconsistent Time Tracking Methods:

Mistake: Using inconsistent methods or tools for time tracking.

Problem: Inconsistency in time tracking methods can lead to confusion, errors in invoicing, and challenges in analyzing time data for project improvement.

Scope Creep Challenges:

Mistake: Failing to monitor and account for scope creep in ongoing projects.

Problem: Scope creep can result in additional hours worked without corresponding compensation, impacting the freelancer's profitability.

Not Communicating Time Constraints:

Mistake: Failing to communicate realistic time constraints to clients.

Problem: Lack of clear communication can lead to misunderstandings, missed expectations, and potential conflicts with clients.

Overworking:

Mistake: Consistently working long hours without proper breaks or time off.

Problem: Overworking can lead to fatigue, decreased productivity, and long-term health issues, impacting the freelancer's overall well-being.

Inefficient Time Management:

Mistake: Poor time management practices, such as procrastination or lack of prioritization.

Problem: Inefficient time management can result in missed deadlines, rushed work, and increased stress levels.

Failure to Learn from Time Data:

Mistake: Neglecting to analyze time data for insights into productivity and efficiency.

Problem: Without learning from time data, freelancers miss opportunities for process improvement and optimization.

Inadequate Planning:

Mistake: Starting a project without a clear plan or timeline.

Problem: Inadequate planning can lead to chaos, missed milestones, and challenges in delivering work on schedule.

To overcome these challenges, freelancers should prioritize accurate time tracking, use reliable tools or software, communicate effectively with clients about time constraints, and regularly assess and improve their time management strategies. Adopting a proactive and strategic approach to time calculation contributes to a freelancer's efficiency, work-life balance, and overall success in the freelancing landscape.

🔔 Managing Time

Time management is a common challenge for freelancers. Here are some mistakes and problems that freelancers often face in managing their time, along with solutions:

1. Lack of Prioritization:

Mistake: Not prioritizing tasks effectively.

Problem: Without clear priorities, freelancers may spend too much time on less critical tasks, leading to delays in crucial project milestones.

Solution: Prioritize tasks based on urgency and importance. Use techniques like the Eisenhower Matrix to categorize tasks as urgent/important, important/not urgent, urgent/not important, or neither.

2. Procrastination:

Mistake: Procrastinating on important tasks.

Problem: Procrastination can lead to rushed work, missed deadlines, and increased stress.

Solution: Break larger tasks into smaller, more manageable steps. Set specific deadlines for each step, use productivity techniques like the Pomodoro Technique, and identify and address the root causes of procrastination.

3. Inefficient Time Tracking:

Mistake: Using inefficient or inconsistent time tracking methods.

Problem: Inaccurate time tracking can lead to billing discrepancies and challenges in assessing project profitability.

Solution: Use reliable time tracking tools or apps to monitor work hours accurately. Establish consistent habits for tracking billable and non-billable time, including breaks and administrative tasks.

4. Overcommitting:

Mistake: Taking on too many projects simultaneously.

Problem: Overcommitting can lead to burnout, reduced quality of work, and missed deadlines.

Solution: Set realistic expectations for project timelines and workloads. Learn to say no when necessary and communicate transparently with clients about realistic delivery timelines.

5. Failure to Set Boundaries:

Mistake: Failing to establish clear boundaries with clients and with personal time.

Problem: Without boundaries, freelancers may face excessive demands, affecting work-life balance and overall well-being.

Solution: Communicate clear working hours, response times, and project scope to clients. Establish dedicated workspaces and schedule regular breaks to maintain a healthy balance.

6. Ignoring Breaks:

Mistake: Skipping breaks or not taking enough time off.

Problem: Ignoring breaks can lead to burnout, decreased productivity, and overall dissatisfaction with freelancing.

Solution: Schedule regular breaks to recharge. Incorporate leisure activities into your routine, and consider taking planned vacations to prevent burnout.

7. Inadequate Planning:

Mistake: Starting projects without a clear plan or timeline.

Problem: Inadequate planning can result in chaos, missed milestones, and challenges in delivering work on schedule.

Solution: Develop project plans with clear timelines and milestones. Break down tasks into smaller, manageable steps, and set realistic deadlines for each.

8. Multitasking Challenges:

Mistake: Attempting to multitask without allocating time effectively.

Problem: Multitasking can lead to inefficiencies, reduced focus, and difficulty in accurately tracking time spent on individual tasks.

Solution: Focus on one task at a time, use productivity tools, and allocate specific time blocks for different types of work.

9. Neglecting Personal Well-being:

Mistake: Neglecting physical and mental well-being.

Problem: Poor health can lead to decreased productivity and overall dissatisfaction.

Solution: Prioritize self-care, including regular exercise, sufficient sleep, and stress management. A healthy freelancer is likely to be a more productive and satisfied professional.

10. Inadequate Communication:

Mistake: Ineffective communication with clients and collaborators.

Problem: Poor communication can lead to misunderstandings, delays, and challenges in managing client expectations.

Solution: Communicate clearly and proactively with clients. Set expectations regarding response times, project milestones, and any potential delays.

By addressing these time management challenges, freelancers can enhance their productivity, maintain a healthy work-life balance, and ensure the successful delivery of projects to the satisfaction of both clients and themselves.

⌛ Work life balance for Freelancers

Maintaining a healthy work-life balance is a common struggle for freelancers. Here are some mistakes and problems that freelancers often face in this regard, along with potential solutions:

1. Blurred Boundaries:

Mistake: Allowing work and personal life to overlap, leading to an "always-on" mentality.

Problem: Blurred boundaries can result in burnout, stress, and difficulty disconnecting from work.

Solution: Establish clear boundaries by setting specific work hours and separating your workspace from personal areas. Communicate these boundaries to clients and family members.

2. Overworking:

Mistake: Consistently working long hours without taking breaks or time off.

Problem: Overworking can lead to fatigue, decreased productivity, and negatively impact physical and mental well-being.

Solution: Set realistic work hours and schedule breaks. Prioritize self-care, and recognize the importance of downtime for recharging.

3. Neglecting Personal Life:

Mistake: Focusing too much on work at the expense of personal relationships and activities.

Problem: Neglecting personal life can lead to feelings of isolation, strained relationships, and decreased overall satisfaction.

Solution: Allocate dedicated time for family, friends, hobbies, and relaxation. Prioritize personal commitments and communicate your work schedule to those around you.

4. Inconsistent Schedule:

Mistake: Having an inconsistent work schedule, making it challenging to plan personal activities.

Problem: Inconsistency can lead to difficulties in maintaining routines and planning leisure time.

Solution: Establish a consistent work schedule that aligns with your natural energy levels. Plan personal activities around this schedule to ensure a balance between work and leisure.

5. Failure to Delegate:

Mistake: Reluctance to delegate tasks or outsource work.

Problem: Freelancers may become overwhelmed by trying to handle every aspect of their business, leading to burnout.

Solution: Identify tasks that can be delegated or outsourced. This could include administrative tasks, marketing, or aspects of project management. This allows freelancers to focus on their core strengths.

6. Unclear Prioritization:

Mistake: Difficulty prioritizing between work and personal commitments.

Problem: Lack of clear priorities can lead to neglecting essential personal tasks or feeling overwhelmed by work demands.

Solution: Prioritize tasks based on urgency and importance. Clearly define work hours and allocate specific time blocks for personal activities.

7. Fear of Missing Opportunities:

Mistake: Fear of turning down work opportunities, leading to overcommitment.

Problem: Overcommitting can result in a lack of time for personal activities and increased stress.

Solution: Evaluate opportunities based on your capacity and workload. Learn to say no when necessary, and communicate transparently with clients about realistic timelines.

8. Lack of Leisure Activities:

Mistake: Failing to engage in leisure activities or hobbies outside of work.

Problem: A lack of leisure activities can contribute to feelings of monotony and reduced overall life satisfaction.

Solution: Schedule time for hobbies, exercise, or activities that bring joy. Engaging in non-work-related pursuits contributes to a more fulfilling and balanced life.

9. Failure to Communicate Boundaries:

Mistake: Not communicating clear boundaries with clients, leading to unrealistic expectations.

Problem: Without clear communication, clients may assume constant availability, disrupting work-life balance.

Solution: Clearly communicate working hours, response times, and any limitations on availability. Set expectations with clients regarding when you will be offline.

10. Inadequate Time Off:

Mistake: Failing to take sufficient time off for vacations or breaks.

Problem: Lack of breaks can contribute to burnout, reduced creativity, and diminished overall well-being.

Solution: Schedule regular breaks and plan vacations to recharge. Recognize the importance of time away from work for maintaining long-term satisfaction and productivity.

By addressing these challenges, freelancers can cultivate a more sustainable work-life balance, fostering not only their professional success but also their overall well-being and satisfaction.

⌨ Freelancing Behavior

Freelancing behavior plays a crucial role in a freelancer's success and client relationships. Here are some common mistakes and problems in freelancing behavior, along with potential solutions:

1. Lack of Professionalism:

Mistake: Behaving unprofessionally in communication or deliverables.

Problem: Lack of professionalism can damage client relationships and harm the freelancer's reputation.

Solution: Maintain a high level of professionalism in all interactions. Respond promptly to emails, communicate clearly, meet deadlines, and deliver high-quality work consistently.

2. Poor Communication:

Mistake: Failing to communicate effectively with clients.

Problem: Poor communication can lead to misunderstandings, delays, and dissatisfaction.

Solution: Establish clear communication channels, update clients regularly on project progress, and be transparent about any challenges or changes. Actively listen to client feedback and address concerns promptly.

3. Ignoring Client Feedback:

Mistake: Disregarding or reacting negatively to client feedback.

Problem: Ignoring feedback can strain relationships and hinder professional growth.

Solution: Embrace constructive feedback as an opportunity for improvement. Listen attentively, appreciate the client's perspective, and demonstrate a willingness to make necessary adjustments.

Overpromising and Underdelivering:

Mistake: Making commitments that cannot be fulfilled.

Problem: Overpromising and underdelivering can erode client trust and harm the freelancer's credibility.

Solution: Set realistic expectations, and only commit to what can be feasibly accomplished. If unexpected challenges arise, communicate proactively and propose solutions.

4. Lack of Accountability:

Mistake: Failing to take responsibility for mistakes or missed deadlines.

Problem: Lack of accountability can lead to strained client relationships and damage the freelancer's reputation.

Solution: Acknowledge mistakes promptly, communicate transparently about any delays, and propose solutions. Taking responsibility demonstrates professionalism and integrity.

5. Inflexibility:

Mistake: Being inflexible in adapting to client needs or changes in project scope.

Problem: Inflexibility can lead to dissatisfaction and strained relationships.

Solution: Demonstrate flexibility and a willingness to adapt to changes in project requirements. Communicate openly about any necessary adjustments and work collaboratively with the client.

6. Unreliable Availability:

Mistake: Inconsistency in availability or responsiveness.

Problem: Unreliable availability can lead to frustration on the client's part and hinder effective collaboration.

Solution: Set clear working hours and communication expectations. Communicate any changes in availability in advance and provide alternative points of contact or response times.

7. Failure to Set Boundaries:

Mistake: Not establishing clear boundaries with clients.

Problem: Lack of boundaries can lead to excessive demands, impacting work-life balance and overall well-being.

Solution: Clearly communicate working hours, response times, and project scope to clients. Set expectations about the level of communication and collaboration.

8. Inadequate Time Management:

Mistake: Poor time management practices.

Problem: Inadequate time management can lead to missed deadlines, rushed work, and dissatisfaction on both sides.

Solution: Implement effective time management techniques, prioritize tasks, and communicate realistic project timelines. Regularly assess and refine time management strategies.

9. Ignoring Contractual Agreements:

Mistake: Neglecting the terms of contractual agreements.

Problem: Ignoring contract terms can lead to disputes and damage the freelancer's professional reputation.

Solution: Familiarize yourself with contract terms, adhere to agreed-upon deliverables, and communicate any necessary adjustments or clarifications in advance.

By cultivating positive freelancing behavior, freelancers can build strong client relationships, establish a reputable professional image, and contribute to their long-term success in the freelancing industry.

◹ Setting Project Scope in The Beginning

Setting the project scope is a critical aspect of freelancing, and freelancers often face challenges in this process. Here are some common mistakes and problems freelancers may encounter when setting project scope, along with potential solutions:

Vague or Undefined Scope:

Mistake: Failing to clearly define the scope of the project from the outset.

Problem: Vague or undefined scope can lead to misunderstandings, scope creep, and disputes with clients.

Solution: Take the time to thoroughly discuss and document the project requirements, objectives, and deliverables with the client. Use a detailed project brief or contract to outline expectations clearly.

Lack of Clarity on Deliverables:

Mistake: Unclear communication regarding the specific deliverables and outcomes expected.

Problem: Lack of clarity can result in client dissatisfaction and potential disagreements on project completion.

Solution: Clearly outline the deliverables, including specifications, formats, and any other relevant details. Provide examples or prototypes if possible to ensure mutual understanding.

Ignoring Client Input:

Mistake: Disregarding or not actively seeking client input during the scoping process.

Problem: Ignoring client input can lead to misalignment between expectations and the final deliverables.

Solution: Involve the client in the scoping process, gather their requirements, and seek their feedback to ensure that the project scope aligns with their vision and goals.

Underestimating Complexity:

Mistake: Underestimating the complexity of the project or the time required.

Problem: Underestimation can lead to missed deadlines, rushed work, and potential client dissatisfaction.

Solution: Conduct a thorough assessment of the project's complexity, potential challenges, and time requirements. Factor in buffer time for unforeseen issues.

Failure to Define Project Phases:

Mistake: Not breaking down the project into manageable phases or milestones.

Problem: Without defined phases, it can be challenging to track progress and manage client expectations.

Solution: Divide the project into clear phases with specific goals and milestones. Provide regular updates to clients upon completing each phase.

Scope Creep:

Mistake: Allowing scope creep, i.e., uncontrolled changes or additions to the project scope.

Problem: Scope creep can lead to project delays, increased workload, and potential disputes.

Solution: Clearly communicate any changes to the scope, and discuss additional fees or timelines associated with scope changes. Use change request forms to formalize modifications.

Inadequate Risk Assessment:

Mistake: Failing to assess potential risks associated with the project.

Problem: Inadequate risk assessment can result in unexpected challenges and difficulties in delivering the project successfully.

Solution: Identify potential risks early in the scoping process and discuss mitigation strategies with the client. Include contingency plans in the project scope.

Unclear Communication of Limitations:

Mistake: Not clearly communicating any limitations, constraints, or dependencies related to the project.

Problem: Lack of transparency can lead to misunderstandings and client dissatisfaction.

Solution: Clearly communicate any limitations or constraints, such as budget restrictions, technology dependencies, or third-party dependencies. Manage client expectations regarding what can and cannot be achieved.

Incomplete Understanding of Client Needs:

Mistake: Assuming a complete understanding of the client's needs without thorough discussions.

Problem: Incomplete understanding can result in misalignment and dissatisfaction with the final deliverables.

Solution: Schedule detailed discussions with the client to understand their vision, goals, and preferences. Ask clarifying questions and seek feedback throughout the scoping process.

Failure to Document Agreements:

Mistake: Neglecting document agreements and scope details in writing.

Problem: Without proper documentation, misunderstandings may arise, and there is no clear reference point for scope-related discussions.

Solution: Create a detailed project contract or agreement that clearly outlines the project scope, deliverables, timelines, and any other relevant terms. Both parties should review and sign the document before starting the project.

By addressing these challenges during the project scoping phase, freelancers can establish a solid foundation for successful project delivery, manage client expectations effectively, and minimize the risk of disputes or misunderstandings.

🖥 Lack Of Client's Response

Dealing with a lack of client response is a common challenge for freelancers. Here are some common issues and potential solutions for freelancers facing this problem:

Unclear Communication Channels:

Problem: Clients may not respond if communication channels are unclear or if there is uncertainty about where to send feedback or inquiries.

Solution: Clearly communicate the preferred communication channels from the beginning. Provide clients with multiple options, such as email, project management tools, or scheduled calls, and confirm their preferences.

Misaligned Expectations:

Problem: Clients may not respond if their expectations were not properly aligned at the beginning of the project.

Solution: Set clear expectations regarding communication frequency and preferred methods during the onboarding or project initiation phase. Ensure that both parties agree on the communication plan.

Client Overwhelm:

Problem: Clients may become overwhelmed with other priorities, leading to delayed responses.

Solution: Proactively manage expectations by discussing the client's availability and workload. Establish realistic timelines for responses and inquire about their preferred communication frequency.

Failure to Follow Up:

Problem: Frequent follow-ups can be perceived as intrusive, but not following up at all may lead to delayed responses.

Solution: Adopt a balanced approach. Send polite and concise follow-up messages at appropriate intervals. Acknowledge the client's time constraints and express a willingness to adjust communication frequencies as needed.

Ineffective Communication:

Problem: If communication lacks clarity or does not address the client's concerns, they may delay responding.

Solution: Ensure that your messages are clear, concise, and address the client's needs or questions. Encourage open communication by inviting feedback and questions.

Unrealistic Response Time Expectations:

Problem: Clients may not respond promptly if they have unrealistic expectations about how quickly they should receive a reply.

Solution: Establish realistic response time expectations early in the project. Clearly communicate your working hours and response times, and set boundaries to manage client expectations.

Failure to Highlight Urgency:

Problem: Clients may not respond promptly if they do not perceive the urgency of the message.

Solution: Clearly communicate the urgency of certain messages or requests. Use appropriate subject lines, urgency indicators, or priority tags to highlight time-sensitive matters.

Lack of Engagement:

Problem: Clients may disengage if they feel their input is not valued or if they do not see progress.

Solution: Foster client engagement by providing regular updates on project progress. Share milestones, achievements, or potential challenges to keep them involved and interested in the project.

Technical Issues:

Problem: Technical issues, such as email delivery problems or communication platform glitches, may hinder client responses.

Solution: Verify that communication channels are functioning correctly. If there are ongoing issues, consider alternative communication methods or platforms.

Inadequate Documentation:

Problem: If important information is not documented or if clients are unsure about project details, they may delay responses.

Solution: Keep project documentation clear and up-to-date. Provide clients with reference materials or summaries to ensure they have the necessary information to respond promptly.

Addressing the lack of client response involves proactive communication, setting clear expectations, and adapting your approach based on the client's preferences and priorities. Open dialogue and a collaborative mindset contribute to a smoother communication process in freelancing.

Chapter 7: Freelance Job-Hunting Skills

In the vast realm of freelancing, mastering the art of job hunting is akin to wielding a key that unlocks doors to countless opportunities.

Freelance job hunting is a skill that goes beyond a simple bid; it involves strategic thinking, effective communication, and a keen understanding of market dynamics.

As we discuss in this chapter, we'll explore the essential skills needed to navigate freelance job platforms, bid on the right projects, and distinguish genuine opportunities from the rest.

Whether you're a seasoned freelancer looking to enhance your job-hunting prowess or a newcomer eager to step into the freelance arena, this chapter will equip you with the insights to stand out and secure projects that align with your expertise and aspirations. Join us on a journey where skillful job hunting becomes a catalyst for a thriving freelance career.

☑ Freelance Job Selection

Freelance job selection is a crucial aspect of successful freelancing. Here are some skills and strategies to enhance your freelance job hunting and selection process:

Define Your Niche:

Skill: Clearly define your freelance niche or specialization.

Strategy: Identify your unique skills and strengths. Tailor your job search to opportunities that align with your expertise to increase the likelihood of successful job selection.

Create a Compelling Profile:

Skill: Craft a compelling freelance profile.

Strategy: Optimize your profiles on freelancing platforms by highlighting your skills, experience, and achievements. Use a professional profile picture and create a concise, engaging bio that showcases your expertise.

Effective Keyword Use:

Skill: Utilize effective keywords in your job search.

Strategy: Understand the keywords relevant to your niche and use them when searching for freelance opportunities. This helps you find jobs that closely match your skills and interests.

Set Clear Job Filters:

Skill: Efficiently use job filters.

Strategy: Use platform-specific filters to narrow down job searches based on criteria such as job type, budget range, and client preferences. This streamlines your search and helps you focus on the most relevant opportunities.

Research Clients:

Skill: Research potential clients before applying.

Strategy: Evaluate clients' profiles, reviews, and previous projects. Look for red flags and ensure that the client's expectations align with your capabilities and working style before submitting a proposal.

Tailor Your Proposals:

Skill: Craft tailored and persuasive proposals.

Strategy: Customize your proposals for each job application. Clearly outline how your skills match the client's needs, showcase relevant experience, and demonstrate enthusiasm for the project. Personalize your approach to stand out.

Effective Communication:

Skill: Demonstrate effective communication skills.

Strategy: Clearly communicate your understanding of the project, ask thoughtful questions, and respond promptly to client messages. This showcases professionalism and increases your chances of being selected.

Portfolio Presentation:

Skill: Showcase your portfolio effectively.

Strategy: Create a portfolio that highlights your best work. Provide diverse examples that demonstrate your skills and versatility. Share your portfolio link in your proposals to give clients a visual representation of your capabilities.

Negotiation Skills:

Skill: Develop negotiation skills.

Strategy: Be prepared to negotiate terms such as project scope, timelines, and rates. Clearly communicate your value while remaining flexible to find mutually beneficial agreements.

Time Management:

Skill: Manage your time efficiently during job hunting.

Strategy: Set aside dedicated time for job searching, proposal writing, and client communication. Avoid spending excessive time on one opportunity if it doesn't align with your goals.

Continuous Learning:

Skill: Embrace continuous learning.

Strategy: Stay updated on industry trends and acquire new skills relevant to your niche. This not only enhances your profile but also opens up opportunities for higher-paying and more challenging projects.

Build Client Relationships:

Skill: Cultivate strong client relationships.

Strategy: Focus on delivering high-quality work, meeting deadlines, and providing excellent customer service. Satisfied clients are more likely to offer repeat business and positive reviews.

By honing these skills and implementing effective strategies, you can navigate the freelance job market with confidence, increase your chances of job selection, and build a successful freelance career.

◉Bidding On the Right Project

Bidding on the right projects is a crucial skill for successful freelancers. Here are some skills and strategies to enhance your ability to bid effectively on freelance projects:

Strategic Project Selection:

Skill: Assessing projects strategically.

Strategy: Prioritize projects that align with your skills, expertise, and interests. Focus on opportunities that contribute to your long-term goals and professional growth.

Understanding Client Needs:

Skill: Analyzing and understanding client needs.

Strategy: Carefully read project descriptions to grasp the client's requirements. Tailor your bid to showcase how your skills and experience directly address their needs.

Competitive Pricing:

Skill: Setting competitive and fair prices.

Strategy: Research market rates for your skills and experience. Price your services competitively while considering the value you provide. Be transparent about your rates in your bids.

Crafting Persuasive Proposals:

Skill: Writing persuasive and customized proposals.

Strategy: Tailor each proposal to the specific project. Clearly articulate how your skills and experience make you the ideal candidate. Address the client's pain points and offer solutions.

Highlighting Relevant Experience:

Skill: Showcasing relevant experience.

Strategy: Emphasize your past work that aligns with the current project. Provide links to relevant portfolio items and describe how your expertise will contribute to the successful completion of the client's project.

Demonstrating Enthusiasm:

Skill: Conveying enthusiasm for the project.

Strategy: Express genuine interest in the client's project in your bid. Use positive language to convey your enthusiasm and commitment to delivering high-quality results.

Effective Communication:

Skill: Communicating effectively with clients.

Strategy: Write clear and concise bids. Be responsive to client inquiries and demonstrate your professionalism. Promptly address any questions or concerns the client may have.

Building Trust:

Skill: Establishing trust with clients.

Strategy: Include client testimonials or references in your bid if applicable. Clearly communicate your reliability, commitment to deadlines, and dedication to client satisfaction.

Differentiating Yourself:

Skill: Setting yourself apart from other freelancers.

Strategy: Identify what makes you unique and emphasize it in your bids. Highlight specific skills, experiences, or approaches that differentiate you from other freelancers.

Researching Clients:

Skill: Researching potential clients.

Strategy: Investigate the client's previous projects, reviews, and overall reputation. Use this information to tailor your bid and demonstrate your understanding of their business.

Understanding Project Scope:

Skill: Assessing project scope accurately.

Strategy: Ensure you have a clear understanding of the project requirements, scope, and deliverables. Ask clarifying questions if needed to avoid misunderstandings.

Timely Follow-ups:

Skill: Following up on bids in a timely manner.

Strategy: Monitor your bids and follow up with clients after submitting a proposal. Express continued interest, address any additional questions, and reiterate your suitability for the project.

By honing these skills and employing effective strategies, you can improve your success rate in bidding on freelance projects. This will not only help you secure more projects but also contribute to building a positive reputation in the freelance marketplace.

Identifying fake vs original project

Identifying fake projects from genuine ones is a critical skill for freelancers to avoid scams and protect their time and resources. Here are some skills and strategies to help freelancers distinguish between fake and original projects:

Thoroughly Read Project Descriptions:

Skill: Analyzing project descriptions.

Strategy: Carefully read and analyze project descriptions for clarity, detail, and coherence. Legitimate projects typically have well-defined requirements and objectives.

Check Client Profiles:

Skill: Evaluating client profiles.

Strategy: Review the client's profile for completeness, past projects, and client feedback. Established and reputable clients are more likely to post genuine projects.

Verify Payment Information:

Skill: Verifying payment details.

Strategy: Be cautious if the client's payment details or methods seem unusual or suspicious. Legitimate clients usually use standard and secure payment methods.

Communication Style:

Skill: Assessing communication style.

Strategy: Pay attention to the client's communication style. Legitimate clients communicate professionally, provide clear instructions, and respond promptly to queries.

Research Client's History:

Skill: Investigating the client's history.

Strategy: Research the client's history on the freelancing platform. If the client has a pattern of creating and abandoning projects, it could be a red flag.

Verify Contact Information:

Skill: Confirming contact information.

Strategy: Check if the client's contact information is accurate and consistent. Legitimate clients provide valid and reachable contact details.

Look for Red Flags:

Skill: Recognizing red flags.

Strategy: Be wary of projects that promise unusually high pay for simple tasks, lack specific details, or have vague requirements. These can be indicators of potential scams.

Research Company Details:

Skill: Researching the client's company.

Strategy: If the project is associated with a company, research the company's details. Legitimate clients often provide information about their business, website, and contact details.

Check for Unusual Requests:

Skill: Identifying unusual requests.

Strategy: Be cautious if the client makes unusual requests, such as requesting personal or financial information outside of the platform, or asking for free work as part of the hiring process.

Evaluate Project Budget:

Skill: Assessing project budget.

Strategy: Be skeptical of projects with exceptionally high budgets that seem disproportionate to the tasks involved. Scammers may use attractive budgets to lure freelancers.

Use Trusted Platforms:

Skill: Choosing trusted freelancing platforms.

Strategy: Stick to reputable freelancing platforms with established security measures. Platforms with robust vetting processes are less likely to host fake projects.

Trust Your Instincts:

Skill: Trusting your instincts.

Strategy: If something feels off or too good to be true, trust your instincts. If a project raises concerns, consider reaching out to the platform's support team for guidance.

By developing these skills and staying vigilant, freelancers can better navigate the freelance job market and avoid falling victim to scams or fake projects. Prioritizing caution and due diligence contribute to a safer and more successful freelancing experience.

? Asking Questions

Asking thoughtful questions is a valuable skill for freelancers during the job hunting process. Here are some skills and strategies to enhance your ability to ask questions effectively:

Understanding Project Requirements:

Skill: Articulating questions to clarify project requirements.

Strategy: Ask specific and targeted questions to gain a clear understanding of the client's expectations, project scope, and deliverables. Seek clarification on any ambiguous or unclear points.

Establishing Communication Expectations:

Skill: Setting communication expectations.

Strategy: Inquire about the client's preferred communication channels, frequency, and expectations. This ensures alignment and helps you establish a communication plan that works for both parties.

Clarifying Budget and Payment Terms:

Skill: Addressing budget and payment-related questions.

Strategy: Ask about the budget range for the project and the client's preferred payment schedule. Clarify any additional costs or potential bonuses. This helps prevent misunderstandings and ensures you are comfortable with the financial aspects.

Discussing Project Timeline:

Skill: Inquiring about project timelines.

Strategy: Ask about the project's timeline, including key milestones and deadlines. Understand the client's expectations regarding project duration and any time-sensitive components.

Exploring Client's Vision:

Skill: Exploring the client's vision for the project.

Strategy: Inquire about the client's goals, vision, and desired outcomes for the project. Understanding their expectations helps you tailor your approach to align with their objectives.

Addressing Technical Requirements:

Skill: Asking technical questions.

Strategy: If the project involves technical aspects, seek details about the required technologies, platforms, or tools. Clarify any technical specifications to ensure you can meet the project's requirements.

Confirming Project Scope:

Skill: Confirming project scope.

Strategy: Ask about any potential changes or additions to the project scope. Clearly define the boundaries of the project to avoid scope creep and ensure alignment between your and the client's expectations.

Inquiring About Revision Policy:

Skill: Discussing the revision process.

Strategy: Inquire about the client's expectations regarding revisions and feedback. Clarify the number of revisions included in the project and the process for addressing feedback.

Understanding Client's Involvement:

Skill: Understanding the client's level of involvement.

Strategy: Ask about the client's preferred level of involvement in the project. Some clients prefer regular updates, while others may prefer a more hands-off approach. Adjust your communication plan accordingly.

Discussing Confidentiality and Ownership:

Skill: Addressing confidentiality and ownership concerns.

Strategy: Inquire about the client's expectations regarding confidentiality and ownership of the work. Clarify any non-disclosure agreements or intellectual property considerations.

Seeking Information About Previous Freelancers:

Skill: Asking about past freelancers.

Strategy: If applicable, inquire about the client's experience with previous freelancers. Understand any challenges or successes to gain insights into their expectations and working style.

Building a Relationship:

Skill: Building rapport through questions.

Strategy: Ask questions that go beyond project details to build a relationship with the client. Inquire about their business, goals, and long-term vision. This demonstrates genuine interest and can lead to stronger collaborations.

By honing these skills and incorporating effective questioning strategies, freelancers can gather essential information, clarify expectations, and establish a solid foundation for successful collaborations with clients. Asking the right questions not only enhances your understanding of the project but also showcases your professionalism and commitment to delivering value.

🐾 Importance Of Professional Response to The Project

The importance of a professional response to a freelance project cannot be overstated. Here are some skills and strategies highlighting why a professional response is crucial during the job-hunting process:

First Impression:

Skill: Making a positive first impression.

Strategy: Your response is often the first interaction a client has with you. A professional and well-crafted response sets a positive tone, demonstrating your commitment and reliability from the outset.

Demonstrating Competence:

Skill: Showcasing your competence.

Strategy: A professional response communicates that you understand the project requirements, have the necessary skills, and are capable of delivering high-quality work. It builds confidence in the client's mind regarding your abilities.

Building Trust:

Skill: Establishing trust with the client.

Strategy: A professional response builds trust by conveying reliability and professionalism. Clients are more likely to choose freelancers who present themselves in a trustworthy and credible manner.

Clear Communication:

Skill: Communicating clearly and concisely.

Strategy: Professional responses are clear, concise, and address all relevant aspects of the project. Clear communication reduces the risk of misunderstandings and ensures that both you and the client are on the same page.

Respecting Client's Time:

Skill: Respecting the client's time.

Strategy: A well-organized and professional response respects the client's time by providing the information they need without unnecessary details. Clients appreciate freelancers who are considerate of their time constraints.

Attention to Detail:

Skill: Demonstrating attention to detail.

Strategy: A professional response is free of typos, grammatical errors, and formatting issues. Attention to detail in your communication reflects your commitment to delivering polished and precise work.

Tailoring Your Response:

Skill: Tailoring your response to the project.

Strategy: Each project is unique, and a professional response demonstrates that you've carefully read the project description. Tailor your response to showcase how your skills align with the specific needs of the client.

Addressing Client's Concerns:

Skill: Addressing client concerns proactively.

Strategy: If the client has mentioned specific concerns or requirements in the project description, a professional response directly addresses those points. This shows that you've paid attention to their needs.

Setting Expectations:

Skill: Setting clear expectations.

Strategy: A professional response includes details about your working process, timelines, and any other relevant information. Setting clear expectations helps prevent misunderstandings and establishes a framework for successful collaboration.

Professional Tone:

Skill: Adopting a professional tone.

Strategy: Use polite and professional language in your response. Avoid overly casual or informal language unless it aligns with the client's communication style. A professional tone contributes to a positive and respectful interaction.

Differentiating Yourself:

Skill: Standing out from other freelancers.

Strategy: A professional response distinguishes you from competitors by showcasing your professionalism, reliability, and commitment to quality. Clients are more likely to choose freelancers who present themselves as serious and dedicated professionals.

Encouraging Further Communication:

Skill: Inviting further discussion.

Strategy: End your response by inviting the client to ask any additional questions or provide more details. Encouraging further communication demonstrates your openness and readiness to discuss the project in greater detail.

In summary, a professional response to a freelance project is not just a formality; it's a strategic step in securing the job. It sets the foundation for a positive client-freelancer relationship and positions you as a reliable and capable professional in the eyes of potential clients.

◿ Time To Put a Premium Bid

Deciding when to put a premium bid on a freelance project is a strategic skill that can significantly impact your success as a freelancer. Here are some skills and strategies to help you determine when to put a premium bid:

High-Value Projects:

Skill: Identifying high-value projects.

Strategy: Assess the potential value of the project to the client. If the project has a high impact on the client's business, such as a critical website development or a major marketing campaign, consider putting a premium bid.

Specialized Expertise:

Skill: Recognizing your specialized expertise.

Strategy: If the project requires unique skills or expertise that you possess, consider putting a premium bid. Clients often recognize and are willing to pay more for freelancers with specialized knowledge.

Urgent or Time-Sensitive Projects:

Skill: Evaluating project urgency.

Strategy: If the client has an urgent or time-sensitive project, and you have the availability to meet tight deadlines, consider putting a premium bid. Clients may be willing to pay more for expedited delivery.

Additional Services or Features:

Skill: Identifying opportunities for additional services.

Strategy: If the project allows for the inclusion of additional services, features, or premium offerings, consider proposing these as part of your bid. Clearly communicate the added value these features bring to the project.

Client's Reputation:

Skill: Researching the client's reputation.

Strategy: If the client has a strong reputation, is well-established, or has a history of valuing quality work, consider putting a premium bid. Such clients are often willing to invest in top-tier freelancers.

Complexity of the Project:

Skill: Assessing project complexity.

Strategy: For projects that are highly complex or require advanced problem-solving skills, consider putting a premium bid. Clients may be willing to pay more for freelancers who can navigate intricate challenges.

Your Portfolio and Track Record:

Skill: Leveraging your portfolio and track record.

Strategy: If you have a strong portfolio and a track record of delivering exceptional results, use this as leverage when putting a premium bid. Clients may be willing to invest in proven expertise.

Demand for Your Services:

Skill: Gauging demand for your services.

Strategy: If there is high demand for your skills in the market, consider putting a premium bid. Clients may recognize the value of securing the services of a freelancer who is in demand.

Limited Availability:

Skill: Communicating limited availability.

Strategy: If you have limited availability due to existing commitments or a busy schedule, consider putting a premium bid. Clients may be willing to pay more for your services if they know you have limited slots.

Project Size and Scope:

Skill: Evaluating project size and scope.

Strategy: Larger projects with extensive scope may warrant a premium bid. Assess the overall size and complexity of the project to determine the level of effort required.

Market Rates and Industry Standards:

Skill: Understanding market rates.

Strategy: Stay informed about market rates and industry standards for your skills. If the project aligns with or exceeds these standards, consider putting a premium bid.

Value Proposition:

Skill: Communicating your value proposition.

Strategy: Clearly articulate the unique value you bring to the project in your bid. Explain how your skills and expertise will benefit the client, justifying the premium bid.

By mastering these skills and considering these strategies, you can make informed decisions on when to put a premium bid, maximizing your earning potential while delivering exceptional value to your clients.

⇧⇩ Choosing Between High Priced Projects Vs Low Priced Projects

Choosing between high-priced and low-priced freelance projects requires a strategic approach to align with your career goals and financial objectives. Here are some skills and strategies to help you make informed decisions when navigating the choice between high-priced and low-priced projects:

Evaluate Your Financial Goals:

Skill: Assessing personal financial goals.

Strategy: Understand your financial needs, including income targets, overhead costs, and savings goals. This assessment will guide your decision-making process when choosing between high and low-priced projects.

Calculate Hourly Rates:

Skill: Calculating your hourly rate.

Strategy: Determine your desired hourly rate based on your financial goals and the time you can realistically dedicate to freelancing. Use this rate as a benchmark when evaluating project offers.

Consider Project Complexity:

Skill: Evaluating project complexity.

Strategy: Assess the complexity of each project and how it aligns with your skill set. More complex projects may justify higher rates, while simpler tasks could be considered for lower-priced projects.

Factor in Time Commitment:

Skill: Estimating time commitment.

Strategy: Consider the time required to complete each project. High-priced projects may be justified if they demand more time and effort, while low-priced projects with shorter timelines may be manageable if they align with your schedule.

Assess Long-Term Potential:

Skill: Evaluating long-term potential.

Strategy: Consider the potential for ongoing work or repeat business. While a high-priced project might offer immediate financial benefits, a lower-priced project with the potential for long-term collaboration could be strategically valuable.

Market Demand for Your Skills:

Skill: Understanding market demand.

Strategy: Gauge the demand for your specific skills in the market. If your skills are in high demand, you may have the flexibility to choose higher-priced projects. In a competitive market, consider the balance between rates and project volume.

Establish a Minimum Rate:

Skill: Setting a minimum acceptable rate.

Strategy: Determine the lowest rate you are willing to accept based on your financial needs and the value you bring to clients. Use this minimum rate as a guideline when evaluating project offers.

Build a Diverse Portfolio:

Skill: Building a diverse project portfolio.

Strategy: Consider the strategic value of including both high and low-priced projects in your portfolio. A diverse portfolio showcases your versatility and attracts a broader range of clients.

Negotiation Skills:

Skill: Negotiating project terms.

Strategy: Develop strong negotiation skills to secure favorable terms, whether it's negotiating a higher rate for a high-priced project or finding a compromise for a lower-priced project that aligns with your goals.

Client Relationship Building:

Skill: Building client relationships.

Strategy: Prioritize building strong relationships with clients, irrespective of project pricing. Satisfied clients may lead to referrals, testimonials, and future opportunities, regardless of the initial project's price.

Value-Based Pricing:

Skill: Implementing value-based pricing.

Strategy: Consider pricing models based on the value you bring to the client rather than solely on time or effort. Communicate the unique value you provide to justify higher rates.

Evaluate Project Benefits:

Skill: Assessing non-monetary benefits.

Strategy: Consider non-monetary benefits such as skill development, networking opportunities, and portfolio enhancement. These factors can contribute to your overall career growth and may influence your decision between high and low-priced projects.

Ultimately, the key is to strike a balance that aligns with your financial goals, skills, and career aspirations. By honing these skills and employing strategic thinking, you can navigate the choice between high-priced and low-priced projects to build a successful and sustainable freelance career.

Chapter 8: Types Of Freelance Marketplaces

Freelance marketplaces can be broadly categorized into traditional and nontraditional types, each offering distinct features and approaches to connecting freelancers with clients. Here's an overview of these two types:

☞Traditional Freelance Marketplaces

Characteristics

1. **Well-Established Platforms:**

Traditional freelance marketplaces are often long-standing, well-established platforms with a history of connecting freelancers and clients.

2. Diverse Range of Services:

These platforms cover a broad spectrum of freelance services, including writing, design, programming, marketing, and more.

3. Escrow Systems:

Many traditional marketplaces use escrow systems, where clients deposit funds that are released to freelancers upon successful project completion.

4. Reviews and Ratings:

They typically incorporate review and rating systems, allowing freelancers and clients to provide feedback based on their experiences.

Examples:

1. Upwork
2. Freelancer
3. Fiverr (while it has traditional aspects, it also blends nontraditional elements)

⏻ Nontraditional Freelance Marketplaces

Characteristics

1. Niche or Industry-Specific:

Nontraditional marketplaces may focus on specific niches or industries, catering to a more targeted audience with specialized needs.

2. Unique Project Structures:

Some nontraditional platforms feature unique project structures, such as competitions, challenges, or collaborative platforms that differ from the standard bidding process.

3. Blockchain and Cryptocurrency:

Some nontraditional platforms leverage blockchain and cryptocurrency technologies for payments, ensuring transparency and security.

4. Innovation in Service Offerings:

Nontraditional marketplaces often bring innovation to the freelance industry by introducing new service models or unconventional ways of connecting freelancers with clients.

Examples:

1. Toptal (specializes in connecting clients with top freelancers in the software development and design fields)
2. 99designs (focuses on graphic design through contests)
3. Gigster (specializes in software development projects)

It's worth noting that the line between traditional and nontraditional freelance marketplaces can sometimes blur, as some platforms incorporate elements from both categories.

Also, the freelance marketplace landscape is dynamic, with new platforms emerging and existing ones evolving to meet the changing needs of freelancers and clients. Freelancers often choose platforms based on their specific skills, preferences, and the types of projects they seek.

❖Types Of Freelance Marketplaces

1. Upwork

Upwork is a well-known and widely used freelance marketplace that falls into the category of traditional freelance platforms. Here are the key characteristics of Upwork:

Scope of Services:

Upwork covers a wide array of freelance services, including writing, design, programming, marketing, administrative support, and more. Freelancers with various skills and expertise can find opportunities on the platform.

Platform Features:

- **Bidding System:**

Upwork operates on a bidding system where freelancers submit proposals in response to clients' job postings. Clients review the proposals and choose the freelancer they want to hire.

- **Escrow System:**

The platform uses an escrow system, ensuring that clients deposit funds for a project before it begins. The funds are held in escrow and released to the freelancer upon successful completion of the project.

Client-Freelancer Interaction:

Messaging and Collaboration Tools: Upwork provides messaging and collaboration tools that allow clients and freelancers to communicate, share files, and collaborate seamlessly within the platform.

Payment Structure:

Upwork charges service fees based on a freelancer's earnings. The fees vary depending on the total billings with a specific client and the freelancer's lifetime billings on the platform.

Profile and Portfolio Building:

Freelancers create profiles that showcase their skills, experience, and portfolio. Clients can review these profiles when deciding whom to hire.

Client Reviews and Ratings:

Upwork incorporates a review and rating system, allowing clients to provide feedback on freelancers' performance after completing a project. Positive reviews contribute to a freelancer's reputation on the platform.

Global Reach:

International Pool of Freelancers and Clients: Upwork facilitates connections between freelancers and clients from around the world. This global reach allows freelancers to access a diverse range of projects and clients.

Job Success Score:

Performance Metric: Upwork uses a Job Success Score (JSS) as a performance metric for freelancers. This score reflects a freelancer's success on the platform, taking into account factors like client satisfaction, completed projects, and long-term relationships.

While Upwork is considered a traditional freelance marketplace, it continues to evolve and adapt to the changing needs of the freelance industry. Freelancers often choose Upwork for its extensive range of opportunities, ease of use, and established reputation within the freelance community.

2. Freelancer.com

Freelancer.com is a prominent freelance marketplace that falls into the category of traditional freelance platforms. Here are the key characteristics of Freelancer.com:

Diverse Range of Services:

Wide Spectrum of Skills: Freelancer.com caters to a diverse range of freelance skills, including writing, graphic design, programming, marketing, data entry, and more. Freelancers with various expertise can find projects that match their skills.

Platform Features:

Bidding System: Like other traditional platforms, Freelancer.com operates on a bidding system where freelancers bid on projects posted by clients. Clients review the bids and select the freelancer they want to hire for the job.

Milestone Payments: Freelancer.com facilitates milestone payments, allowing clients to fund and release payments in increments as predefined project milestones are achieved.

Client-Freelancer Interaction:

Communication Tools: Freelancer.com provides communication tools such as chat and messaging to facilitate interaction between clients and freelancers. This helps in discussing project details and addressing any questions.

Payment Structure:

Project Fees: Freelancer.com charges fees based on the total project value. Both clients and freelancers may encounter fees associated with using the platform, which can vary depending on the membership plan chosen.

Profile and Portfolio Building:

Freelancer Profiles: Freelancers create profiles that showcase their skills, experience, and completed projects. Clients can review these profiles to make informed decisions when hiring.

Client Reviews and Ratings: Freelancer.com incorporates a review and rating system, allowing clients to provide feedback on freelancers' performance. Positive reviews contribute to a freelancer's reputation on the platform.

Global Reach:

International Opportunities: Freelancer.com connects freelancers and clients globally, providing access to a broad pool of projects and talent. This international reach allows freelancers to work with clients from different regions.

Contests and Challenges:

Project Contests: Freelancer.com allows clients to create contests where freelancers submit their work, and the client chooses the winning entry. This adds a unique element to the platform and provides opportunities for freelancers to showcase their skills.

Certifications and Exams:

Skill Testing: Freelancer.com offers skill tests that freelancers can take to validate their proficiency in specific areas. Certifications from these tests can be displayed on a freelancer's profile.

While Freelancer.com shares similarities with other traditional freelance platforms, it has its own distinct features, such as the emphasis on contests and skill testing. Freelancers often choose Freelancer.com based on their specific skills, preferences, and the types of projects they are seeking.

3. Fiverr.com

Fiverr.com is a unique freelance marketplace that has distinctive features setting it apart from traditional platforms. Here are the key characteristics of Fiverr:

Microservices and Gigs:

Micro-Jobs: Fiverr is known for microservices or "gigs," where freelancers offer specific, often small-scale services called gigs, starting at a base price of $5 (hence the name "Fiverr"). While services can be offered at higher prices, the $5 starting point is a defining feature.

Scope of Services:

Wide Range of Creative Services: Fiverr covers a broad spectrum of creative services, including graphic design, writing, video editing, voiceovers, programming, and more.

The platform allows freelancers to showcase their creativity and expertise in various fields.

Package System:

Tiered Service Packages: Fiverr introduces a tiered system where freelancers can offer different packages of their services, each with varying features and pricing. This allows freelancers to provide clients with options that suit their needs and budgets.

No Bidding System:

Service Listings: Unlike traditional bidding platforms, Fiverr freelancers create service listings with a fixed price. Clients can browse these listings, choose the services they need, and make direct purchases.

Communication Tools:

Messaging and Collaboration: Fiverr provides messaging and collaboration tools that allow clients and freelancers to communicate and discuss project details. While communication is facilitated, the platform emphasizes clear service descriptions to minimize the need for extensive back-and-forth.

Payment Structure:

Service Fees: Fiverr charges service fees on completed transactions. Additionally, freelancers have the option to offer additional services, known as "gig extras," at an additional cost.

Profile and Gig Creation:

Freelancer Profiles: Freelancers on Fiverr create profiles showcasing their skills, experience, and the specific services they offer. The emphasis is on creating attractive gig listings that clearly communicate what clients can expect.

Reviews and Ratings:

Client Feedback: Fiverr incorporates a review and rating system where clients can provide feedback on freelancers' performance. Positive reviews contribute to a freelancer's reputation on the platform.

Gig Extras and Add-Ons:

Upselling Opportunities: Fiverr allows freelancers to offer gig extras and add-ons, providing opportunities to upsell additional services or features to clients.

Fiverr Pro:

Professional Services: Fiverr Pro is a premium service that features hand-vetted, high-quality freelancers offering professional-level services. Fiverr Pro freelancers often have higher pricing to reflect their expertise.

Fiverr's model is based on simplicity, allowing freelancers to create standardized service offerings with transparent pricing. It is popular for its accessibility and the ability for freelancers to showcase their skills in a creative and visually appealing manner. Clients looking for specific services can easily find and purchase what they need without the bidding process typical of traditional platforms.

4. Guru.com

Guru.com is a freelance marketplace that combines elements of both traditional and nontraditional platforms.

Here are the key characteristics of Guru.com:

Scope of Services:

Diverse Range of Skills: Guru.com caters to a wide range of freelance skills, including writing, design, programming, marketing, administrative support, and more. Freelancers with various expertise can find projects that align with their skills.

Platform Features:

- **Bidding System:** Guru.com operates on a bidding system, where freelancers submit proposals in response to clients' job postings. Clients review the proposals and select the freelancer they want to hire.

- **Workroom Collaboration:** The platform provides a workroom for freelancers and clients to collaborate on projects, share files, and communicate efficiently.

Payment Structure:

Service Fees: Guru.com charges service fees based on a tiered membership structure. Freelancers can choose from different membership plans, each offering various benefits, and pay fees accordingly.

Work Agreements:

Flexible Agreements: Guru.com allows freelancers and clients to set up flexible work agreements, including hourly or fixed-price contracts. This flexibility accommodates different project types and client preferences.

Profiles and Work Portfolios:

Freelancer Profiles: Freelancers create profiles showcasing their skills, experience, and work history. Clients can review these profiles to make informed decisions when hiring.

Work Portfolios: Freelancers can showcase their work through portfolio sections on their profiles, providing clients with visual representations of their capabilities.

Reviews and Ratings:

Client Feedback: Guru.com incorporates a review and rating system, allowing clients to provide feedback on freelancers' performance. Positive reviews contribute to a freelancer's reputation on the platform.

SafePay Escrow System:

Escrow Payments: Guru.com uses an escrow system called SafePay, where clients fund a project, and payments are released to freelancers upon meeting predefined milestones or project completion.

Membership Levels:

Basic, Basic+, and Professional Memberships: Guru.com offers different membership levels for freelancers, with each level providing varying benefits such as reduced service fees, increased bid limits, and more.

Guru Workroom Mobile App:

Mobile Accessibility: Guru.com offers a mobile app called Guru Workroom, allowing freelancers and clients to manage their projects and communicate on the go.

Guru Enterprise:

Enterprise Solutions: Guru.com provides enterprise solutions for businesses looking to manage multiple projects and teams on the platform. This is suitable for larger-scale freelance collaborations.

Guru.com combines the traditional bidding system with additional features, offering a flexible and user-friendly environment for both freelancers and clients. The tiered membership structure provides freelancers with options to choose a plan that aligns with their preferences and business needs.

PeoplePerHour

PeoplePerHour is a freelance marketplace with unique features that set it apart from traditional platforms. Here are the key characteristics of PeoplePerHour:

Scope of Services:

Hourly and Project-Based Work: PeoplePerHour caters to a variety of freelance services, allowing freelancers to offer both hourly services and project-based work. This dual approach provides flexibility for different types of projects.

Platform Features:

Hourlies and Proposals: Freelancers on PeoplePerHour can offer predefined services called "Hourlies" with fixed prices. Additionally, freelancers can submit custom proposals in response to clients' job postings.

WorkStream Collaboration: The platform provides a WorkStream feature for freelancers and clients to collaborate on projects, share files, and communicate effectively.

Payment Structure:

Service Fees: PeoplePerHour charges service fees based on the total project value. Freelancers are also able to set their own hourly rates for services.

Certification System:

Certified Freelancers: PeoplePerHour has a certification system where freelancers can earn certifications for specific skills. These certifications enhance a freelancer's profile and credibility on the platform.

Profiles and Portfolios:

Freelancer Profiles: Freelancers create profiles showcasing their skills, experience, and certifications. Clients can review these profiles when deciding whom to hire.

Work Portfolios: Freelancers can showcase their work through portfolio sections on their profiles, providing clients with visual representations of their capabilities.

Reviews and Ratings:

Client Feedback: PeoplePerHour incorporates a review and rating system, allowing clients to provide feedback on freelancers' performance. Positive reviews contribute to a freelancer's reputation on the platform.

Escrow Protection:

Escrow Payments: PeoplePerHour uses an escrow system to protect both freelancers and clients. Clients fund projects, and payments are released to freelancers once the project is completed to the client's satisfaction.

Hourlie Extras:

Upselling Opportunities: Freelancers can offer additional services or "Hourlie Extras" to upsell clients and enhance the value of their services.

Mobile Accessibility:

Mobile App: PeoplePerHour offers a mobile app, allowing freelancers and clients to manage their projects, communicate, and collaborate while on the go.

Business Hub:

Business Management Tools: PeoplePerHour provides a Business Hub feature that includes tools for freelancers to manage proposals, invoices, and contracts. This helps freelancers streamline their business operations.

PeoplePerHour's combination of Hourlies, proposals, and certification systems adds a unique dimension to the platform. Freelancers often appreciate the flexibility offered in setting their own prices and showcasing their expertise through certifications. Clients benefit from a diverse pool of freelancers and the option to choose between fixed-price Hourlies and custom project proposals.

5. Craigslist

Craigslist is a classified advertisements website that serves various purposes, including job postings and freelance opportunities. While not a dedicated freelance marketplace like some of the platforms mentioned earlier, Craigslist can still be a source for freelancers to find clients and projects.

Here are some characteristics of using Craigslist for freelancing:

Diverse Job Categories:

Wide Range of Opportunities: Craigslist covers a broad spectrum of job categories, and within those, freelancers can find opportunities for writing, graphic design, web development, marketing, and more.

Local and Remote Opportunities:

Local and Remote Listings: Craigslist includes both local job listings and opportunities for remote work. Freelancers can filter search results based on their location preferences.

Varied Project Types:

One-Time Gigs and Long-Term Jobs: Freelancers may find one-time gigs, short-term projects, or even long-term opportunities on Craigslist, depending on the nature of the listings.

Direct Client Communication:

Direct Interaction: Unlike some traditional freelance platforms, Craigslist often involves direct communication between freelancers and clients. Freelancers may need to initiate contact and negotiate terms directly.

Informal Process:

Less Structured: The process on Craigslist is often less structured than on dedicated freelance platforms. Freelancers and clients may need to rely more on communication and negotiation to establish terms.

No Escrow System:

Payment Arrangements: Craigslist does not provide an escrow system for payments. Freelancers and clients need to agree on payment terms, and payment is typically handled outside the platform.

Local Focus:

Community-Centric: Craigslist often has a community-centric focus, making it suitable for freelancers who prefer local opportunities or building relationships within their community.

Varied Skill Levels:

Entry-Level to Expert Opportunities: Craigslist can have opportunities suitable for freelancers at different skill levels, from those starting out to experienced professionals.

Free and Paid Listings:

Listing Costs: Depending on the location and type of listing, posting a job or services offered on Craigslist can be free or may incur a nominal fee.

While Craigslist offers a diverse range of opportunities, freelancers should exercise caution and due diligence. The platform lacks the structure and safety features found on dedicated freelance marketplaces, and there is a potential for scams or unreliable clients. Freelancers using Craigslist should carefully vet clients, communicate clearly, and establish terms before starting any work.

List Of All Major Freelance Marketplaces And Their Reviews

Here's a list of major freelance marketplaces along with brief one-line reviews:

Upwork:

Review: Upwork is a comprehensive platform with a vast range of freelance opportunities, robust features, and a global user base.

Freelancer.com:

Review: Freelancer.com offers a diverse array of projects with a bidding system, making it suitable for freelancers across various skill sets.

Fiverr:

Review: Fiverr's microservice model and gig-based structure make it user-friendly for both freelancers and clients seeking creative services.

Guru.com:

Review: Guru.com combines traditional bidding systems with flexible work agreements, providing freelancers with diverse project opportunities.

PeoplePerHour:

Review: PeoplePerHour stands out with its combination of fixed-price "Hourlies" and project proposals, offering a unique approach to freelancing.

Toptal:

Review: Toptal specializes in connecting clients with top-tier freelancers in software development, ensuring high-quality talent for complex projects.

Craigslist:

Review: Craigslist, while not dedicated to freelancing, offers a wide range of job opportunities, making it a potential source for freelance work.

99designs:

Review: 99designs focuses on graphic design through contests, providing a platform for clients to receive a variety of design concepts.

SimplyHired:

Review: SimplyHired aggregates job listings, including freelance opportunities, offering a broad range of positions and industries.

Hubstaff Talent:

Review: Hubstaff Talent is a free directory connecting freelancers with clients, emphasizing transparency and direct collaboration.

Catalant (formerly HourlyNerd):

Review: Catalant connects businesses with on-demand business expertise, providing a platform for freelance consultants.

TaskRabbit:

Review: TaskRabbit focuses on local tasks and services, making it suitable for freelancers offering hands-on assistance in various categories.

Truelancer:

Review: Truelancer offers a diverse range of freelance projects with a focus on international opportunities, catering to freelancers across different domains.

Workana:

Review: Workana is a Latin American freelance marketplace that connects clients with freelancers in various fields, emphasizing collaboration.

Crowded:

Review: Crowded is a talent marketplace that connects freelancers with employers, using artificial intelligence to match individuals with suitable projects.

SimplyHired:

Review: SimplyHired aggregates job listings, including freelance opportunities, offering a broad range of positions and industries.

FreeUp:

Review: FreeUp connects businesses with pre-vetted freelancers, specializing in e-commerce, digital marketing, and various other skills.

These brief reviews aim to provide a quick overview of the key features and strengths of each freelance marketplace. It's important for freelancers to explore and choose platforms based on their specific skills, preferences, and the types of projects they are seeking.

Chapter 9: Presenting Yourself

⸙ Present Yourself Professionally

Presenting yourself effectively on freelancing marketplaces is crucial for attracting clients and securing projects.

Here are some tips on how to present yourself professionally:

Create a Complete Profile:

- Fill out all sections of your profile, including your bio, skills, education, and work history.

- Upload a professional profile picture that reflects your personality and approachability.

Craft a Compelling Bio:

- Write a concise and engaging bio that highlights your skills, experience, and what sets you apart.
- Showcase your expertise and describe the value you can bring to clients.

Emphasize Skills and Expertise:

- List your key skills prominently to grab the attention of clients searching for specific talents.
- Highlight any certifications or specialized training that enhances your skills.

Build a Strong Portfolio:

- Showcase your best work through a diverse and well-curated portfolio.

- Include detailed descriptions for each project, explaining your role and the impact of your contributions.

Use a Professional Tone:

- Communicate professionally in your bio, proposals, and messages.
- Check for grammar and spelling errors to maintain a polished image.

Create a Unique Selling Proposition (USP):

- Identify what makes you unique and communicate it clearly.
- Explain how your skills or approach set you apart from other freelancers.

Set Realistic Pricing:

- Determine competitive and realistic pricing for your services.
- Consider your experience, expertise, and the market rates when setting your prices.

Write Persuasive Proposals:

- Customize your proposals for each job, addressing the client's specific needs.
- Clearly outline how your skills and experience make you the ideal candidate for the project.

Include Relevant Keywords:

- Use relevant keywords in your profile and proposals to improve visibility in search results.
- Think about the terms clients might use when searching for your services.

Request and Showcase Client Reviews:

- Request reviews from satisfied clients to build credibility.
- Display positive client feedback prominently on your profile.

Be Responsive and Professional:

- Respond to messages and job invitations promptly.
- Maintain a professional demeanor in all your interactions.

Demonstrate Versatility:

- Highlight your ability to adapt to different project requirements.
- Showcase a range of skills to appeal to a broader client base.

Regularly Update Your Profile:

- Keep your profile up-to-date with your latest skills and accomplishments.
- Add new projects to your portfolio to demonstrate ongoing activity.

Utilize Additional Features:

- Take advantage of any additional features provided by the platform, such as skill tests, certifications, or a professional headline.

By presenting yourself professionally on freelancing marketplaces, you increase your chances of attracting clients, winning projects, and building a successful freelance career. Regularly review and update your profile to reflect your evolving skills and achievements.

🕐 Best Time to Create a Profile

The best time to create a profile on a freelancing marketplace is when you are fully prepared to showcase your skills, experience, and commitment to potential clients. Here are a few considerations for determining the optimal time to create your profile:

When You Have a Strong Portfolio:

Ensure that you have a collection of your best work ready to showcase in your portfolio. This might include samples, case studies, or descriptions of projects you've successfully completed.

After Identifying Your Niche and Skills:

Clearly define your niche and the specific skills you want to offer. This clarity will help you tailor your profile to attract clients looking for your expertise.

Once You Have a Professional Profile Picture:

Choose a professional and friendly profile picture. It's the first visual impression clients will have of you, so make sure it reflects your professionalism.

When You Can Commit to Responsiveness:

Clients often appreciate freelancers who respond promptly. Make sure you can commit to checking messages and notifications regularly before creating your profile.

After Setting Realistic Pricing:

Research market rates for your skills and set realistic pricing for your services. This step is crucial to attracting clients and positioning yourself competitively.

When You Can Write a Compelling Bio:

Craft a well-written bio that highlights your skills, experience, and unique selling points. A compelling bio can make a significant difference in attracting clients.

Once You've Gathered Client Testimonials:

If you have worked with clients outside the platform, gather testimonials that can be included in your profile. Positive feedback enhances your credibility.

When You Can Dedicate Time to Bidding/Proposals:

Plan to spend time regularly bidding on projects or submitting proposals. This proactive approach increases your chances of landing projects.

When You're Ready to Commit to the Platform:

Creating a profile is just the beginning. Be ready to commit to the platform by actively participating, maintaining professionalism, and delivering high-quality work.

When You've Considered Your Availability:

Clearly communicate your availability and turnaround times. Set realistic expectations for clients regarding when you can start and complete projects.

After Researching the Platform:

Take the time to familiarize yourself with the freelancing platform's features, policies, and community guidelines. Understanding the platform's dynamics will help you navigate it effectively.

Remember that first impressions matter, so take the time to present yourself in the best possible light. Once you've addressed these considerations, you'll be well-prepared to create a compelling profile and start your freelancing journey on a positive note.

★ Essentials of Profile

Creating an effective profile is essential for freelancers to attract clients and stand out in a competitive marketplace. Here are the key essentials to include in your freelancing profile:

Professional Profile Picture:

Choose a clear, professional, and friendly profile picture. It adds a personal touch and makes your profile more approachable.

Compelling Headline:

Craft a concise and compelling headline that summarizes your expertise and highlights your unique selling proposition.

Detailed Bio:

Write a comprehensive bio that showcases your skills, experience, and the value you bring to clients. Be specific about your niche and the services you offer.

Skills and Expertise:

List your key skills prominently. Use relevant keywords to enhance your profile's visibility in search results.

Portfolio of Work:

Create a robust portfolio showcasing your best work. Include project descriptions, your role, and the impact of your contributions.

Education and Certifications:

Highlight your educational background and any relevant certifications. This adds credibility to your profile.

Professional Experience:

Provide details about your work history, emphasizing roles and experiences that are relevant to your freelancing services.

Pricing and Payment Preferences:

Clearly outline your pricing structure and payment preferences. This transparency helps clients understand the financial aspects of working with you.

Client Testimonials:

If you have received positive feedback from clients, include testimonials in your profile. Client endorsements build trust with potential clients.

Availability and Time Zone:

Clearly state your availability, including working hours and days. Mention your time zone to manage client expectations regarding communication and project timelines.

Responsive Communication:

Express your commitment to timely and responsive communication. Clients appreciate freelancers who are proactive and communicative.

Link to External Portfolios or Websites:

If applicable, include links to external portfolios, personal websites, or relevant online profiles to provide additional context and showcase your work in more detail.

Languages Spoken:

Specify the languages you are proficient in. This is especially important if language skills are relevant to the services you offer.

Up-to-Date Information:

Regularly update your profile to reflect any changes in skills, experience, or availability. An up-to-date profile signals your active engagement on the platform.

Social Media Links (Optional):

If you maintain professional social media profiles, consider adding links to platforms like LinkedIn to offer clients additional insights into your professional background.

Remember that a well-crafted profile not only attracts clients but also sets the tone for successful collaborations. Tailor your profile to your unique strengths and the specific needs of your target clients.

Create Graphics for Your Profile

Not all marketplaces provide a similar style of profile, but you can create a customized profile for yourself and share the link to clients. Creating a customized profile needs special skills to present yourself in an attractive manner. Creating graphics for your freelancing profile can help make it visually appealing and showcase your professionalism.

Here are some graphics you might consider adding:

Profile Banner:

Design a banner that serves as the header of your profile. Include your name, a tagline, and perhaps some visual elements related to your niche or skills. Some examples are here:

Logo (if applicable):

If you have a personal logo or a brand logo, include it in your profile. This can enhance brand consistency and recognition.

Portfolio Thumbnails:

A thumbnail is a small image representation of a larger image, usually intended to make it easier and faster to look at or manage a group of larger images. A website thumbnail can be used to reinforce a website's brand by incorporating its logo or other distinctive imagery. Design eye-catching thumbnails for your portfolio items. Use visuals that represent the type of work you do.

Infographics:

Create infographics that visually represent your skills, experience, or the process you follow when working on a project. Infographics can quickly convey information in an engaging way.

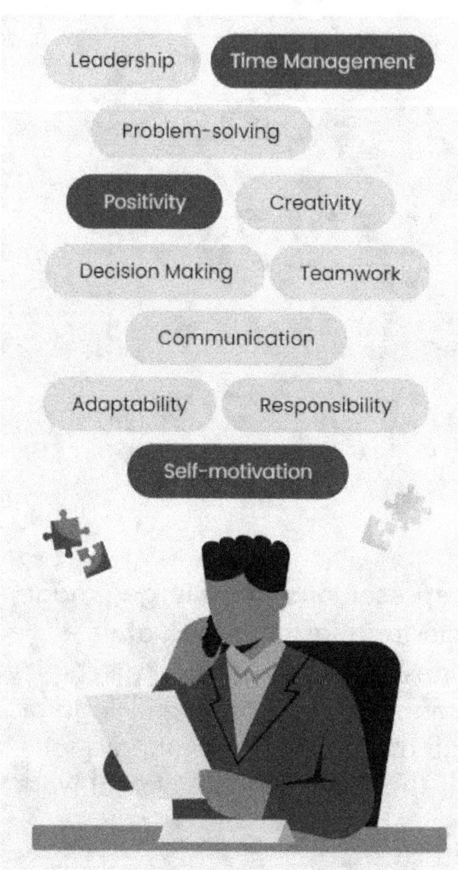

Icons for Skills:

Design icons for each of your key skills. This adds a visual element to the list of skills on your profile and makes it more appealing.

Testimonial Graphics:

Turn positive testimonials into graphics. Use a visually pleasing layout with quotes from satisfied clients, along with their names and titles.

Graphs or Charts:

If you want to showcase data, such as your growth in projects, client satisfaction rates, or any other relevant metrics, design graphs or charts.

Call-to-Action Buttons:

Create visually appealing buttons that serve as calls-to-action. For example, a button leading to your portfolio, a button for contacting you, or a button for hiring you.

Branded Watermark:

If you share visual content or documents, consider adding a subtle branded watermark with your logo or initials.

Custom Backgrounds:

Design custom backgrounds for different sections of your profile. This adds a personal touch and helps break up the visual monotony.

Section Dividers:

Create graphics to serve as dividers between sections of your profile. This adds structure and visual interest to the overall layout.

Skills Badges:

Design badges for your key skills. These can be displayed prominently in your profile to draw attention to your expertise.

Process Flowcharts:

If applicable, create visual flowcharts that illustrate your workflow, or the process clients can expect when working with you.

Clickable Social Media Icons:

Design visually appealing social media icons that are clickable. This makes it easy for clients to connect with you on other platforms.

Mood Boards (for creative professionals):

For creative professionals, consider creating mood boards that showcase your aesthetic preferences, style, or inspiration.

When creating graphics, ensure that they align with your personal brand and the overall theme of your profile. Use consistent colors, fonts, and imagery to maintain a cohesive and professional look. Additionally, ensure that the graphics are optimized for online viewing to ensure fast loading times on the platform.

💳 Payment Verification and Withdrawal Method

Payment verification and withdrawal method are two distinct processes in the context of freelancing platforms.

Let's clarify the differences:

Payment Verification:

Payment verification is the process by which freelancers on a platform confirm or link a valid payment method to their account.

Purpose: This is a security measure to ensure that freelancers have a legitimate means of receiving payments for their services.

Common Methods: Payment verification may involve linking a bank account, credit card, or other payment methods to the freelancers' account on the platform.

Verification Steps: Freelancers often need to provide specific details or documents to verify their payment method, such as bank account information or identification documents.

Outcome: Once the payment method is successfully verified, freelancers can receive payments from clients through the selected method.

Withdrawal Method:

The withdrawal method refers to the process by which freelancers transfer their earned funds from their platform account to their personal accounts.

Purpose: Freelancers use the withdrawal method to access the money they have earned on the platform and transfer it to their preferred financial accounts.

Options: Freelancers can choose from various withdrawal methods offered by the platform, such as bank transfers, PayPal, Payoneer, or other supported payment systems.

Withdrawal Fees and Timelines: Different withdrawal methods may have associated fees or varying processing times. Freelancers should be aware of these details when selecting a withdrawal method.

Flexibility: Freelancers often have the flexibility to choose different withdrawal methods based on their preferences or the most convenient option at a given time.

In short, payment verification is the process of ensuring that freelancers have a valid and secure method for receiving payments on a freelancing platform. Once verified, freelancers can choose a withdrawal method to transfer their earnings from the platform to their personal accounts. While payment verification focuses on the receipt of funds, withdrawal method concerns the process of transferring those funds to the freelancer's chosen financial account.

💰 Setting your payment information

Populating Your Payment Information

Populating your payment information on a freelancing platform is a crucial step for several reasons, and it serves the interests of both freelancers and clients. Here are the main reasons for setting up and populating your payment information:

Facilitates Payment Process:

Reason: By providing your payment information, you enable the platform to process payments efficiently.

Benefit: This streamlines the financial transactions between clients and freelancers, ensuring a smoother and more convenient payment process.

Receives Earnings:

Reason: Payment information is essential for receiving the earnings you generate from completed projects.

Benefit: Without accurate payment details, the platform cannot transfer funds to you. Setting up your payment information ensures you receive your hard-earned money promptly.

Builds Trust with Clients:

Reason: Clients often prefer working with freelancers who have verified and populated payment information.

Benefit: It adds a layer of trust and credibility to your profile. Clients are more likely to hire freelancers with complete payment information as it signifies a commitment to the freelancing relationship.

Ensures Security and Compliance:

Reason: Platforms use payment information to ensure security and compliance with financial regulations.

Benefit: Verifying payment details helps the platform maintain a secure environment for financial transactions and adhere to legal and regulatory requirements.

Enables Automatic Payments:

Reason: Some platforms offer automatic payment features for recurring projects or subscriptions.

Benefit: With populated payment information, you can take advantage of automated payments, saving time and ensuring timely transactions for ongoing work.

Facilitates Dispute Resolution:

Reason: Accurate payment information is essential for resolving any payment-related disputes.

Benefit: In case of discrepancies or disputes, having verified payment details allows the platform to investigate and resolve issues more efficiently.

Complies with Platform Policies:

Reason: Most freelancing platforms require users to provide accurate and up-to-date payment information as part of their terms of service.

Benefit: Complying with platform policies is necessary for continued access to the platform's features and opportunities.

Supports Global Transactions:

Reason: If you work with clients internationally, having populated payment information ensures a seamless cross-border payment process.

Benefit: It facilitates international transactions, allowing you to work with clients from different parts of the world without payment-related complications.

In conclusion, populating your payment information is a fundamental step in establishing a reliable and efficient financial infrastructure on freelancing platforms. It benefits both freelancers and clients by ensuring a secure, trustworthy, and streamlined payment process.

Getting IBAN, Swift code

To obtain your International Bank Account Number (IBAN) and SWIFT/BIC code, you'll need to follow these general steps:

For IBAN:

Contact Your Bank:

Reach out to your bank to request your IBAN. They will provide you with the necessary information related to your account.

Check Bank Statements:

Your IBAN is often available on your bank statements. Review your printed or online statements to find this information.

Online Banking:

Log in to your online banking portal. Many banks provide access to your IBAN through their online platforms.

Visit the Bank:

If you're unable to obtain the IBAN through online channels, visit your bank in person. Speak to a customer service representative who can assist you in retrieving this information.

For SWIFT/BIC Code:

Check with Your Bank:

Contact your bank to inquire about the SWIFT or BIC code associated with your account.

Online Banking:

Like the IBAN, your SWIFT/BIC code may be available through your online banking portal. Log in and explore the available account details.

Bank's Website:

Visit your bank's official website. Many banks provide SWIFT/BIC information on their websites, especially in the international wire transfer or contact sections.

Bank Statement:

Your SWIFT/BIC code might be included in your bank statements, either in paper form or through your online banking account.

Customer Service:

If you're unable to find the SWIFT/BIC code through the above methods, contact your bank's customer service. They can provide you with the accurate code associated with your account.

Additional Tips:

Use the Correct Branch Code:

Depending on your bank, you might also need a branch code or additional information. Ensure that you have all the necessary details for international transactions.

Double-Check Accuracy:

When receiving your IBAN and SWIFT/BIC code, double-check the accuracy of the information provided to avoid any errors in financial transactions.

Keep Information Secure:

Treat your IBAN and SWIFT/BIC code as sensitive information. Only share it with trusted parties involved in financial transactions.

It's important to note that the process may vary depending on your bank and its procedures. If you have difficulties obtaining this information, reaching out directly to your bank's customer service or visiting a local branch is often the most effective way to ensure accuracy.

Populating Bank Wire Information

Populating your bank wire information on a freelancing platform is essential for receiving payments via direct bank transfers. Here's a step-by-step guide on how to populate your bank wire information:

1. Log into Your Freelancing Platform Account:

Access your freelancing platform account using your credentials.

2. Navigate to Payment Settings or Payment Information:

Platforms often have a dedicated section for payment settings, billing, or payment information. Look for a menu option related to payments or financial details.

3. Locate Bank Wire or Direct Transfer Section:

Within the payment settings, find the section specifically for bank wire or direct transfer information. This is where you'll input details for receiving payments directly to your bank account.

4. Input Bank Account Details:

Enter the required information, which typically includes:

Account Holder Name: Your full name as it appears on your bank account.

Bank Name: The name of your bank.

Account Number: Your bank account number.

IBAN (if applicable): International Bank Account Number, if required.

SWIFT/BIC Code: Society for Worldwide Interbank Financial Telecommunication/Bank Identifier Code.

Branch Address (if required): Some platforms may ask for your bank's branch address.

5. Verify the Information:

Double-check the accuracy of the entered details to ensure that there are no errors in your bank wire information.

6. Save or Update Your Settings:

Once you've entered all the necessary details, look for a "Save" or "Update" button to save the information.

7. Set Default Payment Method (if applicable):

Some platforms allow you to set a default payment method. If so, choose bank wire as your default if you prefer this method for receiving payments.

8. Confirm Security Measures (if applicable):

The platform may have additional security measures, such as two-factor authentication, to confirm changes in payment information. Follow any additional steps required to confirm the update.

9. Test a Small Transaction (optional):

If you're unsure about the accuracy of the information, some freelancers prefer to initiate a small transaction first to verify that the bank wire details are correct.

10. Contact Platform Support (if needed):

If you encounter any issues or have questions about populating your bank wire information, don't hesitate to reach out to the customer support of the freelancing platform for assistance.

Remember, the steps and options may vary slightly depending on the specific platform you're using. Always follow the platform's guidelines and policies to ensure a smooth and secure process for updating your payment information.

Chapter 10 : Fiverr

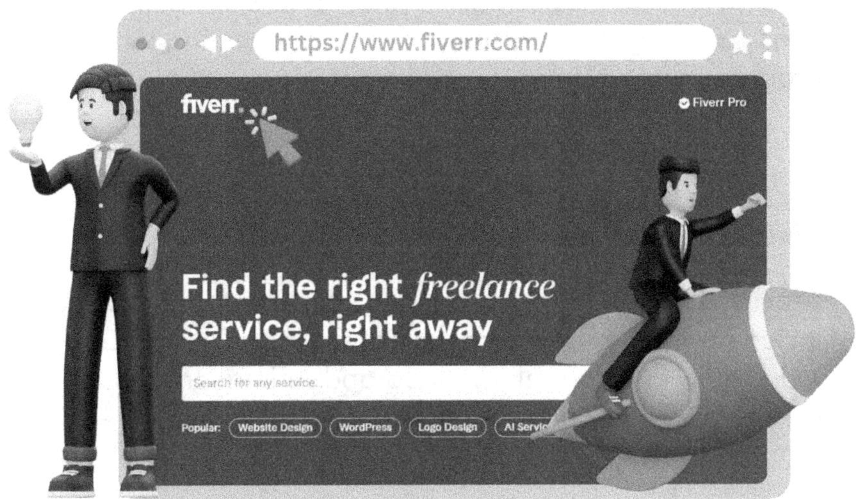

📢 Introduction to Fiverr

Fiverr is a popular online marketplace that connects freelancers with clients who are seeking a wide range of digital services. The platform was founded in 2010 and has since become one of the largest and most diverse freelance marketplaces globally. Fiverr's unique approach lies in its gig-based system, where freelancers offer their services in the form of "gigs" with a starting price of $5, from which the platform derived its name.

key aspects of Fiverr

Gig-Based Marketplace:

Gigs: Freelancers create gigs, which are service listings specifying what they offer, the price, and any additional details. Gigs can range from graphic design and writing to programming and digital marketing.

Diverse Categories:

Services Offered: Fiverr spans a broad spectrum of categories, including Writing and Translation, Graphic Design, Digital Marketing, Programming, Video and Animation, Music and Audio, Business, and many more.

Seller Levels:

Levels: Fiverr has a tiered system for sellers based on performance and customer satisfaction. Sellers start as new sellers and can progress to Level 1, Level 2, and Top Rated Seller, each with added benefits and privileges.

Buyer Requests:

Buyer Requests: Sellers can respond to Buyer Requests, where clients post specific projects they need help with. This allows freelancers to pitch their services directly to potential clients.

Custom Offers and Packages:

Customization: Sellers can create custom offers and packages beyond their basic $5 gig, allowing them to offer additional services or variations at different price points.

Fiverr Pro:

Fiverr Pro: Fiverr offers a premium service called Fiverr Pro, where hand-vetted professionals provide high-quality, premium services for clients who are looking for top-tier freelancers.

Reviews and Ratings:

Feedback System: Fiverr has a review and rating system, allowing both buyers and sellers to leave feedback based on their experience. Positive reviews contribute to a seller's reputation on the platform.

Communication Tools:

Messaging and File Sharing: Fiverr provides built-in communication tools, including messaging and file sharing, to facilitate communication between buyers and sellers throughout the project.

Secure Payment System:

Payment Process: Fiverr handles the payment process securely, ensuring that freelancers receive compensation for their work, and clients get the services they paid for.

Whether you're a freelancer looking to offer your skills or a business seeking professional services, Fiverr provides a platform for diverse digital services with a range of options to suit different needs and budgets.

📖 Profile Details on Fiverr

Fiverr is an online marketplace that connects freelancers with clients, offering a diverse range of digital services. The platform's name is derived from its initial concept of services starting at $5, but it has since evolved to include a variety of price points and service offerings. Freelancers on Fiverr, known as sellers, create "gigs" to showcase their skills and services to potential clients.

Importance of Profile Details on Fiverr

First Impression:

Your Fiverr profile is often the first interaction clients have with you. Complete and detailed profiles create a positive first impression, increasing the likelihood of attracting potential clients.

Professionalism:

A well-crafted profile conveys professionalism. Clients are more likely to trust and hire freelancers who have taken the time to provide comprehensive information about their skills, experience, and expertise.

Showcasing Expertise:

Detailed profile information allows you to showcase your expertise. Clearly outline your skills, areas of specialization, and any certifications or qualifications that demonstrate your proficiency in your field.

Building Trust:

Clients are more likely to trust freelancers with complete profiles. Include details about your background, work history, and any relevant achievements to build trust and credibility.

Customization:

Fiverr profiles allow you to customize your information based on your services. Tailor your profile details to match the specific needs of your target clients, highlighting the skills and services most relevant to them.

Search Visibility:

Fiverr's search algorithm considers the completeness of your profile. A well-filled profile increases your visibility in search results, making it easier for clients to find you when searching for specific services.

Buyer Decision-Making:

Clients often review profiles carefully before making hiring decisions. An informative profile helps clients understand what you offer, your work style, and your commitment to delivering quality services.

Setting Expectations:

Use your profile to set clear expectations for clients. Specify your working hours, response time, and any additional information that helps clients understand how you operate and what they can expect when working with you.

Portfolio Showcase:

Fiverr profiles include a portfolio section where you can showcase samples of your work. Take advantage of this feature to provide visual evidence of your skills and the quality of your services.

Optimized for Keywords:

Use relevant keywords in your profile details to optimize it for search. Think about the terms clients might use when looking for services like yours and incorporate them naturally into your profile.

In summary, a well-crafted Fiverr profile is a powerful tool for attracting clients, building trust, and showcasing your expertise. Take the time to provide comprehensive details that reflect your professionalism and make you stand out in the competitive freelancing marketplace.

♀ Finding Work on Fiverr (Defining Fiverr)

How to create a GIG?

Creating a gig on Fiverr is a straightforward process. Here's a step-by-step guide on how to create a gig:

1. Log In to Your Fiverr Account:

Visit the Fiverr website and log in to your account using your credentials.

2. Navigate to the Selling Dashboard:

Once logged in, go to the "Selling" tab on the top menu to access your selling dashboard.

3. Click on "Gigs":

Within the selling dashboard, click on the "Gigs" option. This will take you to the section where you can create and manage your gigs.

4. Click on "Create a New Gig":

Look for the "Create a New Gig" button. Click on it to start the gig creation process.

5. Choose a Category and Subcategory:

Fiverr has various categories and subcategories. Choose the most relevant category and subcategory for the service you are offering.

6. Select a Gig Title:

Craft a clear and descriptive title for your gig. It should convey what you are offering in a concise manner.

7. Add a Gig Gallery:

Upload images that represent your gig. These could be examples of your work, graphics, or anything that visually showcases what clients can expect.

8. Write a Gig Description:

Write a detailed and engaging description of your gig. Clearly explain what services you are offering, your expertise, and any unique selling points. Be thorough but concise.

9. Add FAQ (Optional):

You have the option to add frequently asked questions (FAQs) to your gig. This can help address common queries from potential clients and provide additional information.

10. Set Gig Pricing:

Set your pricing for the basic gig package. You can offer multiple packages with different features and prices. Specify what clients will get for each package.

11. Add Gig Extras (Optional):

If you want to offer additional services or upgrades, you can add gig extras. This allows clients to customize their order with additional options.

12. Set Delivery Time:

Specify the time it will take you to deliver the basic gig. Be realistic in setting your delivery time to manage client expectations.

13. Add Relevant Tags:

Use relevant tags to help your gig appear in search results. Tags should reflect the keywords clients might use when searching for services like yours.

14. Preview Your Gig:

Before publishing, preview your gig to ensure all details are accurate and visually appealing.

15. Publish Your Gig:

Once you're satisfied with the details, click the "Publish Gig" button to make your gig live on Fiverr.

16. Promote Your Gig (Optional):

After publishing, consider promoting your gig through social media or other channels to increase its visibility.

Congratulations, you've successfully created a gig on Fiverr! Keep in mind that you can always go back and edit your gig details if needed. Regularly updating and optimizing your gig can enhance its performance and attract more clients.

★The Importance of Keywords on Fiverr

Keywords play a crucial role on Fiverr as they are the primary way that clients find relevant services. Understanding the importance of keywords and using them effectively can significantly boost the visibility of your gigs. Here's why keywords matter on Fiverr:

Search Visibility:

Fiverr's search algorithm relies on keywords to match clients with relevant gigs. Using the right keywords increases the likelihood of your gig appearing in search results when clients are looking for services like yours.

Targeting Your Audience:

Keywords help you target your specific audience. Think about the terms or phrases potential clients might use when searching for services in your niche. Incorporate these keywords into your gig title, description, and tags.

Competition Analysis:

Researching and strategically using keywords allows you to analyze your competition. Identify high-performing gigs in your category, observe their keyword usage, and adapt your approach accordingly.

Gig Optimization:

Incorporating relevant keywords in your gig title, description, and tags optimizes your gig for search. This ensures that Fiverr's algorithm can accurately categorize and display your gig to clients seeking specific services.

Credibility and Trust:

Using precise and relevant keywords builds credibility. When clients see that your gig is aligned with their search terms, it instills confidence and trust in your services, increasing the likelihood of them clicking on your gig.

Understanding Client Language:

Clients may use different terms or phrases to describe the same service. Using a variety of keywords allows you to speak the language of potential clients and cater to a broader range of search queries.

Gig Discoverability:

Keywords contribute to the discoverability of your gig. The more accurately you describe your services using relevant keywords, the easier it is for clients to find you amidst the vast pool of gigs on Fiverr.

Adapting to Trends:

Stay informed about industry trends and the evolving language clients use. Regularly update your gig keywords to reflect changing preferences and emerging terms in your field.

Strategic Tagging:

Fiverr allows you to add tags to your gig. These tags are essential keywords that further enhance your gig's visibility. Choose tags that directly relate to your services and align with popular search terms.

Improved Conversion Rates:

When your gig appears in relevant searches, you are more likely to attract clients genuinely interested in your services. This targeted exposure can lead to higher conversion rates and increased orders.

In summary, keywords are a fundamental element in Fiverr's search and discovery process. By carefully selecting and strategically incorporating keywords, you can optimize your gig for search visibility, attract the right audience, and ultimately increase your chances of securing freelance opportunities on the platform.

🎥The Importance of Video for Your Gigs

Adding a video to your Fiverr gig can significantly enhance its appeal and effectiveness. Here are several reasons highlighting the importance of including a video in your gig:

Increased Engagement:

Videos capture attention more effectively than text or images alone. A well-made video can engage potential clients and encourage them to explore your gig further.

Showcasing Your Skills:

A video allows you to visually showcase your skills and the quality of your work. It provides a dynamic and interactive way to demonstrate what clients can expect from your services.

Building Trust and Credibility:

Seeing and hearing a freelancer through a video can create a sense of trust and credibility. Clients may feel more confident in hiring someone whose personality and expertise are showcased in a video.

Explaining Complex Services:

If your services are complex or require additional explanation, a video can help simplify and clarify the details. It provides an opportunity to walk clients through your process and offerings.

Personal Connection:

Videos allow you to establish a personal connection with potential clients. Sharing a bit about yourself, your work environment, or your creative process can create a more personalized and relatable experience.

Highlighting Unique Selling Points:

Use the video to highlight the unique aspects of your services that set you apart from competitors. Whether it's your approach, creativity, or specific skills, a video can effectively communicate your unique selling points.

Increased Visibility in Fiverr Search:

Fiverr's algorithm often prioritizes gigs with videos in search results. Having a video can improve the visibility of your gig and make it more likely to appear in relevant searches.

Encouraging Client Interaction:

A video can encourage clients to interact with your gig by watching, liking, and sharing. The more engagement your gig receives, the more likely it is to be promoted by Fiverr's algorithm.

Improving Conversion Rates:

Gigs with videos tend to have higher conversion rates. When clients can see your work in action and understand your services better, they are more likely to make a purchasing decision.

Comprehensive Gig Preview:

A video allows you to provide a comprehensive preview of your services. You can showcase multiple examples of your work, explain different packages, and give clients a better overall understanding of what you offer.

Remember to keep your video concise, focused, and professionally produced. Clearly communicate the value of your services and encourage viewers to take action. Whether it's a demonstration of your skills, a brief introduction, or a showcase of your portfolio, a well-crafted video can significantly enhance the effectiveness of your Fiverr gig.

🖂 Extra Offer (time constraint) To charge More Money

Offering extra services with a time constraint, commonly known as "Express" or "Fast Delivery" options, can be a strategic approach to attract more clients and increase your earnings on Fiverr. Here's how you can effectively utilize this feature:

1. Identify Services Suitable for Fast Delivery:

Choose services within your expertise that can be delivered quickly without compromising quality. This could include simple tasks, quick consultations, or services that naturally lend themselves to faster turnaround times.

2. Set Realistic Timeframes:

When offering an express or fast delivery option, it's crucial to set realistic timeframes. Consider the complexity of the service and your own workload to ensure you can consistently meet the specified delivery times.

3. Highlight the Express Option in Your Gig:

Clearly communicate the availability of express or fast delivery in your gig description. Use attention-grabbing phrases like "Get Your Project Done in 24 Hours!" to attract clients looking for quick turnaround.

4. Charge a Premium for Fast Delivery:

Since fast delivery is a premium service, consider charging an additional fee for this option. Clients willing to pay extra for quick turnaround are likely to appreciate the convenience and urgency.

5. Offer Tiers with Varied Delivery Times:

Provide different packages or tiers with varied delivery times. For example, offer a standard delivery time, an express option for quicker delivery at an additional cost, and a premium option for even faster delivery with added benefits.

6. Showcase Previous Fast Delivery Successes:

If you have successfully delivered projects quickly in the past, showcase these achievements in your portfolio or gig description. Testimonials or reviews that mention your speed and efficiency can build credibility.

7. Use Urgency in Gig Descriptions:

Create a sense of urgency in your gig descriptions by emphasizing limited availability or special discounts for fast delivery. This can encourage clients to take immediate action.

8. Optimize Keywords for Quick Turnaround:

Include keywords related to fast delivery in your gig title, description, and tags. This will make your gig more visible to clients specifically searching for quick turnaround services.

9. Provide Clear Communication Channels:

Clearly outline communication channels to maintain transparency with clients. Inform them about the importance of timely communication for faster project completion.

10. Set Expectations Clearly:

Clearly communicate what clients can expect with the fast delivery option. Be transparent about the services included, the delivery process, and any limitations to avoid misunderstandings.

11. Deliver High-Quality Work:

While speed is essential, never compromise on the quality of your work. Delivering high-quality results within a short timeframe enhances client satisfaction and builds a positive reputation.

12. Promote the Fast Delivery Option:

Actively promote your fast delivery option on your social media channels, Fiverr profile, and other platforms where potential clients might discover your services.

By strategically offering express or fast delivery options, you not only cater to clients with urgent needs but also create an additional revenue stream for your freelancing business on Fiverr. Remember, balancing speed and quality is key to building a reputation for reliability and excellence.

⚡ The Importance of Meeting Timelines (deliverables)

Meeting timelines or deliverables is of utmost importance in freelancing for several compelling reasons:

Client Satisfaction:

Timely delivery of work contributes significantly to client satisfaction. Clients appreciate freelancers who respect deadlines, as it allows them to plan and execute their projects seamlessly.

Professionalism and Reliability:

Consistently meeting deadlines is a reflection of your professionalism and reliability as a freelancer. It builds trust with clients, establishing you as someone they can depend on for timely and quality work.

Building a Positive Reputation:

Word-of-mouth is powerful in the freelance industry. By consistently meeting deadlines, you build a positive reputation that can lead to repeat business and referrals from satisfied clients.

Client Retention:

Freelancers who consistently meet timelines are more likely to retain clients. Clients appreciate reliability, and those who have positive experiences with your punctuality are likely to return for future projects.

Earning Trust and Respect:

Meeting deadlines earns you the trust and respect of clients. It demonstrates your commitment to their projects and showcases your ability to manage time effectively.

Reducing Stress and Pressure:

Timely completion of tasks helps in reducing stress and pressure on both you and the client. Procrastination and missed deadlines can lead to last-minute rushes, negatively impacting the quality of work.

Encouraging Positive Feedback:

Clients are more likely to leave positive feedback and testimonials when you consistently deliver work on time. Positive feedback enhances your profile on freelancing platforms and attracts more clients.

Maintaining Professional Relationships:

Meeting timelines is crucial for maintaining positive professional relationships. In freelancing, where communication is often virtual, being reliable in terms of timelines is a key factor in fostering good relationships with clients.

Enhancing Efficiency and Productivity:

Adhering to deadlines requires effective time management. By consistently meeting timelines, you enhance your efficiency and productivity, allowing you to take on more projects and increase your earning potential.

Avoiding Penalties and Disputes:

Some freelancing platforms have penalties for missed deadlines, and clients may dispute payments if work is not delivered as agreed. Meeting timelines helps you avoid these potential issues and maintain a positive standing on the platform.

Demonstrating Commitment:

Timely delivery communicates your commitment to the success of the client's project. It shows that you take their work seriously and are dedicated to providing value within the agreed-upon timeframe.

In fact, meeting timelines is not just a professional expectation; it is a fundamental aspect of building a successful freelancing career. It positively impacts client relationships, your reputation, and your overall success in the competitive freelance marketplace.

💬 Importance Of Employer's Feedback

The importance of employer feedback on Fiverr cannot be overstated, as it plays a pivotal role in shaping your reputation, attracting new clients, and building trust within the freelancing community. Here are several reasons highlighting the significance of employer feedback:

Reputation Building:

Positive employer feedback contributes directly to building a strong reputation on Fiverr. It serves as a public endorsement of your skills, professionalism, and the quality of your work.

Trust and Credibility:

Potential clients often rely on feedback and reviews to gauge the trustworthiness and credibility of freelancers. Positive feedback signals to new clients that you have a history of delivering satisfactory results.

Competitive Edge:

In a competitive freelancing marketplace, positive employer feedback sets you apart from others offering similar services. Clients are more likely to choose a freelancer with a proven track record of success.

Increased Visibility:

Fiverr's search algorithm considers the feedback and reviews a freelancer receives. Positive feedback can enhance your gig's visibility in search results, making it more likely to attract potential clients.

Client Confidence:

Employers are more confident in hiring freelancers with a track record of positive feedback. Knowing that others have had successful experiences with your services instills confidence in new clients considering your gig.

Portfolio Enhancement:

Positive feedback serves as a valuable addition to your portfolio. As clients browse through your gigs, seeing positive reviews provides them with concrete evidence of your ability to meet expectations.

Building Long-Term Relationships:

Frequent positive feedback can lead to long-term relationships with clients. Satisfied clients are more likely to return for additional projects, contributing to the sustainability of your freelancing business.

Feedback as a Learning Tool:

Constructive criticism in feedback offers an opportunity for improvement. Use feedback—both positive and constructive—as a learning tool to refine your skills and enhance the overall client experience.

Platform Trustworthiness:

Fiverr, as a platform, relies on the feedback system to maintain a trustworthy environment. Positive feedback helps build the platform's reputation as a reliable marketplace for quality freelancers.

Mitigating Risks:

Employers often read feedback before making hiring decisions. Positive feedback helps mitigate the perceived risks associated with hiring a freelancer, encouraging more clients to choose your services.

Encouraging Repeat Business:

Clients who leave positive feedback may become repeat clients. The positive experience they had with your services increases the likelihood of them returning for future projects.

Word-of-Mouth Marketing:

Positive employer feedback acts as a form of word-of-mouth marketing. Clients may share their positive experiences with others, indirectly promoting your services to a broader audience.

To maximize the impact of employer feedback, consistently deliver high-quality work, communicate effectively, and strive to exceed client expectations. The accumulation of positive feedback over time becomes a valuable asset in your freelancing career on Fiverr.

⚓ Promoting Your GIG On Fiverr

Promoting your gig on Fiverr is essential to attract more clients and increase your visibility in the marketplace. Here are effective strategies to promote your gig on Fiverr:

Optimize Your Gig:

Start by optimizing your gig details. Use a clear and descriptive title, write a compelling gig description, and choose relevant tags. This optimization helps your gig appear in relevant search results.

Create a Professional Profile:

Your Fiverr profile is a key element in attracting clients. Ensure your profile is complete, professional, and showcases your skills. Use a clear profile picture and provide information that builds trust with potential clients.

Utilize Keywords:

Incorporate relevant keywords in your gig title, description, and tags. Think about the terms potential clients might use when searching for services similar to yours. This helps improve your gig's visibility in search results.

Offer Special Promotions:

Consider offering special promotions, discounts, or bundled services to attract new clients. Fiverr allows you to create custom offers, and promoting these special deals can make your gig more appealing.

Create an Eye-Catching Gig Gallery:

Use high-quality images in your gig gallery that showcase your work. Visuals are powerful, and an eye-catching gallery can grab the attention of potential clients browsing through Fiverr.

Highlight Unique Selling Points:

Clearly communicate the unique aspects of your services that set you apart from others. Whether it's your approach, expertise, or additional offerings, make sure potential clients understand what makes your gig special.

Promote Through Social Media:

Leverage your social media channels to promote your Fiverr gig. Share links to your gig, showcase your work, and encourage your network to spread the word. Social media promotion can significantly increase your gig's visibility.

Participate in Fiverr Forums:

Engage with the Fiverr community by participating in forums. Share your expertise, answer questions, and showcase your work. Active participation in the community can lead to increased visibility for your gig.

Ask for Reviews and Testimonials:

Encourage satisfied clients to leave reviews and testimonials on your gig. Positive feedback builds trust with potential clients and contributes to the overall success of your gig.

Use Fiverr Promoted Gigs:

Fiverr offers a Promoted Gigs feature that allows you to pay for increased visibility. You can set a daily budget, and Fiverr will display your gig in prominent positions, increasing its chances of being seen by potential clients.

Offer a Variety of Packages:

Provide different packages or tiers for your services to cater to a broader audience. Clients appreciate having options, and offering packages at various price points can attract a diverse range of clients.

Regularly Update Your Gig:

Keep your gig information up to date. If you acquire new skills, update your gig to reflect them. Regularly updating your gig shows that you are actively engaged and committed to providing valuable services.

Remember that promoting your gig is an ongoing process. By consistently implementing these strategies, you can increase your chances of attracting clients and growing your freelancing business on Fiverr.

The Importance of Multiple Gigs

Creating and managing multiple gigs on platforms like Fiverr can be strategically beneficial for freelancers. Here are several reasons highlighting the importance of having multiple gigs:

Diversifying Your Offerings:

Multiple gigs allow you to diversify the services you offer. This not only attracts a broader range of clients with different needs but also minimizes the impact of market fluctuations in a specific niche.

Catering to Different Audiences:

Each gig can target a specific audience or demographic. By tailoring your gigs to different client needs or industries, you increase your chances of attracting a diverse clientele.

Expanding Your Reach:

Having multiple gigs increases your visibility on the platform. When potential clients search for services, having a variety of gigs increases the likelihood that one of your offerings will match their needs.

Showcasing Specialized Skills:

If you possess a range of skills, multiple gigs allow you to showcase each skillset individually. This helps you stand out as an expert in specific areas and positions you as a versatile freelancer.

Taking Advantage of Trends:

Freelancing trends may evolve over time. By having multiple gigs, you can adapt to emerging trends and cater to the changing needs of clients. This flexibility can give you a competitive edge.

Maximizing Earning Potential:

Offering a variety of services allows you to maximize your earning potential. Clients with different budgets and requirements may be interested in different gigs, enabling you to generate income from various sources.

Increasing Conversion Opportunities:

Multiple gigs provide more opportunities for clients to discover and engage with your services. If one gig doesn't resonate with a particular client, they may find another gig that better suits their needs.

Building a Robust Portfolio:

Each gig contributes to your overall portfolio. A robust portfolio showcasing a variety of skills and successful projects enhances your credibility and attracts clients who value a well-rounded freelancer.

Adapting to Market Demand:

Markets can be dynamic, and client demands may change. Having multiple gigs allows you to adapt to shifts in demand and align your offerings with what clients are actively seeking.

Testing and Optimization:

You can use multiple gigs as an opportunity to test different strategies. Monitor the performance of each gig, analyze client engagement, and optimize based on the data you gather to refine your approach.

Creating a Niche Presence:

If you have expertise in different niches, multiple gigs help you establish a presence in each niche. This can make you more visible to clients specifically searching for services within those niches.

Enhancing Branding:

Each gig contributes to your overall freelancer brand. By maintaining consistency in branding across your gigs, you create a unified and professional image that resonates with clients.

Having multiple gigs offers freelancers strategic advantages, including diversification, expanded reach, and the ability to adapt to market trends. It provides a comprehensive approach to showcasing your skills, attracting clients, and maximizing your success on freelancing platforms.

💰 Funds Withdrawal Method (Payoneer)

Withdrawing funds from Fiverr using Payoneer is a straightforward process. Here's a step-by-step guide on how to set up and use Payoneer for funds withdrawal on Fiverr:

Setting Up Payoneer on Fiverr

1. **Create a Payoneer Account:**

If you don't have a Payoneer account, go to the Payoneer website and sign up. Follow the registration process, providing the required information.

2. Link Payoneer to Fiverr:

- Log in to your Fiverr account.
- Go to the "Earnings" tab on the top menu.
- Select "Fiverr Revenue Card."
- Click on the "Link Payoneer" button.
- Complete the Payoneer Setup

You'll be redirected to the Payoneer website to complete the setup.

Follow the instructions to link your Fiverr account to your Payoneer account.

Withdrawing Funds Using Payoneer

1. Access Earnings Page:

Log in to your Fiverr account.

Go to the "Earnings" tab.

Initiate Withdrawal:

Under the "Available for Withdrawal" section, click on "Withdraw."

Select Payoneer as Withdrawal Method:

Choose Payoneer as your preferred withdrawal method.

2. Enter Withdrawal Amount:

Enter the amount you want to withdraw. Note that there may be a minimum withdrawal amount.

3. Confirm Withdrawal:

Confirm the withdrawal details and click "Review Withdrawal."

4. Review and Confirm:

Review the withdrawal details and click "Confirm Withdrawal."

5. Wait for Processing:

Fiverr will process your withdrawal, and the funds will be sent to your Payoneer account.

Receiving Funds in Payoneer

1. Check Payoneer Balance:

Log in to your Payoneer account.

Once the funds are processed, they will be available in your Payoneer balance.

2. Withdraw to Bank Account:

From your Payoneer account, you can withdraw the funds to your linked bank account.

3. Use Payoneer Card (Optional):

If you have a Payoneer card, you can also use it to make purchases or withdraw cash from ATMs.

Important Notes:

- Payoneer may charge fees for certain transactions, so be aware of the fee structure.
- Ensure that the details on both your Fiverr and Payoneer accounts match to avoid any withdrawal issues.
- Fiverr may take a few days to process the withdrawal, and the actual time for funds to reach your Payoneer account depends on various factors, including processing times and your location.
- Always refer to the latest information on Fiverr and Payoneer websites for any updates or changes to the withdrawal process and fees.

💣 Fiverr: Disputes

Disputes on Fiverr can arise when there is a disagreement or issue between a buyer and a seller regarding a completed order. Fiverr provides a resolution process to help resolve disputes and ensure fair outcomes for both parties. Here's a guide on how to handle disputes on Fiverr:

1. Communication:

Before escalating the issue, try to communicate with the other party to understand their perspective and find a resolution. Many disputes can be resolved through open communication.

2. Dispute Resolution Center:

If communication does not lead to a resolution, you can use Fiverr's Dispute Resolution Center.

Go to the order page and click on the "Resolution Center" button.

3. Initiate Dispute:

Provide a clear description of the issue and why you believe a dispute is necessary.

You can choose between options such as "I'm not satisfied with the delivery" or "I did not receive my order."

4. Fiverr Mediation:

Once a dispute is initiated, Fiverr's support team may mediate between the buyer and seller to understand both sides of the argument.

Provide any relevant evidence or documentation to support your case.

5. Resolution:

Fiverr will review the case and make a decision. The resolution may involve a refund, partial refund, or another agreed-upon solution.

Both the buyer and seller will be notified of the resolution.

6. Refund Process:

If a refund is granted, it will be processed back to the original payment method.

Note that Fiverr may retain a portion of the funds for platform fees.

Tips for Handling Disputes

1. Document Everything:

Keep records of all communication, delivery messages, and any files exchanged during the order process. This documentation can be valuable in presenting your case.

2. Be Transparent:

Clearly explain your perspective in the dispute, providing factual information and evidence to support your claims.

3. Stay Professional:

Maintain a professional and respectful tone in all communications. Emotional language can hinder the resolution process.

4. Understand Fiverr's Terms of Service:

Familiarize yourself with Fiverr's Terms of Service, especially sections related to disputes, cancellations, and refunds.

5. Set Realistic Expectations:

Both buyers and sellers should set realistic expectations regarding deliverables, timelines, and the scope of work to minimize the chances of disputes.

Remember that Fiverr's Dispute Resolution Center is in place to ensure fair outcomes, and the platform strives to provide a resolution that considers the interests of both parties involved in the dispute.

Chapter11: Freelancers.com, Skrill, PeoplePerHour

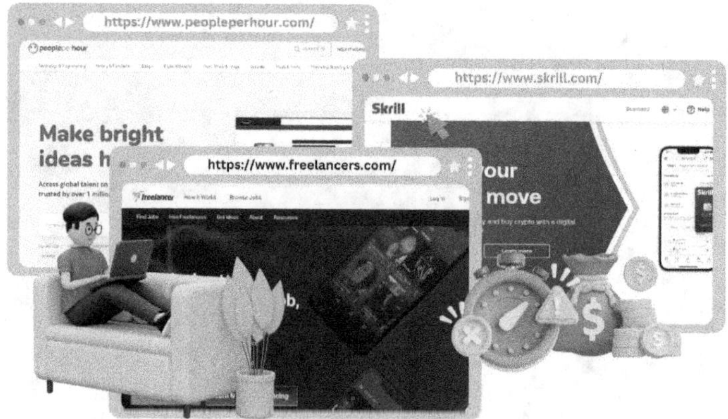

≡ Introduction to Freelancer.com

Freelancer.com is a prominent online platform that connects businesses and individuals with freelancers from around the world. Established in 2009, Freelancer.com has grown into one of the largest freelance marketplaces, offering a diverse range of services and opportunities for both employers and freelancers. The platform facilitates the exchange of skills, allowing freelancers to showcase their expertise and businesses to find the right talent for their projects.

Key Features of Freelancer.com

Diverse Services:

Freelancer.com covers a wide array of services, including writing, graphic design, programming, marketing, data entry, and much more. This diversity makes it suitable for a broad range of industries and projects.

Global Talent Pool:

Freelancer.com connects employers with a global pool of freelancers, providing access to talent from various countries and cultural backgrounds. This global reach enables businesses to find specialized skills that may not be readily available locally.

Project Variety:

Projects on Freelancer.com vary in size and complexity, ranging from small one-time tasks to large, ongoing projects. This flexibility allows freelancers to take on projects that align with their skills and interests.

Bidding System:

Freelancers bid on projects by submitting proposals outlining their expertise, approach, and estimated costs. Employers review these proposals and select the freelancer they believe is the best fit for their project.

Secure Payments:

The platform offers a secure payment system that protects both employers and freelancers. Payments can be made through various methods, including credit cards and milestone payments.

Milestone Payments:

Freelancer.com employs a milestone payment system, where payments are released in stages based on the completion of specific project milestones. This ensures that freelancers are compensated as they make progress on the project.

Rating and Reviews:

After completing a project, both employers and freelancers have the opportunity to leave reviews and ratings. This feedback system helps build trust and reputation within the Freelancer.com community.

Contests:

Employers can also run contests to crowdsource creative solutions. Freelancers submit their entries, and the employer selects the winning submission.

Skills Testing:

Freelancer.com offers skills testing to help freelancers showcase their proficiency in specific areas. Employers can use these test results as an additional factor when making hiring decisions.

Mobile App:

Freelancer.com provides a mobile app, allowing users to manage their projects, submit proposals, and communicate on the go.

Freelancer.com continues to be a dynamic platform that empowers freelancers to find meaningful work and enables businesses to access a diverse pool of talented professionals. As with any freelance marketplace, success often depends on effective communication, professionalism, and delivering high-quality work.

Freelancer: Bidding On Projects, Bid Types and Requesting Milestone's Payment

Bidding on projects on Freelancer.com is a key aspect of securing freelance work. Here's a guide on how to bid on projects, the types of bids available, and how to request milestone payments:

Bidding on Projects

1. **Search for Projects:**

Explore the "Browse Projects" section on Freelancer.com to find projects that match your skills and interests.

2. **Review Project Details:**

Carefully read the project description, requirements, and any attachments provided by the employer. Understand the scope of work and deadlines.

3. **Prepare a Proposal:**

Craft a compelling proposal that addresses the specific needs of the project. Outline your relevant skills, experience, and how you plan to approach the task.

4. Set a Competitive Bid:

Enter a bid amount that reflects the value of your services and is competitive within the context of the project. Consider factors such as the complexity of the task, time commitment, and your expertise.

5. Submit Proposal:

Once your proposal is ready, submit it to the employer by clicking the "Submit a Proposal" button. You may have the option to attach additional files or provide samples of your previous work.

6. Engage in Communication:

Monitor your proposal for any messages from the employer. Be responsive and engage in professional communication to clarify any questions or discuss project details.

Types of Bids

1. Fixed Price Bid:

Propose a fixed amount for the entire project. This is suitable for well-defined tasks with clear deliverables.

2. Hourly Rate Bid:

Specify your hourly rate and estimate the number of hours required to complete the project. This is ideal for ongoing or more flexible projects.

3. Contest Entry:

For contests, you can submit your entry as a bid. Employers may choose the winning entry and award the prize.

Requesting Milestone Payments

1. Understanding Milestones:

Milestones are stages or deliverables within a project. Employers can fund and release payments for each milestone achieved.

2. Discuss Milestones:

During the bidding process or project discussion, clarify and agree with the employer on the project milestones. Outline the tasks and deadlines associated with each milestone.

3. Create Milestones:

Once awarded the project, work with the employer to create milestones on the project page. Specify the amount to be funded for each milestone.

4. Request Milestone Payment:

When you reach a milestone, request payment by clicking on the "Request Milestone Payment" button. The employer will be prompted to release the funds for that specific milestone.

5. Completion and Final Payment:

Continue to complete milestones and request payments until the project is finished. After the final milestone, request the remaining payment for the completion of the entire project.

6. Maintain Professionalism:

Communicate openly and professionally with the employer throughout the milestone and payment process. Provide updates on your progress and address any concerns promptly.

Using a combination of effective bidding strategies and clear milestone planning can increase your chances of winning projects on Freelancer.com and ensure a smooth payment process.

Freelancer: Payment Integration and Withdrawal Methods

Freelancer.com offers various payment integration options and withdrawal methods to facilitate transactions between freelancers and employers. Here's an overview of payment integration and withdrawal methods on Freelancer.com:

Payment Integration

1. Freelancer Payments:

Freelancer.com has its own payment system, allowing clients to fund projects and freelancers to receive payments directly on the platform.

2. Credit/Debit Cards:

Clients can make payments using credit or debit cards. Freelancers can link their credit/debit cards to receive payments.

3. PayPal:

PayPal is a widely used payment option. Freelancers can link their PayPal accounts to receive payments, and clients can use PayPal for project funding.

4. Skrill:

Skrill is another e-commerce platform that facilitates online payments. Freelancers can link their Skrill accounts for withdrawal.

5. Bank Transfers:

Clients have the option to make payments through bank transfers. Freelancers can also withdraw funds directly to their bank accounts.

6. Local Payment Methods:

Freelancer.com supports various local payment methods depending on the user's location. These may include regional payment gateways and services.

Withdrawal Methods:

1. Bank Withdrawal:

Freelancers can withdraw funds directly to their bank accounts. It is a common and convenient withdrawal method.

2. PayPal:

Freelancers can withdraw funds to their linked PayPal accounts, providing a quick and accessible withdrawal option.

3. Skrill:

Skrill can be used as a withdrawal method for freelancers who prefer this platform.

4. Freelancer Prepaid Card:

Freelancer.com offers a prepaid card that freelancers can use to withdraw funds from ATMs or make purchases where cards are accepted.

5. Local Currency Withdrawals:

Depending on the country, Freelancer.com may offer local currency withdrawal options to avoid currency conversion fees.

Withdrawal Process:

1. Access Withdrawal Page:

Freelancers can access the "Withdraw" or "Withdraw Funds" page on Freelancer.com.

2. Choose Withdrawal Method:

Select the preferred withdrawal method from the available options.

3. Enter Withdrawal Details:

Enter the necessary details, such as bank account information or PayPal email address.

4. Enter Withdrawal Amount:

Specify the amount to be withdrawn. Note that there may be minimum withdrawal limits.

5. Review and Confirm:

Review the withdrawal details and confirm the transaction.

6. Processing Time:

The processing time for withdrawals may vary depending on the chosen withdrawal method. Bank transfers and card withdrawals may take a few business days, while online payment platforms like PayPal and Skrill are usually quicker.

It's essential for users to be aware of any associated fees with each payment method and withdrawal option. Freelancer.com provides detailed information on fees and withdrawal processes in their Help and Support section. Users should also stay updated on any changes or additions to payment and withdrawal methods made by the platform.

☑ Introduction to Skrill

Skrill is a digital wallet that offers you the safety and convenience of paying online just with your email address and password. You can upload and withdraw your funds whenever you need them and use them at your favorite websites.

Account Creation and Payment Method Integration

Creating a Skrill account and integrating payment methods is a straightforward process. Skrill is an online payment platform that allows users to send and receive money, make online purchases, and more. Here's a step-by-step guide on how to create a Skrill account and integrate payment methods:

Creating a Skrill Account:

1. **Visit the Skrill Website:**

Go to the official Skrill website: https://www.skrill.com/.

2. **Sign Up:**

Click on the "Register" or "Sign Up" button. You may find this option in the top right corner of the website.

3. Provide Personal Information:

Fill in the required fields with your personal information, including your email address, full name, country of residence, and desired account currency.

4. Create a Password:

Choose a secure password for your Skrill account.

5. Verification:

Skrill may ask you to verify your email address. Check your email for a verification link and follow the instructions.

6. Additional Verification (Optional):

Depending on your location and the services you plan to use, Skrill may require additional verification steps, such as providing identification documents.

7. Login to Your Skrill Account:

Once verified, log in to your Skrill account using your email address and password.

Integrating Payment Methods:

1. Navigate to the "Settings" Section:

Once logged in, go to the "Settings" section. This is typically represented by a gear icon.

2. Add a Payment Method:

Look for the option to add a payment method. Skrill supports various payment methods, including credit/debit cards and bank accounts.

3. Link Credit/Debit Card:

If you're adding a credit or debit card, enter the card details as prompted. This may include the card number, expiration date, and security code.

4. Verify the Payment Method:

Skrill may require you to verify the payment method. This can involve a small charge to your card that you need to confirm or entering a code sent by Skrill.

5. Link Bank Account:

If you're adding a bank account, enter the necessary details. Skrill may also require verification through a small deposit to your bank account.

6. Explore Additional Options:

Skrill offers additional features such as a prepaid Mastercard and the ability to connect cryptocurrency wallets. Explore these options if they align with your needs.

7. Review and Confirm:

Review the details of your linked payment methods and confirm the integration.

Using Skrill for Transactions:

1. Sending Money:

To send money using Skrill, navigate to the "Send" section, enter the recipient's email address, and the amount you wish to send.

2. Receiving Money:

When someone sends you money, it will appear in your Skrill account balance.

3. Making Online Purchases:

Use your Skrill account to make online purchases at websites that accept Skrill as a payment method.

4. Withdrawing Funds:

Skrill allows you to withdraw funds to your linked bank account or credit/debit card.

Remember to check Skrill's fee structure for transactions and withdrawals, as fees may apply depending on the type of transaction and the payment method used.

⧗ Introduction to PeoplePerHour

PeoplePerHour is an online freelancing platform that connects businesses with freelancers offering a wide range of skills and services. Launched in 2007, PeoplePerHour has become a prominent platform for both freelancers seeking work opportunities and businesses looking to hire skilled professionals. The platform operates on a project-based model, allowing businesses to post projects, and freelancers to bid on those projects based on their expertise and capabilities.

Key Features of PeoplePerHour

1. Project-Based Model:

Businesses can post projects outlining their requirements, and freelancers submit proposals or "hourlies" specifying the services they offer.

2. Diverse Freelancer Skills:

PeoplePerHour covers a broad spectrum of skills and services, including writing, graphic design, programming, marketing, SEO, social media management, and more.

3. Hourlies:

Freelancers can create "hourlies," which are fixed-price services or packages that clients can purchase directly without the need for bidding.

4. Search and Discovery:

Users can search for freelancers based on skills, location, or specific project requirements. The platform also provides recommendations based on user preferences.

5. Workstream Communication:

PeoplePerHour features a dedicated workstream for each project, facilitating communication between clients and freelancers. This allows for real-time updates, file sharing, and discussions.

6. Secure Payments:

The platform ensures secure payments through its payment system. Clients fund the project, and freelancers are paid once the work is completed and approved.

7. Feedback and Ratings:

Clients and freelancers can leave feedback and ratings for each other after the completion of a project, helping build reputations and trust within the community.

8. Escrow System:

PeoplePerHour employs an escrow system, holding client funds until the project is successfully completed. This provides assurance to both parties.

9. Custom Offers:

Freelancers can send custom offers to clients based on their project requirements. This allows for personalized proposals beyond standard bidding.

10.Certification and Qualifications:

Freelancers can showcase their certifications and qualifications on their profiles, giving clients insight into their expertise.

11.Mobile App:

PeoplePerHour offers a mobile app, allowing users to manage their projects, submit proposals, and communicate while on the go.

How It Works:

1. Post a Project:

Businesses post details about their project, including the scope of work, budget, and timeline.

2. Freelancer Bids:

Freelancers submit proposals or hourlies in response to posted projects, detailing how they can meet the client's needs.

3. Client Selection:

Clients review proposals, freelancer profiles, and ratings before selecting the freelancer they want to work with.

4. Work Commences:

Once a freelancer is selected, work begins, and communication takes place within the platform's workstream.

5. Payment and Feedback:

Payment is made through the platform, and both parties can leave feedback and ratings based on their experience.

PeoplePerHour offers a dynamic and efficient environment for freelancers and businesses to collaborate, making it a popular choice in the freelancing landscape. Users can leverage its features to find skilled professionals or secure freelance opportunities in various industries.

PeoplePerHour: Requesting Milestones and Raising Invoice

PeoplePerHour follows a project-based model where freelancers and clients collaborate on specific tasks or projects. Here's a guide on how to request milestones and raise invoices on PeoplePerHour:

Requesting Milestones:

1. Project Discussion:

Once a client and freelancer agree on the scope of work, deadlines, and other project details, the next step is to set up milestones.

2. Navigate to Workstream:

The project's workstream is the central communication hub. Navigate to the project's workstream to discuss and set up milestones.

3. Discuss Milestone Details:

In the workstream, discuss and agree on the specific tasks or deliverables that will constitute each milestone. Clarify the timeline for completing each milestone.

4. Create Milestones:

Freelancers can create milestones by going to the project's page and selecting the "Create Milestone" option. Specify the milestone title, description, due date, and amount.

5. Client Approval:

Clients will receive notification about the proposed milestones. They can review the details and either approve or request modifications.

6. Modify if Necessary:

If the client requests changes to the proposed milestones, freelancers can make the necessary adjustments based on the client's feedback.

7. Approval and Funding:

Once the client approves the milestones, they need to fund the total milestone amount. This is typically done by depositing the funds into an escrow account on PeoplePerHour.

8. Start Working:

With the milestones funded and approved, freelancers can begin working on the tasks associated with each milestone.

Raising Invoice:

1. Milestone Completion:

When a freelancer completes the tasks associated with a milestone, they can mark the milestone as completed in the workstream.

2. Navigate to Invoices:

Go to the "Invoices" section on the project page to create and raise an invoice.

3. Select Milestone:

Choose the milestone for which you want to raise an invoice. Confirm that the tasks associated with the milestone are completed and delivered to the client's satisfaction.

4. Create Invoice:

Click on the "Create Invoice" option and enter the details, including the invoice amount, any additional notes, and any files related to the completed milestone.

5. Submit Invoice:

Once the invoice details are filled out, submit the invoice for client review.

6. Client Approval:

Clients will receive a notification about the submitted invoice. They can review the details and either approve the invoice or request modifications.

7. Payment Release:

If the client approves the invoice, the funds held in escrow for that milestone are released to the freelancer.

8. Repeat for Subsequent Milestones:

Repeat the process for each milestone as the freelancer progresses through the project.

PeoplePerHour's system of milestones and invoices helps ensure that freelancers are paid for their work in stages, providing security for both parties involved in the project. The platform facilitates transparent communication and efficient payment processes throughout the project lifecycle.

Chapter 12: Upwork

📄 Upwork: Introduction

Upwork is one of the largest and most well-known online freelancing platforms that connects businesses and individuals with skilled freelancers. Originally formed by the merger of oDesk and Elance in 2014, Upwork has since become a go-to platform for both clients seeking freelance talent and freelancers looking for work opportunities.

Key Features of Upwork

Diverse Skill Categories:

Upwork covers a vast range of skill categories, including writing, graphic design, programming, marketing, virtual assistance, and more. This diversity makes it suitable for a wide array of projects and industries.

Global Talent Pool:

Upwork provides access to a global pool of freelancers, allowing clients to find talent from different parts of the world. This global reach enables businesses to tap into specialized skills that may not be readily available locally.

Project-Based Model:

Clients post projects on Upwork, specifying their requirements, budget, and timeline. Freelancers then submit proposals or bids, outlining their skills and approach to the project.

Bidding System:

Freelancers bid on projects by submitting proposals. Clients review these proposals and select the freelancer they believe is the best fit for their project.

Hourly and Fixed-Price Contracts:

Upwork supports both hourly and fixed-price contracts. Hourly contracts are based on tracked hours, while fixed-price contracts involve a set payment for the entire project.

Upwork Work Diary:

For hourly contracts, Upwork offers a Work Diary feature that tracks the freelancer's work hours and takes periodic screenshots to provide transparency to the client.

Secure Payments:

Upwork handles secure payments through its platform. Clients fund the project, and freelancers are paid according to the agreed-upon terms.

Escrow System:

Upwork employs an escrow system for fixed-price contracts, where client funds are held until the freelancer completes the project and the client approves the work.

Feedback and Ratings:

Clients and freelancers can leave feedback and ratings for each other after the completion of a project. This helps build reputations within the Upwork community.

Search and Filters:

Upwork provides advanced search and filtering options, allowing clients to find freelancers based on specific criteria such as skills, location, and past work history.

Mobile App:

Upwork offers a mobile app that enables users to manage their projects, submit proposals, and communicate on the go.

How It Works

Post a Job:

Clients post detailed job listings, specifying the project requirements, budget, and timeline.

Freelancer Bids:

Freelancers review job listings and submit proposals, detailing their skills and how they plan to approach the project.

Client Selection:

Clients review proposals, freelancer profiles, and may conduct interviews before selecting the freelancer they want to work with.

Work Commences:

Once a freelancer is selected, work begins. Communication and project management take place within the Upwork platform.

Payment and Feedback:

Payment is made through Upwork, and both parties can leave feedback and ratings based on their experience.

Upwork continues to be a dynamic platform, offering a vast and diverse marketplace for freelancers and clients to connect and collaborate on a wide range of projects. Users can leverage its features to find skilled professionals or secure freelance opportunities in various industries.

☑ Upwork: Benefits

Upwork offers several benefits to both freelancers and clients, making it a popular and effective platform for online freelancing. Here are some key advantages of using Upwork:

Benefits for Freelancers

1. Global Reach:

Freelancers on Upwork have access to a global marketplace, allowing them to connect with clients from different parts of the world. This broad reach increases opportunities for finding diverse and high-paying projects.

2. Diverse Skill Categories:

Upwork covers a wide range of skill categories, from writing and graphic design to programming and marketing. Freelancers with various skills can find suitable projects that match their expertise.

3. Flexible Work Arrangements:

Freelancers can choose between hourly and fixed-price contracts based on their preferences and the nature of the project. This flexibility enables freelancers to adapt to different client needs.

4. Transparent Work Diary:

For hourly contracts, Upwork provides a Work Diary feature that tracks work hours and takes screenshots periodically. This transparency helps build trust between freelancers and clients.

5. Secure Payments:

Upwork handles secure payments through its platform, ensuring that freelancers are paid for their work. The platform also offers an escrow system for fixed-price contracts, providing financial security.

6. Opportunities for Growth:

Successful completion of projects and positive client feedback can contribute to a freelancer's reputation on Upwork. As freelancers build a strong profile, they have the potential to attract more clients and higher-paying projects.

7. Networking and Connections:

Upwork serves as a networking platform where freelancers can connect with clients and other freelancers. Building a professional network can lead to additional work opportunities.

Benefits for Clients

1. Access to a Global Talent Pool:

Clients can tap into a diverse and global pool of freelancers, allowing them to find skilled professionals with specific expertise that may not be readily available locally.

2. Cost-Effective Solutions:

Upwork provides clients with cost-effective solutions, as they can choose freelancers based on their budget and project requirements. Clients can also compare different proposals before making a hiring decision.

3. Flexible Hiring Models:

Clients have the flexibility to hire freelancers on an hourly basis or for fixed-price contracts. This adaptability accommodates different project scopes and client preferences.

4. Transparent Communication:

Upwork's platform facilitates transparent communication between clients and freelancers. The workstream feature allows for real-time updates, file sharing, and efficient project management.

5. Quality Assurance:

Client reviews and ratings provide valuable insights into a freelancer's work history and performance. This helps clients make informed decisions when selecting freelancers for their projects.

6. Efficient Payment Process:

Upwork streamlines the payment process for clients, ensuring that funds are securely held in escrow until the project is successfully completed and approved.

7. Wide Range of Services:

Upwork covers a broad spectrum of services, making it suitable for clients with diverse project requirements. Whether it's design, development, writing, or marketing, clients can find freelancers with the right skills.

Upwork's platform offers a balance of flexibility, transparency, and efficiency, making it a preferred choice for both freelancers and clients in the world of online freelancing.

👍 Upwork: When to Start

Starting a business on Upwork can be a strategic move for both freelancers and clients. Here are some considerations for when to start doing business on Upwork:

Considerations For Freelancers

1. Skill Development:

Before joining Upwork, ensure that you have honed your skills and have a solid understanding of your chosen field. Clients on Upwork expect high-quality work, so being proficient in your area of expertise is crucial.

2. Portfolio Preparation:

Create a portfolio showcasing your best work. This allows potential clients to evaluate your skills and determine if you're a good fit for their projects.

3. Profile Optimization:

Take the time to optimize your Upwork profile. Include a professional photo, write a compelling bio, and highlight your skills and experience. A well-crafted profile increases your chances of attracting clients.

4. Research Rates:

Research the average rates for freelancers in your field on Upwork. Price your services competitively based on your skill level and experience, keeping in mind that competitive rates can attract more clients.

5. Understand Upwork Policies:

Familiarize yourself with Upwork's policies, terms of service, and community guidelines. Adhering to Upwork's rules ensures a positive experience for both freelancers and clients.

6. Prepare for Consistency:

Consistency is key on Upwork. Be prepared to dedicate regular time to search for projects, submit proposals, and communicate with clients. Building a successful freelance career takes time and effort.

Considerations For Clients

1. Project Clarity:

Clearly define your project requirements, scope, and expectations before posting a job on Upwork. This ensures that freelancers understand the task and can provide accurate proposals.

2. Budget Determination:

Set a realistic budget for your project. Upwork offers a range of freelancers with different rates, and setting a suitable budget attracts quality proposals.

3. Review Freelancer Profiles:

Take the time to review freelancer profiles thoroughly. Look for relevant skills, experience, and client feedback. A well-documented profile indicates a freelancer's professionalism.

4. Understand Upwork's Fee Structure:

Familiarize yourself with Upwork's fee structure. Upwork charges a percentage of the total project value, and clients should factor this into their budget planning.

5. Effective Communication:

Communication is vital on Upwork. Clearly articulate your project requirements, respond promptly to freelancer inquiries, and maintain open communication throughout the project.

6. Prepare for the Hiring Process:

Be prepared to review proposals, conduct interviews, and make hiring decisions. The hiring process may take time, especially if you're looking for the right fit for your project.

General Considerations

1. Market Research:

Conduct market research within your industry on Upwork. Understand the demand for your skills or the availability of freelancers offering the services you need.

2. Read Upwork Resources:

Explore Upwork's resources, tutorials, and blogs. Upwork provides valuable information to help both freelancers and clients navigate the platform successfully.

3. Network and Connect:

Network with other freelancers and clients on Upwork. Building a network can lead to additional opportunities and collaborations.

4. Upwork Membership:

Consider the benefits of an Upwork Plus or Business membership. These memberships offer additional features such as improved visibility and proposal insights.

Ultimately, the right time to start doing business on Upwork is when you are well-prepared, have a clear understanding of the platform's dynamics, and are committed to delivering quality work or finding the right talent for your projects.

Upwork: Profile Setup

Setting up a strong and professional profile on Upwork is crucial for attracting clients and securing freelance opportunities.

Here's a step-by-step guide to setting up your profile on Upwork:

1. Create Your Account:

Go to the Upwork website and sign up for a new account. Provide the necessary information, including your name, email address, and password.

2. Complete Your Profile:

Once you've created your account, you'll be prompted to complete your profile. Fill in all the required fields, including your full name, profile title, and a professional profile photo. Choose a clear and friendly photo that reflects your professionalism.

3. Write a Compelling Overview:

Craft a compelling overview that summarizes your skills, experience, and what you can offer clients. Highlight your expertise, unique selling points, and the value you bring to potential projects. Keep it concise and engaging.

4. Add Relevant Skills:

List your skills in the "Skills" section. Upwork allows you to select up to 10 skills that best represent your capabilities. Choose skills that align with your expertise and the services you plan to offer.

5. Complete Employment History:

Provide details about your employment history, including your past roles, responsibilities, and achievements. If you're a new freelancer, focus on relevant experiences or projects you've worked on independently.

6. Education and Certifications:

Include your educational background and any relevant certifications. This helps clients understand your qualifications and expertise.

7. Create a Portfolio:

Upwork allows you to showcase your work through a portfolio. Add samples of your previous work, such as writing samples, design projects, or any work that demonstrates your skills. This visual representation enhances your profile.

8. Set Your Hourly Rate or Project Rate:

Determine your pricing strategy. You can either set an hourly rate or a fixed-price for projects. Research the average rates in your field on Upwork to ensure your rates are competitive.

9. Availability and Location:

Indicate your availability for new projects and your location. Upwork allows you to specify if you're open to short-term or long-term projects.

10. Upwork Tests:

Consider taking Upwork skill tests to showcase your proficiency in specific areas. These tests can help validate your skills and make your profile stand out.

11. Languages Spoken:

Specify the languages you speak fluently. This is particularly important if you offer services that require language proficiency.

12. Complete the Identity Verification:

Upwork may require you to complete an identity verification process. Follow the provided instructions to verify your identity, which adds an extra layer of trust to your profile.

13. Review and Proofread:

Before publishing your profile, carefully review all the information you've entered. Ensure there are no typos, and the content is clear and professional.

14. Publish Your Profile:

Once you're satisfied with your profile, click the "Publish" button. Your profile will now be visible to clients searching for freelancers with your skills.

15. Optimize for Keywords:

Use relevant keywords in your profile to improve its discoverability. Clients often search for specific skills, so including relevant keywords can increase your chances of being found.

Remember to update your profile regularly, especially as you gain more experience and complete new projects. A well-maintained and up-to-date profile increases your visibility and credibility on Upwork.

8 Upwork: Badges

Upwork badges are visual indicators that showcase specific achievements, skills, or qualifications on a freelancer's profile. These badges help freelancers stand out to clients and demonstrate their expertise. Here are some of the key badges available on Upwork:

Top Rated:

The Top Rated badge is awarded to freelancers who consistently provide high-quality work, maintain a high job success score, and adhere to Upwork's guidelines. This badge signifies a freelancer's reliability and professionalism.

Top Rated Plus:

Top Rated Plus is an extension of the Top Rated badge, recognizing freelancers who have demonstrated sustained excellence on the platform. It may come with additional benefits, such as increased visibility.

Rising Talent:

The Rising Talent badge is for new freelancers who have shown promise early in their Upwork career. It provides recognition for their skills and potential, helping them attract clients more easily.

Expert-Vetted:

Freelancers who have been vetted by Upwork's Talent Success team and demonstrated exceptional skills in their field may receive the Expert-Vetted badge. This badge is a mark of excellence and expertise.

Identity Verified:

The Identity Verified badge indicates that a freelancer has completed Upwork's identity verification process. This adds an extra layer of trust for clients, as the freelancer's identity has been confirmed.

Freelancer Plus:

Freelancer Plus is a subscription plan that freelancers can opt for on Upwork. It includes features like additional connects, improved visibility, and a more prominent placement in search results.

Job Success:

The Job Success badge reflects a freelancer's overall success on Upwork. It takes into account factors like client satisfaction, project success, and the completion of milestones.

Skill Certifications:

Upwork offers skill certifications for various technologies and tools. Freelancers who pass these tests receive a badge indicating their proficiency in that particular skill.

Languages:

Freelancers can receive language badges indicating their proficiency in specific languages. This can be important for clients seeking freelancers with multilingual capabilities.

Connects Usage:

Upwork provides badges related to the usage of connects, which are used to submit proposals for projects. For example, a badge may indicate if a freelancer has a high response rate to invitations.

It's important for freelancers to earn and display relevant badges on their profiles to enhance their credibility and attract clients. Clients, on the other hand, can use these badges as a quick way to assess a freelancer's qualifications and achievements. Regularly updating skills, completing certifications, and maintaining a high level of professionalism contribute to earning and retaining these badges on Upwork.

🗀 Upwork: Project Catalog

The Upwork Project Catalog is a feature that allows clients to find and purchase predefined services or "gigs" directly from freelancers without going through the traditional hiring process. It simplifies the process for clients who need specific, well-defined tasks or services completed quickly.

Here's an overview of the Upwork Project Catalog:

How Upwork Project Catalog Works

Predefined Services:

Freelancers create predefined service offerings or "gigs" with clear descriptions, deliverables, and prices. These services are typically specific and well-defined.

Browse and Purchase:

Clients can browse the Project Catalog to find services that match their needs. The catalog includes a variety of services across different categories, such as writing, design, marketing, and more.

Transparent Pricing:

Each service in the catalog comes with a transparent pricing structure, allowing clients to know the cost upfront before making a purchase.

No Proposals or Interviews:

Unlike traditional Upwork projects, clients using the Project Catalog can directly purchase services without going through the proposal and interview process. This streamlines the hiring process for quick and straightforward tasks.

Instant Start:

Once a client purchases a service from the catalog, the freelancer can begin working on the task immediately. This can be beneficial for clients who need a fast turnaround.

Client Reviews:

After the service is completed, clients can leave reviews for the freelancers. Positive reviews can enhance a freelancer's reputation and attract more clients.

Tips for Freelancers Using the Project Catalog

Create Well-Defined Gigs:

Clearly define your services with detailed descriptions, specific deliverables, and transparent pricing. This helps clients understand exactly what they'll get.

Competitive Pricing:

Set competitive prices for your services to attract clients. Consider the value you're providing and the market rates for similar services.

Highlight Your Expertise:

Emphasize your expertise and skills in your gig descriptions. Showcase what makes you the right freelancer for the task.

Prompt Communication:

Be prompt in communicating with clients who purchase your services. Clear communication contributes to a positive client experience.

Deliver High-Quality Work:

Consistently deliver high-quality work to clients. Positive reviews can lead to more clients discovering and purchasing your services.

Tips for Clients Using the Project Catalog

Clearly Define Needs:

Clearly define your needs when browsing the Project Catalog. Look for services that align with your specific requirements.

Review Freelancer Profiles:

Before purchasing a service, review the freelancer's profile, including their reviews, skills, and past work. This helps ensure you're selecting a qualified freelancer.

Understand Deliverables:

Understand the deliverables outlined in the service description. Make sure they meet your expectations before making a purchase.

Provide Clear Instructions:

When making a purchase, provide clear instructions to the freelancer. Clear communication sets the stage for a successful project.

The Project Catalog is a valuable feature for both freelancers and clients, offering a streamlined and efficient way to complete specific tasks without the need for extensive project proposals and interviews. It's particularly useful for small, well-defined projects that can be quickly executed.

✪ Upwork: Specialized Profile

A specialized profile on Upwork allows freelancers to showcase their expertise in a specific niche or skill set. This feature enables freelancers to create a profile tailored to a particular type of work or industry, making it easier for clients to find them for relevant projects. Here's how to set up a specialized profile on Upwork:

Creating a Specialized Profile

Log In to Upwork:

Log in to your Upwork account. If you don't have an account, you'll need to sign up.

Access Your Profile:

Once logged in, go to your Upwork profile. You can find this by clicking on your profile picture in the top right corner and selecting "Profile."

Create Specialized Profile:

In the "Overview" section of your profile, look for the "Create a specialized profile" option. Click on it to get started.

Choose a Niche:

Select the niche or skill set for which you want to create a specialized profile. This could be a specific service you offer, industry expertise, or a unique set of skills.

Customize Profile Sections:

Customize the sections of your specialized profile to highlight relevant information. This may include a tailored overview, skills, work history, and portfolio items specific to the chosen niche.

Add Portfolio Items:

Upload portfolio items that showcase your work in the chosen niche. This could be samples of previous projects, case studies, or any relevant materials that demonstrate your expertise.

Set Pricing:

Specify your pricing for services related to the specialized profile. This helps clients understand the cost associated with hiring you for projects within that specific niche.

Review and Publish:

Review all the information in your specialized profile to ensure accuracy and completeness. Once satisfied, click the "Publish" button to make your specialized profile visible to clients.

Tips for Optimizing Your Specialized Profile

Be Specific:

Clearly define the niche or skill set you're focusing on. The more specific and targeted your specialized profile is, the better it will resonate with clients looking for those specific skills.

Highlight Relevant Experience:

Emphasize your relevant experience in the chosen niche. Showcase projects you've completed, achievements, and any certifications or qualifications that strengthen your expertise.

Use Keywords:

Incorporate relevant keywords in your specialized profile to improve its visibility in search results. Think about terms clients might use when looking for someone with your skills.

Showcase Results:

Highlight the results you've achieved in your chosen niche. Whether it's increased sales, improved efficiency, or any other measurable outcome, demonstrating your impact adds credibility.

Regularly Update:

Keep your specialized profile up to date. As you complete new projects or gain additional skills, update your profile to reflect your latest accomplishments.

Request Endorsements:

If you've worked with clients in your specialized niche on Upwork, consider requesting endorsements. Positive feedback from previous clients can boost your credibility.

A specialized profile is a powerful tool for freelancers looking to attract clients in a specific area of expertise. By tailoring your profile to showcase your skills and experience in a targeted manner, you increase your chances of being discovered by clients seeking precisely what you offer.

⊕ **Upwork: Connects policy.**

Upwork Connects are a form of virtual currency on the Upwork platform that freelancers use to submit proposals for job opportunities posted by clients. The Connects system helps ensure a fair and efficient process for freelancers to apply for projects. Here's an overview of Upwork's Connects policy:

How Connects Work

Connects Allocation:

Freelancers receive a certain number of free Connects each month as part of their membership. Upwork Basic members receive a limited number of free Connects, while Plus and Business members receive additional Connects.

Connects Purchase:

If freelancers need more Connects beyond their allocated amount, they have the option to purchase additional Connects. This is done through the Upwork platform, and the cost varies based on the freelancer's location.

Connects Expiry:

Connects have a validity period, and they expire if not used within a certain timeframe. Freelancers need to keep track of their Connects and ensure they are used before expiration.

Submitting Proposals

Connects Requirement:

To submit a proposal for a job posting, freelancers need to use a certain number of Connects. The number of Connects required varies depending on the nature of the job and the budget set by the client.

Connects Refund:

If a freelancer submits a proposal but the client doesn't hire anyone for the job or cancels the job, the Connects used for that proposal are refunded to the freelancer's account.

Upwork Plus and Business Membership

Additional Connects:

Upwork Plus and Business members receive additional Connects as part of their membership benefits. This allows them to submit more proposals and increases their visibility to clients.

Rolling Connects:

Upwork Plus members have the advantage of having their unused Connects roll over to the next month, up to a certain limit. This provides flexibility for freelancers who may have a variable workload.

Tips for Using Connects Effectively

Choose Relevant Jobs:

Be selective when choosing which jobs to apply for. Focus on opportunities that align with your skills and experience to increase your chances of getting hired.

Craft Quality Proposals:

Invest time in creating personalized and high-quality proposals for each job application. Tailor your proposals to the specific requirements of the job posting.

Monitor Connects Usage:

Keep track of your Connects usage and expiration dates. This ensures that you use your allocated Connects efficiently and do not miss out on potential opportunities.

Evaluate Job Budgets:

Consider the budget set by clients for a particular job. Ensure that it aligns with your own expectations and is worth the investment of Connects.

Utilize Membership Benefits:

If you have an Upwork Plus or Business membership, take advantage of the additional Connects and any other benefits offered. This can enhance your overall experience on the platform.

Understanding and managing Upwork Connects is essential for freelancers to effectively apply for jobs and maximize their chances of securing projects. By using Connects strategically and adhering to Upwork's policies, freelancers can navigate the platform successfully.

▢ Upwork: Membership Plans and Their Perks

Upwork offers different membership plans, each tailored to the needs of freelancers on the platform. These plans come with various perks designed to enhance the freelancing experience. Here are the Upwork membership plans and their associated perks:

1. Basic (Free) Membership:

Perks:

- Upwork Basic is the free membership plan available to all users.

- Freelancers receive a limited number of free Connects each month to submit proposals for jobs.
- Access to the Upwork platform and job postings.

2. Upwork Plus Membership:

Perks:

- Upwork Plus is a paid membership plan that includes all the benefits of the Basic plan.
- Additional Connects: Upwork Plus members receive a higher number of free Connects each month.
- Roll-Over Connects: Unused Connects can roll over to the next month, up to a certain limit.
- Visibility Boost: Upwork Plus members get enhanced visibility in the Upwork marketplace.
- Dedicated Customer Support: Priority access to customer support for quicker assistance.

3. Upwork Business Membership:

Perks:

- Upwork Business is designed for agencies and larger freelance teams.
- All benefits of Upwork Plus.
- Team Management: The ability to build and manage a team of freelancers.
- Consolidated Billing: Simplified billing for multiple team members.
- Premium Customer Support: Priority access to premium customer support.
- Enhanced Reporting: Additional reporting features for better team management.

Important Notes:

- Membership plans and perks may be subject to change by Upwork, so it's advisable to check the Upwork website for the most up-to-date information.
- Upwork frequently updates and refines its features and plans to meet the evolving needs of its users.

How to Upgrade Your Membership

To upgrade your membership on Upwork, log in to your account and go to the "Membership & Connects" page. From there, you can choose the plan that best suits your needs and follow the prompts to upgrade.

Remember to review the specific perks and details of each plan to determine which one aligns with your freelancing goals and preferences. Whether you're a solo freelancer or part of a larger team, Upwork's membership plans provide options to enhance your experience on the platform.

🕐 Upwork: Difference Between Fixed and Hourly Jobs

On Upwork, freelancers and clients have the option to choose between fixed-price (fixed-rate) and hourly jobs when posting or bidding on projects. Each type of job has its own characteristics, and the choice between them depends on the nature of the work and the preferences of the parties involved. Here are the key differences between fixed and hourly jobs on Upwork:

Fixed-Price (Fixed-Rate) Jobs

Payment Structure:

Agreed Fixed Amount: In fixed-price jobs, the client and freelancer agree on a fixed amount for the entire project. This amount is specified in the project contract.

Milestones:

Breakdown of Work: Fixed-price jobs often involve breaking down the project into milestones. Each milestone corresponds to a specific deliverable, and payment is released upon the successful completion of each milestone.

Payment Protection:

Escrow System: Upwork uses an escrow system for fixed-price jobs. Clients fund the escrow before the project begins, providing a level of payment protection for both parties.

Project Scope:

Well-Defined Scope: Fixed-price jobs are suitable for projects with well-defined scopes of work, where the deliverables and expectations are clear from the outset.

Billing and Payments:

Payment on Completion: Freelancers receive payment when they complete and submit the agreed-upon work, and the client approves the milestone.

Hourly Jobs

Payment Structure:

Hourly Rate: In hourly jobs, freelancers and clients agree on an hourly rate for the freelancer's work. The client is billed based on the actual hours worked.

Time Tracking:

Upwork Time Tracker: Freelancers use the Upwork Time Tracker tool to log their working hours. Screenshots and activity levels are often recorded to provide transparency.

Payment Protection:

Upwork Guarantee: Hourly jobs benefit from the Upwork Hourly Protection, ensuring that freelancers are paid for hours worked. Clients are billed based on the tracked time.

Project Scope:

Flexible Scope: Hourly jobs are suitable for ongoing or less defined projects where the scope may evolve over time. It's ideal for tasks that require ongoing collaboration and adjustments.

Billing and Payments:

Weekly Billing: Clients are billed weekly based on the freelancer's logged hours. Payments are made automatically through Upwork.

Choosing Between Fixed and Hourly Jobs

Nature of Work:

Choose fixed-price jobs for well-defined projects with clear deliverables. Opt for hourly jobs when the scope is flexible, ongoing, or may evolve.

Client Preferences:

Some clients may prefer the certainty of fixed pricing, while others may appreciate the flexibility and transparency of hourly billing.

Freelancer's Expertise:

Freelancers may prefer one model over the other based on their working style and the type of services they offer.

Risk Management:

Fixed-price jobs may involve more upfront risk for freelancers, as they need to complete milestones to receive payment. Hourly jobs offer more immediate compensation for hours worked.

Ultimately, the choice between fixed and hourly jobs depends on the specific requirements of the project and the preferences of the client and freelancer. Upwork provides flexibility to accommodate various working arrangements.

▤ Upwork: Work Diary

The Upwork Work Diary is a tool designed for hourly jobs on the platform. It allows freelancers to track their work hours and provides clients with visibility into the work being done. Here's an overview of the Upwork Work Diary:

Key Features

Time Tracking:

Freelancers use the Upwork Time Tracker, a desktop application, to log their work hours. The tool captures screenshots periodically and records the activity level on the freelancer's computer.

Hourly Billing:

The Work Diary is specifically associated with hourly jobs. It helps ensure that freelancers are accurately compensated for the time they spend on a project.

Screenshots:

The Time Tracker captures screenshots of the freelancer's screen at intervals. This provides clients with a visual record of the work being done.

Activity Levels:

The tool measures the freelancer's activity level based on keyboard and mouse movements. This helps provide additional context to the client about the freelancer's engagement during tracked hours.

Manual Time:

Freelancers can also enter manual time entries for work that may not be easily captured by screenshots, such as phone calls or off-computer tasks.

Privacy Features:

Freelancers have control over which activities are visible to clients. They can mark certain activities as private to respect privacy concerns.

Payment Assurance:

The Work Diary, along with the Upwork Hourly Protection, assures freelancers that they will be paid for the hours they've worked if the client approves the time.

How It Works

Start Work:

Freelancers initiate the Upwork Time Tracker when they begin working on a project. This tool runs in the background and captures relevant data.

Screenshots and Activity Levels:

The Time Tracker captures screenshots at predetermined intervals, providing a visual representation of the freelancer's work. Activity levels are also recorded.

Stop Work:

Freelancers stop the Time Tracker when they finish their work for the day or on a specific task. They can add manual time entries for any additional work that may not be captured by the screenshots.

Client Review:

Clients can review the Work Diary to see the logged hours, screenshots, and activity levels. They have the option to dispute hours if needed.

Payment:

Once the client approves the hours worked, the freelancer is paid for the tracked time. The funds are automatically transferred through Upwork.

Tips for Freelancers

Use the Time Tracker Consistently:

Consistent use of the Time Tracker ensures accurate tracking of billable hours.

Add Manual Time Entries:

If you perform tasks away from the computer or have non-computer-based work, add manual time entries to capture that time.

Review Privacy Settings:

Adjust privacy settings to ensure that confidential or private activities are not visible to clients.

Communicate with Clients:

Keep open communication with clients about your work and the tracked hours to build trust.

The Upwork Work Diary is a valuable tool for both freelancers and clients engaged in hourly jobs. It provides transparency, accountability, and a structured way to track and compensate freelancers for their time and effort.

✉ Upwork: Handling Invites.

Handling invites on Upwork refers to the process of managing invitations from clients to bid on their projects. Freelancers receive invites based on their skills, expertise, and profile visibility. Here's a guide on how to handle invites effectively:

1. Notification and Review:

When a client sends you an invitation, Upwork will notify you via email and within your Upwork account. Take the time to review the details of the project and the client's requirements.

2. Evaluate Project Suitability:

Assess whether the project aligns with your skills, availability, and interests. Consider the project scope, timeline, and budget to determine if it's a good fit for you.

3. Check Client's Profile and Reviews:

Examine the client's Upwork profile and any reviews from other freelancers. This provides insights into their communication style, reliability, and whether they've had successful collaborations on the platform.

4. Respond Promptly:

Clients often invite multiple freelancers, so it's crucial to respond promptly. Even if you're not interested, it's courteous to decline the invitation rather than leaving the client waiting.

5. Ask Questions:

If the project details are not fully clear, feel free to ask the client questions for clarification. Clear communication at this stage can help both parties understand each other's expectations.

6. Negotiate Terms:

If you're interested in the project but need more information or want to discuss terms, negotiate professionally. This may include discussing rates, project milestones, or any other relevant details.

7. Accept or Decline:

Once you've gathered enough information and are ready to commit or decline, take action accordingly. If you accept, follow up with the client to discuss project details further.

8. Manage Your Invitations:

Upwork provides a dedicated section for invites in your dashboard. Regularly check and manage your invitations to ensure you're aware of all opportunities.

9. Communication Etiquette:

Maintain professional and courteous communication. Even if you decline an invitation, express your gratitude for the opportunity and provide a brief explanation if possible.

10. Set Preferences:

In your Upwork settings, you can define your preferences for receiving invites. Specify your availability, desired project types, and other criteria to receive more relevant invites.

11. Update Profile:

Regularly update your Upwork profile to reflect your skills, experience, and availability. A well-maintained profile increases your visibility and the likelihood of receiving invites for projects that match your expertise.

Handling invites on Upwork is a strategic process that involves evaluating opportunities, communicating effectively, and making decisions that align with your freelancing goals. By managing invites professionally, you can build positive relationships with clients and increase your chances of securing projects that suit your skills and preferences.

★★★ Upwork: Feedback and Reviews

Feedback and reviews are crucial aspects of a freelancer's profile on Upwork. They provide a transparent and public record of a freelancer's performance and reliability. Here's a comprehensive guide to understanding and managing feedback and reviews on Upwork:

1. Importance of Feedback:

Feedback is a key factor that clients consider when hiring freelancers. Positive feedback builds credibility and trust, making it more likely for a freelancer to secure future projects.

2. Types of Feedback:

- **Public Feedback:** Public comments and ratings visible on a freelancer's profile.
- **Private Feedback:** Clients can provide private feedback that is not displayed publicly but is shared with the freelancer. This helps freelancers understand areas for improvement.

3. How Feedback Works:

After completing a contract, both the freelancer and client have the opportunity to leave feedback. Clients rate freelancers on a scale from 1 to 5 stars and can provide additional written comments.

4. Responding to Feedback:

Freelancers have the option to respond to feedback publicly. This is an opportunity to express gratitude for positive feedback or address any concerns raised in negative feedback. A thoughtful and professional response can mitigate the impact of negative feedback.

5. Maintaining a Positive Rating:

Consistently delivering high-quality work, meeting deadlines, and maintaining good communication are key to receiving positive feedback. It's crucial to prioritize client satisfaction.

6. Private Feedback Insights:

Freelancers receive private feedback even if the overall public feedback is positive. This information can be valuable for self-improvement and understanding client perspectives.

7. Handling Negative Feedback:

In cases of negative feedback, it's essential to respond diplomatically and address any concerns raised by the client. Demonstrating a commitment to resolving issues can reflect positively on a freelancer.

8. Asking for Feedback:

After completing a successful project, freelancers can politely ask clients for feedback. Many clients appreciate the reminder and are willing to leave positive feedback.

9. Frequency of Feedback:

The frequency of feedback on a freelancer's profile depends on the number of contracts completed. As a freelancer accumulates more completed contracts, their overall rating becomes a weighted average of all feedback received.

10. Impact on Job Success Score (JSS):

Feedback is a component of the Job Success Score (JSS), which is a metric that measures a freelancer's overall success on Upwork. Maintaining a high JSS is important for securing more opportunities on the platform.

11. Continuous Improvement:

Use feedback as a tool for continuous improvement. Identify patterns in feedback to enhance skills, communication, and overall service quality.

12. Client Recommendations:

Clients can provide recommendations on a freelancer's profile. Positive recommendations serve as additional endorsements of a freelancer's skills and professionalism.

13. Encourage Happy Clients to Leave Feedback:

If a client expresses satisfaction with your work, politely encourage them to leave feedback. Positive reviews contribute to a strong profile.

Understanding the role of feedback and reviews on Upwork is essential for freelancers aiming to build a reputable and successful presence on the platform. By consistently delivering high-quality work and maintaining positive client relationships, freelancers can earn favorable feedback that enhances their professional standing.

☠ Upwork: How to identify Scam.

Identifying potential scams on Upwork is crucial to protecting yourself and your freelance business. Scammers often target freelancers with promises of high-paying jobs or other opportunities. Here are some tips on how to identify potential scams on Upwork:

Unrealistic Payment Offers:

Be wary of job postings that offer exceptionally high payments for simple tasks. If an offer seems too good to be true, it may be a scam.

Incomplete Job Descriptions:

Scam job postings may lack detailed information about the project, client, or specific requirements. Legitimate clients typically provide clear project descriptions.

Communication Outside of Upwork:

Avoid clients who insist on communicating exclusively outside of Upwork, such as through personal email or messaging platforms. All communication related to a project should take place on the Upwork platform.

Urgent Payment Requests:

Be cautious if a client requests payment or personal information urgently. Scammers often create a sense of urgency to pressure freelancers into providing sensitive information.

Check Client History:

Review the client's history on Upwork. If the client has a new or incomplete profile, and especially if they haven't hired other freelancers, exercise caution.

Grammar and Spelling Errors:

Poorly written job descriptions, messages, or client profiles with numerous grammar and spelling errors can be a red flag. Legitimate clients typically present themselves professionally.

Request for Upfront Payment:

Scammers may request upfront payments or fees before starting the project. Legitimate clients typically follow Upwork's payment system.

Unusual Payment Methods:

Be cautious if the client suggests using unconventional payment methods or platforms not associated with Upwork. Stick to Upwork's payment system for security.

Verify Identity:

If a client's identity seems questionable, ask for more information or clarification. Legitimate clients are usually willing to provide additional details about their company or project.

Research the Company:

If the client represents a company, research the company's website and online presence. Scammers may use fake company details.

Trust Your Instincts:

If something feels off or if you have doubts about the legitimacy of a job offer, trust your instincts and proceed with caution. It's better to decline a potential scam than risk your security.

Check Upwork's Safety Guidelines:

Familiarize yourself with Upwork's safety guidelines and recommendations for avoiding scams. Upwork provides valuable information on recognizing and reporting scams.

Remember that Upwork has security measures in place, but freelancers also play a crucial role in staying vigilant and identifying potential scams. If you encounter suspicious activity, report it to Upwork immediately to protect yourself and other freelancers on the platform.

☹ Upwork: Handling Disputes

Handling disputes on Upwork is an important aspect of freelancing, especially when disagreements arise between freelancers and clients. Upwork provides a dispute resolution process to address issues and find a fair resolution.

Here's a guide on how to handle disputes on Upwork:

1. Open Communication:

Before escalating a situation, try to resolve the issue through open and respectful communication. Discuss concerns, expectations, and potential solutions with the client or freelancer.

2. Review Contract and Terms:

Revisit the contract terms and project details. Ensure that both parties are clear on the agreed-upon scope of work, deadlines, and payment terms.

3. Use Upwork Messages:

If a dispute arises, use Upwork's messaging system to communicate. This ensures that all communication is documented on the platform.

4. Request Milestone or Hourly Review:

For fixed-price contracts, request a milestone review if you believe you've completed the work as per the agreement. For hourly contracts, ensure that you've logged accurate hours and have supporting documentation.

5. Upwork Dispute Resolution:

If communication doesn't resolve the issue, consider using Upwork's dispute resolution process. Upwork provides a system for both clients and freelancers to file a dispute.

6. Submit Evidence:

When filing a dispute, provide clear and detailed evidence to support your case. This may include messages, files, screenshots, or any other relevant information that can help Upwork understand the situation.

7. Upwork Mediation:

Upwork's mediation team will review the evidence provided by both parties. They will work to mediate a fair resolution that aligns with the terms of the contract and Upwork policies.

8. Be Patient:

The dispute resolution process may take some time. Be patient and allow Upwork to thoroughly investigate and address the issue.

9. Accept Upwork's Decision:

Once Upwork makes a decision, both parties are expected to accept it. Upwork's decision is final in most cases.

10. Learn from the Experience:

Use the dispute resolution process as an opportunity to learn and improve. Understand the factors that led to the dispute and take steps to prevent similar issues in the future.

11. Provide Feedback:

After the resolution, consider providing feedback on the client or freelancer's profile. Honest feedback helps other users on the platform make informed decisions.

12. Review Upwork Policies:

Familiarize yourself with Upwork's policies on disputes and conflict resolution. Knowing the platform's rules can help you navigate situations more effectively.

13. Legal Action (if Necessary):

In extreme cases, where the dispute is not resolved through Upwork's platform, consider seeking legal advice. However, this is usually a last resort, as Upwork's dispute resolution process is designed to handle most conflicts.

Handling disputes professionally and following Upwork's established processes helps maintain the integrity of the platform and ensures a fair resolution for both freelancers and clients. Open communication, documentation, and adherence to Upwork's policies are key components of a successful dispute resolution process.

➲ Upwork: Direct Contracts

On Upwork, direct contracts refer to agreements between a freelancer and a client outside of Upwork's platform. Upwork strongly discourages direct contracts, as it poses risks to both freelancers and clients and violates the platform's Terms of Service. Here are key points to consider regarding direct contracts on Upwork:

1. Platform Violation:

Conducting work outside of Upwork without using the platform's features, such as hourly tracking or fixed-price milestones, violates Upwork's Terms of Service. This can result in penalties or account suspension.

2. Risk of Non-Payment:

Upwork's platform provides payment protection for freelancers through the escrow system. Direct contracts expose freelancers to a higher risk of non-payment since they don't benefit from Upwork's payment security features.

3. Loss of Upwork Benefits:

Freelancers who engage in direct contracts miss out on the benefits and features provided by Upwork, including access to a large client base, built-in communication tools, and the dispute resolution process.

4. Impact on Job Success Score (JSS):

Successfully completed contracts on Upwork contribute to a freelancer's Job Success Score (JSS), a metric that influences a freelancer's visibility on the platform. Direct contracts don't contribute to the JSS.

5. Communication on the Platform:

Upwork encourages all communication and project management to occur within the platform. Messaging, file sharing, and milestone creation should be conducted through Upwork to ensure a transparent and documented process.

6. Payment Security:

Upwork's escrow system ensures that freelancers are paid for their work. Direct contracts lack this security measure, exposing freelancers to the risk of delayed or non-payment.

7. Client Protections:

Clients also benefit from using Upwork, as it provides them with a pool of verified and skilled freelancers. Engaging in direct contracts may expose clients to risks such as unreliable freelancers or disputes without Upwork's mediation process.

8. Reporting Violations:

If you come across a client or freelancer attempting to conduct work outside of Upwork, it's advisable to report the violation to Upwork's support team. This helps maintain the integrity of the platform.

9. Educate Clients:

Clients may not be aware of the risks associated with direct contracts. Freelancers can educate their clients on the benefits of using Upwork's platform, including payment security and access to a diverse pool of freelancers.

10. Professionalism and Trust:

Building a professional and trustworthy profile on Upwork contributes to long-term success. Clients often prefer freelancers who adhere to Upwork's policies and demonstrate a commitment to professionalism.

It's crucial for freelancers and clients to understand and respect Upwork's policies regarding direct contracts. Engaging in work outside of the platform can lead to negative consequences, and it's in the best interest of both parties to utilize Upwork's features for a secure and transparent freelance experience.

☑ Upwork: Finding the Right Jobs.

Finding the right jobs on Upwork is essential for freelancers to build a successful and fulfilling career. Here are some strategies to help freelancers identify and secure the most suitable projects on the platform:

1. Optimize Your Profile:

Ensure your Upwork profile is complete, highlighting your skills, experience, and expertise. Use a professional profile picture and write a compelling and detailed overview.

2. Define Your Niche:

Identify your niche or specialization. Clients often prefer freelancers who excel in a specific area. Clearly communicate your expertise in your profile.

3. Set Realistic Goals:

Define your career goals and the type of projects you want to work on. This will guide your job search and help you filter through relevant opportunities.

4. Use Upwork's Search Filters:

Utilize Upwork's advanced search filters to narrow down job listings based on criteria such as job type, budget, and client history. This helps you find projects that align with your skills and preferences.

5. Save Job Searches:

Save customized job searches with specific filters to easily revisit and apply to relevant opportunities regularly.

6. Create Job Alerts:

Set up job alerts for specific keywords or categories. Upwork will notify you when new jobs matching your criteria are posted.

7. Regularly Check Job Feed:

Browse the Upwork job feed regularly to discover new opportunities. New jobs are posted frequently, and being proactive in your search increases your chances of finding the right projects.

8. Apply Strategically:

Don't apply to every job. Focus on quality over quantity. Tailor your applications to showcase how your skills align with the client's needs.

9. Review Client Profiles:

Before applying, review the client's Upwork profile. Check their hiring history, feedback from freelancers, and overall reputation. This helps you gauge the credibility of the client.

10. Check Payment History:

Review the client's payment history on Upwork. Clients with a history of paying freelancers promptly are more likely to be reliable.

11. Write a Customized Proposal:

Craft personalized proposals for each job application. Clearly outline how your skills and experience make you the ideal candidate for the project.

12. Highlight Relevant Experience:

Emphasize your relevant experience in your proposal. Clients are more likely to hire freelancers who have demonstrated expertise in similar projects.

13. Build a Strong Portfolio:

Showcase your best work in your Upwork portfolio. A compelling portfolio can attract clients and set you apart from other freelancers.

14. Network and Collaborate:

Connect with other freelancers and clients on Upwork. Building a network can lead to referrals and collaborations on interesting projects.

15. Seek Long-Term Relationships:

Look for clients who are interested in long-term collaborations. Building ongoing relationships with clients can provide a steady stream of work.

By combining these strategies, freelancers can optimize their job search on Upwork and increase the likelihood of finding projects that align with their skills, goals, and preferences. Regularly updating your profile and staying active in the Upwork community contribute to a successful and rewarding freelancing experience.

❧ Upwork: Effective bids for the right jobs

Crafting effective bids on Upwork is crucial for freelancers to stand out and win the right jobs. Here are some strategies to create compelling bids that increase your chances of securing the projects that align with your skills and goals:

1. Read the Job Description Thoroughly:

Before submitting a bid, carefully read the job description to understand the client's requirements. Tailor your bid to showcase how your skills and experience meet their needs.

2. Address the Client by Name:

If the client's name is mentioned in the job post, use it in your bid. Personalizing your response shows that you've taken the time to understand the job.

3. Start with a Greeting:

Begin your bid with a friendly greeting to create a positive first impression. Be professional and courteous in your communication.

4. Express Genuine Interest:

Demonstrate genuine interest in the project by expressing enthusiasm. Clients are more likely to hire freelancers who are enthusiastic about their work.

5. Highlight Relevant Experience:

Showcase your relevant experience and skills in your bid. Clearly explain how your background makes you the ideal candidate for the job.

6. Provide Specific Examples:

Offer specific examples of past projects or achievements that demonstrate your expertise. This helps the client visualize your capabilities.

7. Address Client's Pain Points:

Identify and address any pain points mentioned by the client in the job description. Show how your skills can alleviate their challenges.

8. Propose Solutions:

If applicable, propose solutions to the client's problems or challenges. This demonstrates your proactive approach and problem-solving abilities.

9. Be Transparent About Your Availability:

Clearly communicate your availability and any potential constraints. Clients appreciate freelancers who are transparent about their schedules.

10. Include Relevant Keywords:

Use keywords related to the job in your bid. This not only makes your bid more searchable but also demonstrates your understanding of the project.

11. Provide a Realistic Timeline:

Offer a realistic timeline for completing the project. Clients appreciate freelancers who set clear expectations regarding delivery dates.

12. Specify Your Rate:

Clearly state your rate for the project. Be transparent about your pricing to avoid any misunderstandings later in the hiring process.

13. Ask Clarifying Questions:

If there are any uncertainties in the job description, ask clarifying questions. This shows that you are attentive and committed to delivering the best results.

14. Proofread Your Bid:

Before submitting, proofread your bid to ensure it is free of grammatical errors and typos. A polished and professional bid enhances your credibility.

15. End with a Call to Action:

Conclude your bid with a call to action, inviting the client to discuss the project further or ask any additional questions. This encourages further communication.

Remember, the goal is to demonstrate your value and make it easy for the client to see why you're the best fit for the job. By tailoring your bids to each job, showcasing your skills, and maintaining professionalism, you increase your chances of winning the right projects on Upwork.

⛶ Upwork: Client Retention

Client retention on Upwork is crucial for building a sustainable and successful freelancing business. Here are some strategies to enhance client retention and foster long-term relationships:

1. Deliver High-Quality Work:

Consistently provide high-quality work that exceeds client expectations. Clients are more likely to return if they are impressed with the results.

2. Effective Communication:

Maintain clear and open communication throughout the project. Update clients on progress, ask for feedback, and address any concerns promptly.

3. Meet Deadlines:

Adhere to project deadlines and deliverables. Timely delivery builds trust and reliability, key factors in retaining clients.

4. Understand Client Needs:

Take the time to understand the client's goals, preferences, and expectations. Tailor your work to align with their specific needs.

5. Proactive Problem-Solving:

Anticipate potential issues and proactively address them. Clients appreciate freelancers who can navigate challenges and offer solutions.

6. Provide Value Beyond Expectations:

Go the extra mile by offering additional value or insights that may not have been explicitly requested. This demonstrates your commitment to client success.

7. Build a Personal Connection:

Foster a personal connection with clients. Share relevant updates about your work, and express genuine interest in their business.

8. Seek Feedback:

Regularly seek feedback from clients on your performance. Use constructive criticism to improve and refine your approach.

9. Offer Retainer Agreements:

If appropriate, discuss the possibility of a retainer agreement for ongoing work. This provides stability for both you and the client.

10. Provide Regular Updates:

Keep clients informed about your availability, skills, and any new services you offer. Regular updates maintain engagement.

11. Flexible Collaboration:

Be flexible in your collaboration. Adapt to changes in the project scope or client requirements to demonstrate your versatility.

12. Stay Updated on Industry Trends:

Stay informed about industry trends and changes. Share relevant insights with clients to position yourself as a knowledgeable and valuable partner.

13. Express Gratitude:

Express gratitude for the opportunity to work together. Simple gestures, such as a thank-you note, can leave a positive impression.

14. Offer Discounts or Incentives:

Consider offering loyalty discounts or special incentives for clients who continue to work with you. This encourages them to maintain a long-term relationship.

15. Resolve Issues Professionally:

In the event of conflicts or misunderstandings, address them professionally and find mutually agreeable solutions. A positive resolution can strengthen the client-freelancer relationship.

16. Maintain a Professional Profile:

Regularly update your Upwork profile with new skills, achievements, and projects. A professional and updated profile enhances your credibility.

17. Networking and Referrals:

Network within your industry and ask satisfied clients for referrals. Word-of-mouth recommendations can lead to new opportunities and client retention.

18. Celebrate Milestones:

Acknowledge and celebrate project milestones with clients. This helps build a positive and collaborative working relationship.

By implementing these strategies, freelancers can foster client retention, build a positive reputation, and create a foundation for long-term success on Upwork. Building strong client relationships is not only beneficial for the current project but can also lead to repeat business and referrals.

👁 Upwork: Identify Good Clients

Identifying good clients on Upwork is essential for freelancers to ensure a positive and mutually beneficial working relationship. Here are some indicators to help freelancers identify good clients on the platform:

1. Clear Project Descriptions:

Good clients provide detailed and clear project descriptions. They articulate their needs, expectations, and project scope, demonstrating a thoughtful approach.

2. Positive Client History:

Check the client's history on Upwork, including their feedback and ratings from previous freelancers. A positive track record suggests a reliable and professional client.

3. Responsive Communication:

Good clients are responsive to messages and inquiries. They value effective communication and are willing to discuss project details, requirements, and expectations.

4. Verified Payment:

Look for clients who have verified payment methods on Upwork. This adds a layer of security and indicates a commitment to the platform's payment process.

5. Reasonable Budgets:

Good clients offer realistic and reasonable budgets for the scope of work. They understand the value of quality work and are willing to invest appropriately.

6. Clear Milestones:

When posting fixed-price projects, good clients break down the project into clear and achievable milestones. This demonstrates a structured and organized approach to the project.

7. Hiring History:

Clients with a history of hiring and successfully working with freelancers are often reliable. Check if the client has ongoing or completed projects with positive feedback.

8. Detailed Profile:

A good client often has a detailed and well-filled profile. Look for clients who provide information about their business, industry, and project requirements.

9. Reasonable Expectations:

Good clients have realistic expectations about project timelines, deliverables, and outcomes. They understand the complexities of the work and are willing to collaborate for success.

10. Positive Communication Tone:

Analyze the tone of communication in the job post and messages. Good clients communicate professionally and respectfully, fostering a positive working relationship.

11. Consistent Hiring:

Clients who consistently hire freelancers for various projects may be reliable. It indicates an ongoing need for services and a willingness to establish long-term relationships.

12. Previous Repeat Hires:

Look for clients who have a history of rehiring freelancers. Repeat hires suggest satisfaction with previous collaborations and a willingness to continue working together.

13. Upfront about Requirements:

Good clients are transparent about their requirements and expectations. They provide clear guidelines and information, reducing the likelihood of misunderstandings.

14. Check Upwork Reviews:

Explore reviews and testimonials from other freelancers who have worked with the client. Positive reviews from peers can be a strong indicator of a good client.

15. Engagement in Upwork Community:

Some good clients actively participate in the Upwork community. They may have a detailed profile, participate in forums, or engage in discussions, showcasing their commitment to the platform.

Freelancers should assess these factors collectively to identify good clients on Upwork. While no client-freelancer relationship is without challenges, these indicators can help freelancers make informed decisions about the clients they choose to work with, ultimately leading to more positive and successful collaborations.

Upwork: Reach Out Existing Clients

Reaching out to existing clients on Upwork is a strategic approach to maintaining relationships, securing repeat business, and garnering positive feedback. Here are some effective ways to reach out to your existing clients on the platform:

1. Express Appreciation:

Begin your message by expressing gratitude for the opportunity to work with them. A simple "thank you" goes a long way in fostering a positive relationship.

2. Follow Up on Completed Projects:

If you've recently completed a project for the client, follow up to ensure they are satisfied with the results. Seek feedback and inquire if there's anything else you can assist them with.

3. Share Updates or New Skills:

If you've acquired new skills or certifications, inform your clients. Highlight how these additional skills can benefit their projects and contribute to their success.

4. Offer Ongoing Support:

Reiterate your availability for ongoing support. Let clients know that you're ready to assist with any future projects or tasks they may have.

5. Provide Relevant Insights:

Share industry insights or trends that may be relevant to their business. Position yourself as a valuable resource and someone who stays informed about their industry.

6. Propose New Ideas:

Suggest new ideas or improvements for their projects. Clients appreciate freelancers who proactively contribute to the success of their businesses.

7. Offer Exclusive Discounts:

Consider offering exclusive discounts for your services as a token of appreciation for their continued collaboration. This can be an incentive for them to hire you again.

8. Highlight Success Stories:

Share success stories or positive outcomes from previous projects you've worked on together. This reinforces the value you bring to their business.

9. Inquire About Future Projects:

Politely inquire if they have upcoming projects where your skills could be beneficial. Express your interest in contributing to their ongoing success.

10. Share Relevant Content:

If you come across articles, resources, or content that may interest your clients, share it with them. This demonstrates that you're thinking about their business beyond project work.

11. Solicit Feedback:

Ask for feedback on your collaboration. Constructive feedback can help you improve, and positive feedback can be used as testimonials for your Upwork profile.

12. Invite to Connect Outside of Upwork:

If appropriate, invite your clients to connect with you on professional networks or via email. This allows you to stay in touch even if the project is not currently active on Upwork.

13. Celebrate Milestones:

Recognize any milestones or achievements in their business. Celebrate these successes together, reinforcing the positive bond between freelancer and client.

14. Remind of Upcoming Availability:

If you have periods of increased availability, inform your clients in advance. This gives them an opportunity to plan projects around your schedule.

15. Encourage Referrals:

Politely ask if they know of any colleagues or contacts who might benefit from your services. Client referrals can lead to new opportunities.

16. Update Portfolio and Profile:

Regularly update your Upwork portfolio and profile with new achievements, skills, or completed projects. This keeps your profile fresh and appealing to clients.

When reaching out to existing clients, aim for genuine and personalized communication. Tailor your messages to each client's specific situation and needs. Building strong and lasting relationships with clients is not just about completing projects; it's about maintaining open communication, offering ongoing support, and positioning yourself as a valuable partner in their success.

Upwork: Upselling

Upselling on Upwork involves offering additional services or enhancements to existing clients, providing them with more value and increasing your earnings. Here are some strategies for effectively upselling on the platform:

1. Assess Client Needs:

Understand your client's business and project requirements thoroughly. Identify areas where additional services or improvements could benefit them.

2. Propose Relevant Add-Ons:

Tailor your upsell offers to address specific needs or challenges the client may be facing. Propose services that complement the work you've already done.

3. Highlight Your Expertise:

Showcase your expertise in the proposed upsell services. Demonstrate how your skills can further contribute to the success of their projects or business.

4. Offer Package Deals:

Create bundled packages that include your existing services along with the upsell. Package deals can be appealing to clients looking for comprehensive solutions.

5. Provide Clear Benefits:

Clearly articulate the benefits of the upsell. Explain how it will save them time, improve efficiency, or enhance the overall quality of the project.

6. Set a Limited-Time Offer:

Create a sense of urgency by setting a limited-time offer for the upsell. This encourages clients to make a decision sooner rather than later.

7. Showcase Past Successes:

Reference past successful collaborations and highlight instances where similar upsell services have delivered positive results.

8. Offer Consultation Sessions:

Propose consultation sessions to discuss their broader business goals or upcoming projects. Position yourself as a strategic partner in their overall business strategy.

9. Provide a Discount or Incentive:

Offer a discount or special incentive for the upsell. This can be a percentage off the total cost or an additional service at no extra charge.

10. Explain Cost-Benefit Ratio:

Clearly explain the cost-benefit ratio of the upsell. Help clients understand the value they will receive in proportion to the additional investment.

11. Ask for Feedback:

Before presenting the upsell, ask for feedback on your existing services. Use this opportunity to address any concerns and position the upsell as a solution.

12. Upsell Through Progress Updates:

Introduce the upsell concept during project updates or milestone discussions. This keeps the conversation focused on project improvement and growth.

13. Customize Upsell Offers:

Customize upsell offers based on the client's unique needs. Avoid generic proposals and tailor your suggestions to their specific situation.

14. Cross-Sell Related Services:

Identify related services that could enhance the client's overall experience. Cross-selling allows you to offer complementary services that add value.

15. Upsell in Phases:

If the upsell involves a series of services, consider proposing it in phases. This allows clients to adopt the enhancements gradually.

16. Follow Up After Project Completion:

Send a follow-up message after completing a project, expressing your interest in their continued success. Use this as an opportunity to introduce the upsell.

17. Create a Seamless Transition:

Ensure that the upsell integrates seamlessly with your existing services. Clients are more likely to accept if they perceive a natural progression in their project.

By adopting these upselling strategies, freelancers on Upwork can enhance their client relationships, provide additional value, and increase their earning potential. Upselling is not just about selling more; it's about understanding and addressing the evolving needs of your clients to become a trusted and valuable partner in their success.

ⓘ Upwork: Policies

Upwork has various policies in place to ensure a fair and secure environment for both freelancers and clients. It's important for freelancers to be aware of and adhere to these policies to maintain a positive experience on the platform. Here are some key Upwork policies:

1. Terms of Service:

Freelancers and clients must agree to Upwork's Terms of Service when creating an account. This document outlines the rules and guidelines for using the platform.

2. Payment Protection:

Upwork has Payment Protection in place to ensure freelancers are paid for the work they complete. This includes hourly contracts with the Work Diary tool and fixed-price contracts with milestones.

3. Feedback and Ratings:

Upwork encourages honest and constructive feedback from both freelancers and clients. However, the platform has policies against feedback manipulation or coercion.

4. Identity and Profile Policies:

Freelancers are required to use their real identities on Upwork. Creating multiple accounts or using false information is against Upwork's policies.

5. Code of Conduct:

Upwork has a Code of Conduct that outlines expected behavior for freelancers and clients. This includes professionalism, respectful communication, and compliance with laws and regulations.

6. Prohibited Services:

Upwork prohibits certain services, including illegal activities, academic writing, and services that violate intellectual property rights. Freelancers should be aware of these restrictions.

7. Payment Verification:

Freelancers are required to verify their payment methods to receive payments on Upwork. This is part of the platform's security measures.

8. Communication Outside of Upwork:

Upwork discourages freelancers and clients from taking communication and transactions outside of the platform. This is to ensure the protection of both parties and adherence to Upwork's policies.

9. Upwork Connects Policy:

Upwork uses a Connects system for freelancers to submit proposals for jobs. Each proposal consumes a certain number of Connects. Freelancers need to be aware of the Connects policy and manage their Connects accordingly.

10. Service Fees:

Upwork charges service fees on earnings. Freelancers should be familiar with the fee structure to understand how fees are calculated and deducted from their payments.

11. Identity Verification:

Upwork may request freelancers to undergo identity verification, especially if there are concerns or discrepancies related to their account information.

12. Intellectual Property:

Upwork has policies in place to protect intellectual property rights. Freelancers and clients should respect copyright laws and ownership of work.

13. Violations and Reporting:

Upwork provides mechanisms for reporting policy violations. Users can report any suspicious or inappropriate activity to uphold the integrity of the platform.

Freelancers should regularly review Upwork's policies to stay informed about any updates or changes. Adhering to these policies not only ensures a positive experience on Upwork but also contributes to a trustworthy and secure freelancing environment for all users.

👪 Upwork: Agency and Its Pros and Cons

Upwork agencies are a feature that allows groups of freelancers to collaborate under a single agency profile. Here are the pros and cons of using Upwork agencies:

Pros:

1. Team Collaboration:

Agencies allow freelancers with complementary skills to collaborate on projects. This can provide clients with a broader range of services.

2. Single Agency Profile:

Agencies have a single profile on Upwork, making it easier for clients to find and hire a team with diverse skills.

3. Centralized Communication:

Clients can communicate with the entire agency through a centralized channel, streamlining communication and project management.

4. Unified Portfolio:

Agencies can showcase a unified portfolio that highlights the collective skills and expertise of the team members.

5. Shared Workload:

Workload can be distributed among agency members based on their expertise, ensuring that tasks are assigned to the most qualified individuals.

6. Increased Visibility:

Agencies may receive more visibility on Upwork, attracting clients who are specifically looking for team-based solutions.

7. Scalability:

Agencies can scale their operations by adding new members as needed, allowing for flexibility in handling larger or more complex projects.

Cons:

1. Revenue Distribution:

Managing revenue distribution among agency members can be complex. Deciding on a fair and transparent system for compensating team members is crucial.

2. Communication Challenges:

Coordinating communication among team members may pose challenges, especially if members are located in different time zones or have varying schedules.

3. Client Dependence:

Agencies may become dependent on a few key clients. If a major client leaves, it can impact the entire agency's revenue.

4. Shared Reputation:

The reputation of an agency is shared among its members. Negative feedback for one member can affect the overall agency rating.

5. Administrative Overhead:

Managing an agency involves administrative tasks such as coordinating work, handling payments, and resolving conflicts, which can add additional responsibilities.

6. Client Preferences:

Some clients may prefer working with individual freelancers rather than agencies. Agencies need to effectively communicate the benefits of their team approach.

7. Limited Flexibility:

Agencies may have less flexibility compared to individual freelancers in terms of negotiating rates or changing contract terms.

8. Quality Control:

Ensuring consistent quality across different team members can be a challenge. Agencies need to implement quality control measures to maintain high standards.

9. Upwork Agency Fee:

Upwork charges an additional fee for agency contracts. This fee is in addition to the standard service fees and can impact the overall earnings of the agency.

Agencies on Upwork can be beneficial for freelancers looking to collaborate and offer a broader set of services. However, careful planning and effective communication are essential to overcome the challenges associated with managing a team. Freelancers considering forming or joining an agency should weigh the pros and cons to determine if it aligns with their goals and working preferences.

🗣 Upwork: Forum and Communities

Upwork provides forums and communities where freelancers and clients can connect, share experiences, and seek advice. These platforms facilitate discussions, networking, and the exchange of valuable information. Here are the main forum and community features on Upwork:

1. Upwork Community:

The Upwork Community is an online forum where users can discuss various topics related to freelancing, the Upwork platform, and the gig economy. It's a space for freelancers and clients to connect, share insights, and seek advice.

2. Categories and Subcategories:

The forum is organized into categories and subcategories, covering a wide range of subjects. This includes discussions on freelancing basics, using Upwork tools, industry-specific topics, and more.

3. Announcements:

Upwork uses the community to make important announcements, updates, and share information about new features or changes to the platform.

4. Freelancer Success Stories:

The community features success stories from freelancers who have achieved notable milestones on Upwork. This serves as inspiration and provides insights into successful freelancing journeys.

5. Tips and Best Practices:

Users often share tips, best practices, and strategies for success on Upwork. These discussions cover topics such as writing effective proposals, setting competitive rates, and building a strong profile.

6. Q&A Section:

The community includes a Q&A section where users can ask specific questions and receive answers from fellow freelancers and Upwork moderators. It's a helpful resource for troubleshooting issues or seeking advice.

7. Upwork Events:

Upwork occasionally organizes virtual events, webinars, and Q&A sessions within the community. These events provide opportunities for users to interact with Upwork representatives and industry experts.

8. Freelancer Forum and Client Forum:

The community is divided into separate sections for freelancers and clients. This ensures that discussions are relevant to each group's needs and concerns.

9. Moderation and Guidelines:

Upwork's community forums have moderators who enforce guidelines to maintain a positive and respectful environment. Users are expected to adhere to community rules to ensure productive discussions.

10. Networking Opportunities:

Users can network with fellow freelancers and clients within the community. This can lead to collaborations, partnerships, and the exchange of professional insights.

11. Industry-Specific Discussions:

Some sections of the community focus on industry-specific discussions, allowing users to connect with others in their field and share insights relevant to their niche.

12. Freelancer Resources:

Upwork's community often shares links to helpful resources, articles, and guides aimed at supporting freelancers in their professional development.

Participating in Upwork's forums and communities can be valuable for both freelancers and clients. It offers a platform for learning, networking, and staying updated on industry trends and changes within the Upwork platform. Users are encouraged to engage respectfully, share their experiences, and contribute to the community's collaborative spirit.

Chapter 13: Realtime Project Hunting

📄 Case Study-01 : Realtime Project Hunting on Upwork

Background

Sarah, a seasoned freelance graphic designer, found herself seeking a more efficient way to secure projects on Upwork. Faced with stiff competition and the need for a steady flow of work, she decided to implement a real-time project hunting strategy.

Objective:

Sarah's primary goal was to increase her project acquisition rate by identifying and bidding on relevant projects as soon as they were posted. Real-time project hunting aimed to give her a competitive edge in a fast-paced freelancing environment.

Methodology

1. Alerts and Notifications:

Sarah set up custom alerts and notifications on Upwork based on her preferred criteria. This included project categories, budgets, and keywords related to her expertise. She ensured these alerts were configured to be delivered in real-time.

2. Dedicated Workspace:

To respond quickly, Sarah designated a specific time each day for real-time project hunting. During this period, she focused solely on browsing new project listings and submitting proposals.

3. Prepared Proposal Templates:

To save time during the real-time hunting window, Sarah created a set of well-crafted proposal templates. These templates were adaptable to different project requirements, allowing her to respond promptly without compromising quality.

4. Rapid Proposal Submission:

As soon as a relevant project appeared, Sarah quickly reviewed the details and tailored her pre-prepared proposal template. This streamlined the submission process and enabled her to be among the first freelancers to express interest.

5. Continuous Monitoring:

Sarah consistently monitored her Upwork dashboard for new project listings throughout the designated time. The goal was to maintain an active presence and promptly engage with potential clients.

6. Dynamic Adjustments:

Sarah regularly reviewed and adjusted her alert settings based on the performance of her real-time strategy. This included refining keywords, updating budget filters, and experimenting with different project categories.

Results

1. Increased Proposal Visibility:

Sarah's real-time approach significantly increased the visibility of her proposals. By being among the first to submit, her proposals were more likely to be seen by clients during the crucial early stages of project evaluation.

2. Higher Response Rates:

Clients, appreciating the swift response, were more inclined to engage with Sarah. This led to an increase in positive interactions, interviews, and invitations to submit proposals for additional projects.

3. Improved Success Rate:

Sarah's success rate on Upwork improved as a direct result of her real-time project hunting strategy. She secured a higher number of projects compared to the period before implementing this approach.

4. Enhanced Client Relationships:

The real-time engagement allowed Sarah to build stronger relationships with clients. Timely communication and quick proposal turnaround contributed to positive client experiences.

5. Time-Efficient Workflow:

The prepared proposal templates and dedicated real-time hunting periods streamlined Sarah's workflow. She maximized her efficiency, spending less time on project discovery and more time on high-value activities.

Conclusion

Sarah's case demonstrates the impact of real-time project hunting on a freelancing marketplace. By adopting a proactive and responsive approach, she not only increased her project acquisition rate but also enhanced client relationships and improved overall success on Upwork. This case highlights the importance of agility and strategic planning in a competitive freelancing environment.

📄 Case Study-02 : Agile Project Hunting on Freelancer.com

Background

John, a freelance web developer, faced challenges securing consistent projects on Freelancer.com due to the platform's dynamic and competitive nature. Determined to boost his project acquisition, he implemented an agile project hunting strategy.

Objective:

John aimed to optimize his project hunting process by staying agile and responsive to new opportunities. The goal was to increase his project win rate and establish a steady stream of work on Freelancer.com.

Methodology

1. Customized Project Filters:

John configured advanced project filters on Freelancer.com, focusing on his specific skills, preferred project types, and budget ranges. These filters were designed to ensure he received real-time notifications for projects aligned with his expertise.

2. Mobile App Utilization:

Recognizing the importance of speed, John installed and configured the Freelancer.com mobile app. This allowed him to receive instant project notifications and submit proposals on-the-go, ensuring he could engage with projects promptly.

3. Responsive Proposal Templates:

John created a set of responsive proposal templates that could be quickly tailored to different project requirements. These templates allowed him to submit proposals rapidly without sacrificing the quality of his responses.

4. Continuous Engagement:

John committed to consistent and continuous engagement with the platform. Rather than waiting for specific time windows, he checked for new projects several times a day to stay ahead of the competition.

5. Adaptability and Experimentation:

John regularly reviewed and adjusted his project filters based on the changing nature of the platform. He experimented with different combinations of keywords and filters to refine his approach continually.

Results

1. Swift Proposal Submissions:

John's agile approach enabled him to submit proposals swiftly after project postings. This responsiveness increased the visibility of his proposals and positioned him as an early contender for projects.

2. Improved Win Rate:

By being one of the first freelancers to engage with clients, John noticed a significant improvement in his project win rate. Clients appreciated the prompt response and showed a preference for proactive freelancers.

3. Enhanced Mobile Accessibility:

The use of the Freelancer.com mobile app proved crucial in maintaining agility. John could respond to project notifications instantly, even when away from his computer, giving him a competitive edge.

4. Diversified Project Portfolio:

The agile project hunting strategy allowed John to diversify his project portfolio. He could quickly adapt to changing client needs and explore a wider range of projects within his expertise.

5. Time-Efficient Workflow:

John's approach optimized his workflow, allowing him to spend more time on project execution and client communication. The efficiency gained from agile project hunting contributed to overall productivity.

Conclusion

John's case illustrates the positive impact of an agile project hunting strategy on Freelancer.com. By embracing responsiveness, adaptability, and continuous engagement, he achieved a higher project win rate and established a more resilient and dynamic freelancing workflow. This case underscores the importance of staying agile in project acquisition on competitive freelancing platforms.

🗎 Case Study-03 : Proactive Project Scouting On Fiverr

Background

Emily, a freelance content writer specializing in technology and marketing, faced challenges in securing consistent projects on Fiverr. Motivated to take a more proactive approach, she implemented a strategy focused on proactive project scouting.

Objective:

Emily's primary goal was to break through the competition on Fiverr by actively seeking out projects that matched her skills and expertise. The objective was to increase her project acquisition rate and build a more predictable income stream.

Methodology

1. Customized Search Alerts:

Emily leveraged Fiverr's search alert feature to receive instant notifications for newly posted projects related to her niche. She customized the alerts based on relevant keywords and specific project requirements.

2. Strategic Gig Positioning:

Recognizing the importance of visibility, Emily strategically positioned her gigs on Fiverr to attract clients looking for her specific expertise. She optimized gig titles, descriptions, and tags to align with popular search queries in her industry.

3. Continuous Niche Research:

Emily committed time to continuous niche research within her industry. By staying informed about emerging trends and client needs, she could proactively position herself as an expert in sought-after areas.

4. Early Communication with Prospective Clients:

Upon receiving alerts for potential projects, Emily initiated early communication with clients. She sent personalized messages expressing her interest, showcasing relevant samples of her work, and highlighting how her skills aligned with the project requirements.

5. Tailored Offer Packages:

Emily created tailored offer packages that provided clients with clear choices based on their project scope and budget. This proactive approach allowed clients to see the value she could bring to their projects.

Results

1. Increased Visibility and Inquiries:

Emily's proactive project scouting strategy significantly increased the visibility of her gigs. Clients started reaching out to her with inquiries, appreciating the proactive approach and personalized communication.

2. Higher Conversion Rate:

By engaging with clients at an early stage, Emily observed a higher conversion rate from inquiries to actual projects. The personalized communication and tailored offers resonated well with clients, leading to more successful collaborations.

3. Diversified Project Portfolio:

The proactive approach enabled Emily to diversify her project portfolio. By actively seeking out a variety of projects within her niche, she could showcase her versatility and attract clients with different content needs.

4. Established Expertise:

Consistent proactive engagement allowed Emily to position herself as an expert in her niche. Clients recognized her as a go-to freelancer for specific types of projects, contributing to her reputation on Fiverr.

5. Predictable Income Stream:

Emily's proactive strategy resulted in a more predictable income stream. By consistently securing projects aligned with her expertise, she could better plan and manage her freelancing business.

Conclusion

Emily's case highlights the effectiveness of proactive project scouting on Fiverr. By combining customized search alerts, strategic gig positioning, and early communication with clients, she not only increased her visibility but also established herself as an expert with a predictable and diversified income stream. This case emphasizes the importance of taking a proactive stance in project acquisition on freelance platforms.

📄 Case Study-04 : Strategic Niche Positioning on PeoplePerHour

Background

Alex, a freelance digital marketer, faced challenges in standing out among the diverse talent pool on PeoplePerHour. In a quest to differentiate himself and attract clients in his specific niche, he implemented a strategic niche positioning strategy.

Objective:

Alex aimed to carve a niche for himself within the digital marketing landscape on PeoplePerHour. The primary goal was to be recognized as an expert in a specific area, increase visibility within that niche, and ultimately secure more projects aligned with his expertise.

Methodology

1. Niche Identification:

Alex conducted a thorough self-assessment to identify his unique strengths and interests within digital marketing. He narrowed down his focus to a specific niche – content marketing for tech startups – where he had both expertise and a genuine passion.

2. Optimized Profile and Portfolio:

Alex revamped his PeoplePerHour profile to reflect his specialization in content marketing for tech startups. He optimized his profile headline, summary, and portfolio to showcase relevant skills, experiences, and successful projects in this niche.

3. Tailored Gig Offers:

Instead of offering generic digital marketing services, Alex created specialized gig offers tailored to the content marketing needs of tech startups. Each offer highlighted his expertise, unique selling points, and the specific value he could bring to clients in this niche.

4. Targeted Proposal Approach:

When submitting proposals for projects, Alex adopted a targeted approach. He crafted personalized proposals that emphasized his niche expertise, shared relevant case studies, and demonstrated a deep understanding of the challenges and goals specific to tech startups.

5. Content Marketing Strategy:

To further establish his niche positioning, Alex implemented a content marketing strategy. He regularly published blog posts on PeoplePerHour, sharing insights, tips, and success stories related to content marketing for tech startups.

Results

1. Niche Authority and Recognition:

Alex's strategic niche positioning resulted in increased authority and recognition within the content marketing niche for tech startups on PeoplePerHour. Clients began associating him with expertise in this specific area.

2. Higher Conversion Rates:

The targeted approach in proposals, combined with specialized gig offers, led to higher conversion rates. Clients seeking content marketing services for tech startups were more likely to choose Alex based on his niche expertise.

3. Quality Leads and Projects:

By aligning his profile, gigs, and proposals with a specific niche, Alex attracted higher-quality leads. He started receiving project invitations and inquiries from clients specifically looking for a content marketing expert in the tech startup domain.

4. Community Engagement:

Alex's content marketing strategy also contributed to increased community engagement. Other freelancers and clients within the niche recognized him as a valuable contributor, further enhancing his visibility and credibility.

5. Consistent Project Flow:

The strategic niche positioning resulted in a consistent flow of projects within the targeted niche. Alex could rely on a steady stream of projects that matched his expertise, contributing to a more stable freelancing business.

Conclusion

Alex's case underscores the importance of strategic niche positioning on PeoplePerHour. By identifying and showcasing his expertise in content marketing for tech startups, he not only differentiated himself in a competitive market but also attracted higher-quality leads and projects. This case emphasizes the impact of aligning one's freelancing profile with a specific niche to enhance visibility and success on platform-specific markets.

Chapter 14: Finding Work on Traditional Marketplaces.

This chapter is about how to find Work on Traditional marketplaces (Guru, upwork, freelancer.com). The first step is to Identifying Projects on Traditional Freelance Marketplaces.

⚲ Identifying Projects on Traditional Freelance Marketplaces

Finding work on traditional freelance marketplaces like Guru, Upwork, and Freelancer.com involves a systematic approach to identifying suitable projects. Here are key steps to help you navigate and identify potential projects:

1. Profile Optimization:

Begin by optimizing your freelancer profile. Clearly articulate your skills, experiences, and areas of expertise. Use a professional profile picture and write a compelling summary that showcases your unique value proposition.

2. Define Your Niche:

Clearly define your niche or specialization. Clients often prefer freelancers with specific expertise in their desired field. This can help you stand out and attract projects that align with your skills.

3. Set Up Relevant Keywords:

Utilize the search and filter features on the platforms. Set up relevant keywords related to your skills, industry, or specific services you offer. This helps narrow down your search and find projects that match your expertise.

4. Browse Job Categories:

Explore the various job categories available on the platform. Traditional marketplaces typically have a range of categories covering different industries and skill sets. Look for categories that align with your skills and interests.

5. Use Advanced Filters:

Take advantage of advanced filters provided by the platforms. You can filter projects based on criteria such as budget, project type, client history, and project duration. This allows you to focus on projects that meet your preferences.

6. Saved Searches and Alerts:

Save relevant searches and set up job alerts. This ensures you receive notifications for new projects that match your criteria. Saved searches can be a time-saving feature, allowing you to quickly access projects of interest.

7. Regularly Check Job Feeds:

Stay active on the job feeds or job boards of the platforms. New projects are regularly posted, and being proactive in checking the feeds allows you to be among the first to apply, increasing your chances of being noticed by clients.

8. Read Project Descriptions Carefully:

When identifying potential projects, carefully read the project descriptions. Look for projects that clearly outline the scope, requirements, and expectations. Ensure that the project aligns with your skills and capabilities.

9. Check Client Feedback and Ratings:

Evaluate the client's history and reputation. Traditional marketplaces often provide feedback and ratings for clients. Choose projects posted by clients with positive reviews, as this indicates a higher likelihood of a successful collaboration.

10. Submit Tailored Proposals:

Craft personalized and tailored proposals for each project you apply to. Clearly address how your skills and experience make you the ideal candidate for the project. Tailored proposals demonstrate your genuine interest and understanding of the client's needs.

11. Network and Build Relationships:

Engage with the platform's community and participate in relevant forums or groups. Building relationships with other freelancers and clients can open up opportunities for collaboration and referrals.

By following these steps and maintaining an active presence on traditional freelance marketplaces, you can effectively identify and pursue projects that match your skills and contribute to a successful freelancing career.

ॐ Importance of Understanding Client's Brief

Understanding the client's brief is a critical aspect of finding work on traditional freelance marketplaces like Guru, Upwork, and Freelancer.com. It not only enhances your chances of winning projects but also contributes to successful and long-lasting client relationships. Here's why understanding the client's brief is essential:

1. **Accurate Proposal Submission:**

By thoroughly understanding the client's brief, you can ensure that your proposal accurately addresses their needs and requirements. This increases the chances of your proposal standing out among others and being considered by the client.

2. **Customized Solutions:**

Every client has unique challenges and goals. Understanding the brief allows you to tailor your solutions to the specific needs of the client. This customization demonstrates your commitment to providing value and solving their particular problems.

3. **Building Trust and Confidence:**

Clients appreciate freelancers who take the time to understand their projects. When you show a deep understanding of the client's brief in your communication and proposals, you build trust and confidence. Clients are more likely to hire freelancers they trust to deliver on their vision.

4. **Effective Communication:**

Clear and effective communication is crucial in freelancing. Understanding the client's brief enables you to communicate more effectively. You can ask relevant questions, provide clarifications, and demonstrate your expertise in a way that resonates with the client.

5. Alignment with Client's Goals:

Clients are seeking freelancers who align with their project goals. By understanding the brief, you can showcase how your skills and experience directly contribute to achieving the client's objectives. This alignment makes you a valuable asset to the client's project.

6. Avoiding Misunderstandings:

Misunderstandings can lead to project delays, revisions, and dissatisfaction. A thorough understanding of the client's brief helps you avoid misinterpretations and ensures that your deliverables meet the client's expectations from the start.

7. Efficient Project Planning:

Understanding the client's brief allows you to plan your project more efficiently. You can accurately estimate the time, resources, and effort required to complete the project, leading to realistic timelines and expectations.

8. Showcasing Relevance and Expertise:

When you demonstrate a deep understanding of the client's industry, business, and challenges, you position yourself as a relevant and knowledgeable freelancer. Clients are more likely to choose freelancers who showcase expertise specific to their needs.

9. Higher Client Satisfaction:

Ultimately, understanding the client's brief contributes to higher client satisfaction. When you deliver exactly what the client is looking for, on time and within budget, you create a positive experience that can lead to repeat business and positive reviews.

10. Differentiation in a Competitive Market:

Traditional freelance marketplaces are often competitive. Understanding the client's brief allows you to differentiate yourself from other freelancers by showing a genuine interest in the project and a commitment to delivering exceptional results.

In summary, the importance of understanding the client's brief cannot be overstated in the freelancing world. It forms the foundation for successful collaborations, positive client experiences, and the overall growth of your freelancing career on traditional marketplaces.

Summarizing client's brief

Summarizing a client's brief effectively is a crucial skill when finding work on traditional freelance marketplaces such as Guru, Upwork, and Freelancer.com. It involves distilling the key information from the client's project description to demonstrate your understanding and present a concise overview of your proposed approach. Here's a guide on how to summarize a client's brief:

1. **Thorough Reading:**

Begin by carefully reading the client's brief multiple times. Understand the project requirements, goals, and any specific instructions provided. Pay attention to details such as project scope, deadlines, and the client's expectations.

2. Identify Key Components:

Identify the key components of the client's brief, including the main objectives, deliverables, and any challenges mentioned. Highlight essential details that will guide your proposal and help you address the client's needs effectively.

3. Clarify Ambiguities:

If any part of the client's brief is unclear or ambiguous, seek clarification. Send a polite and concise message to the client asking for additional information or clarification on specific points. This proactive approach demonstrates your commitment to understanding the project.

4. Create an Outline:

Structure your summary in an organized manner. Create an outline that includes sections such as project overview, key requirements, milestones, and any questions or clarifications you may have. This will help you present the information in a clear and coherent format.

5. Use Client's Language:

Mirror the client's language and terminology in your summary. This shows that you've paid attention to their communication style and that you can seamlessly integrate into their project environment.

6. Highlight Relevant Experience:

Draw connections between the client's brief and your relevant experience. Mention specific projects or skills that align with the client's requirements. This helps to establish your credibility and reassure the client that you have the expertise to handle their project.

7. Demonstrate Understanding:

Explicitly state that you understand the client's requirements. Summarize the key points in a sentence or two to reassure the client that you've grasped the essence of the project. This demonstrates your attention to detail and commitment to delivering precisely what they're looking for.

8. Propose a Solution:

In your summary, briefly outline your proposed approach to the project. Mention how you plan to tackle the key challenges or meet the project objectives. This gives the client a glimpse into your thought process and problem-solving abilities.

9. Invite Further Discussion:

Conclude your summary by expressing your enthusiasm for the project and inviting further discussion. Let the client know that you're available to answer any questions or provide additional information. This encourages communication and sets the stage for ongoing collaboration.

10. Proofread Carefully:

Before submitting your summary, proofread it carefully to ensure clarity, coherence, and correctness. A well-written and error-free summary reflects professionalism and attention to detail.

By mastering the art of summarizing client's briefs, you enhance your ability to communicate effectively and stand out among freelancers competing for the same projects on traditional freelance marketplaces.

ⓘ Policies of Freelancing Marketplaces: Upwork, Guru, and Freelancer

Upwork Policies

1. Terms of Service:

Upwork provides a comprehensive Terms of Service document that outlines the rules and conditions for using the platform. Freelancers and clients are required to adhere to these terms to maintain a fair and secure environment.

2. Membership Plans:

Upwork offers different membership plans, including free and paid options. Each plan comes with its own set of features and benefits. Freelancers and clients should be familiar with the details of their chosen membership plan.

3. Connects System:

Upwork employs a Connects system where freelancers need to use Connects to submit proposals for jobs. The number of Connects required varies based on the type of job. Understanding and adhering to the Connects system is crucial for freelancers.

4. Payment Protection:

Upwork provides Payment Protection for hourly and fixed-price contracts. This ensures that freelancers are paid for the work they complete. Freelancers should familiarize themselves with Upwork's policies regarding payment protection.

5. Feedback and Ratings:

Upwork encourages clients and freelancers to provide feedback and ratings after completing a project. Positive reviews enhance a freelancer's profile, while clients are rated based on their interactions. Understanding the importance of feedback is essential for building a reputable profile.

Guru Policies

1. Terms of Service:

Guru has its Terms of Service that users must agree to when using the platform. This document outlines the rights and responsibilities of freelancers and clients, ensuring a transparent and fair working relationship.

2. Workroom and Work Agreements:

Guru uses Workrooms for project collaboration. Freelancers and clients can create Work Agreements that detail the terms of the project. Understanding how to effectively use Workrooms and create Work Agreements is crucial for successful project management.

3. SafePay System:

Guru employs a SafePay system for hourly and fixed-price projects. SafePay acts as an escrow service, holding funds until the agreed-upon work is completed. Freelancers should be familiar with SafePay and how it ensures payment security.

4. Guru Work Collections:

Freelancers can create Work Collections to showcase their portfolio. Understanding how to curate and present Work Collections helps freelancers attract clients by highlighting their skills and previous work.

5. Freelancer Work Summaries:

Freelancers are encouraged to provide Work Summaries for completed projects. This feature allows freelancers to describe their contributions and showcase their expertise. Understanding how to effectively use Work Summaries contributes to a freelancer's online presence.

Freelancer.com Policies

1. User Agreement:

Freelancer.com has a User Agreement that outlines the terms and conditions for using the platform. Users must adhere to these terms to ensure a secure and fair freelancing environment.

2. Milestone Payments:

Freelancer.com uses Milestone Payments for fixed-price projects. Understanding how to set up and manage Milestone Payments is crucial for freelancers to ensure they receive compensation for completed project milestones.

3. Freelancer Levels:

Freelancer.com has a freelancer level system that categorizes users based on their performance and activity on the platform. Advancing through levels unlocks additional features and benefits. Freelancers should understand the criteria for each level.

4. Contests:

Freelancer.com allows clients to create contests where freelancers submit entries, and the client selects the winning entry. Understanding how contests work and how to participate is important for freelancers interested in this type of project.

5. Bid Upgrades:

Freelancers can use Bid Upgrades to enhance the visibility of their proposals. These upgrades come at an additional cost and can help freelancers stand out when bidding on projects.

Understanding and adhering to the policies of freelancing marketplaces such as Upwork, Guru, and Freelancer is crucial for a successful and secure freelancing experience. This includes familiarity with user agreements, payment systems, and features unique to each platform.

◈ What gets your profile banned?

Each freelancing platform, including Upwork, Guru, and Freelancer, has specific policies and guidelines that users must follow. Violating these policies can result in consequences, ranging from warnings to the suspension or banning of user profiles. Here are some common actions that could lead to your profile being banned on these platforms:

Upwork

1. Submitting Fraudulent Information:

Providing false or misleading information in your Upwork profile, such as fake credentials, experience, or portfolio items, can lead to a ban.

2. Misrepresentation:

Misrepresenting your skills, qualifications, or experience to clients is a violation of Upwork's policies. Be truthful and accurate in presenting your capabilities.

3. Multiple Accounts:

Creating and managing multiple Upwork accounts without proper authorization is against Upwork's policies. Freelancers should have only one account.

4. Violating Intellectual Property Rights:

Using copyrighted material without permission or violating intellectual property rights in any way can lead to account suspension.

5. Inappropriate Behavior:

Engaging in inappropriate or offensive behavior, harassment, or discrimination on the platform can result in disciplinary action, including profile suspension.

Guru

1. False Information:

Providing false or misleading information in your Guru profile, such as fake credentials, qualifications, or work history, is a violation of Guru's policies.

2. Plagiarism:

Submitting plagiarized work or misrepresenting someone else's work as your own is against Guru's policies.

3. Communication Violations:

Engaging in abusive or inappropriate communication with clients, freelancers, or Guru support staff can lead to profile suspension.

4. Payment Violations:

Violating payment terms, such as attempting to bypass Guru's SafePay system or engaging in fraudulent payment activities, can result in a ban.

5. Unauthorized Account Use:

Allowing others to use your Guru account or using someone else's account without permission is a breach of Guru's policies.

Freelancer.com

1. Fake Credentials:

Providing inaccurate or fraudulent information in your Freelancer.com profile, such as false credentials, certifications, or skills, can lead to account suspension.

2. Bidding Violations:

Engaging in bid manipulation, spamming, or using automated tools to bid on projects inappropriately is a violation of Freelancer.com's policies.

3. Payment Fraud:

Attempting to manipulate or defraud the payment system, including creating fake transactions, can result in a ban.

4. Multiple Accounts:

Maintaining multiple Freelancer.com accounts without proper authorization is against the platform's policies.

5. Inappropriate Content:

Uploading or sharing inappropriate content, including offensive language, images, or materials, can lead to disciplinary action.

It's crucial for freelancers to thoroughly read and understand the policies of each platform they use and to conduct themselves in a professional and ethical manner to avoid profile bans. If in doubt, referring to the specific terms of service and guidelines provided by each platform is recommended.

⚲ How To Get Your Profile Unbanned?

If your profile on freelancing platforms like Upwork, Guru, or Freelancer has been banned, getting it unbanned involves following the platforms' respective appeal processes. Here are general steps you can take:

1. Review Platform Policies:

Before taking any action, carefully review the platform's terms of service and policies. Understand the specific reasons for the ban to address them appropriately.

2. Identify the Violation:

Clearly identify the violation that led to the profile ban. This could be related to false information, inappropriate behavior, multiple accounts, or other policy breaches.

3. Contact Support:

Upwork:

Visit the Upwork Help Center and submit a support ticket explaining the situation. Clearly outline your understanding of the violation, express your commitment to adhering to Upwork's policies, and request a review of your profile.

Guru:

Use the "Contact Us" or support options provided by Guru to reach out to their customer support team. Clearly explain the circumstances surrounding the ban and ask for guidance on how to resolve the issue.

Freelancer.com:

Contact Freelancer.com support through their Help Center or support channels. Provide a detailed explanation of the situation, express your willingness to comply with platform policies, and request a review of your profile.

4. Apologize and Provide Clarifications:

In your communication with the support team, offer a sincere apology for any unintentional violations and provide clarifications on how you plan to prevent such issues in the future. Demonstrating understanding and responsibility can work in your favor.

5. Demonstrate Corrective Actions:

Outline any corrective actions you have taken to address the issues leading to the profile ban. This may include updating your profile information, improving communication practices, or resolving any outstanding concerns.

6. Be Professional and Polite:

Maintain a professional and polite tone in all communications. Avoid being confrontational or defensive. Clearly express your commitment to maintaining a positive and compliant presence on the platform.

7. Follow Up:

If you don't receive a response promptly, consider following up through the platform's support channels. Reiterate your commitment to compliance and request a status update on your profile review.

8. Learn from the Experience:

Use the situation as an opportunity to learn and grow. Understand the platform's policies thoroughly, and ensure you comply with them going forward. Regularly check and update your profile information to reflect accurate and truthful details.

It's important to note that the success of profile unbanning requests depends on the severity of the violation and the platform's policies. Platforms may have different processes, so always refer to the specific guidelines provided by each platform for the most accurate information.

⚡ Managing Freelance Marketplace Dispute with Employer

When to get out of a dispute?

Managing a dispute with an employer on a freelance marketplace can be challenging, and deciding when to get out of a dispute depends on various factors. Here are some considerations to help you determine when it might be appropriate to consider exiting a dispute:

Communication Breakdown:

If communication with the employer has reached a point where it is no longer productive and both parties are unable to find common ground, it may be an indication that resolving the dispute through continued communication is unlikely.

Repeated Violations of Freelancer Rights:

If the employer repeatedly violates the agreed-upon terms, fails to provide necessary information or resources, or engages in unethical behavior, it may be a sign that continuing the relationship is not in your best interest.

Unreasonable Demands:

If the employer is making demands that are clearly beyond the scope of the initial agreement, and attempts to negotiate a reasonable compromise have been unsuccessful, it may be a signal to consider exiting the dispute.

Lack of Progress:

If the dispute resolution process on the freelance platform is not making progress, and there are no signs of a resolution in sight, it may be worth reassessing the situation.

Impact on Your Well-being:

If the dispute is causing significant stress, anxiety, or other negative impacts on your well-being, it may be important to prioritize your mental and emotional health.

Legal or Ethical Concerns:

If the employer's actions raise legal or ethical concerns, it may be in your best interest to disengage from the dispute. Consult with legal professionals if necessary.

Assessment of Potential Losses:

Evaluate the potential losses, including time, effort, and potential income, against the likelihood of a favorable resolution. If the dispute is causing substantial losses with little chance of recovery, exiting may be a reasonable choice.

Platform Guidelines:

Review the guidelines and policies of the freelance platform. Some platforms may have specific recommendations or requirements for handling disputes, and understanding these guidelines can inform your decision.

Consultation with Platform Support:

If the dispute resolution process on the platform is not progressing, consider reaching out to the platform's support team for guidance. They may provide insights or assistance in navigating the situation.

Reviewing Terms of Agreement:

Revisit the initial terms of agreement and evaluate whether the employer is adhering to those terms. If there are clear violations that are not being addressed, it may be an indication to consider leaving the dispute.

Ultimately, the decision to get out of a dispute should be based on a careful assessment of the specific circumstances and your overall well-being. It may also be helpful to seek advice from trusted colleagues, mentors, or legal professionals before making a final decision.

Chapter 15 : Inspirational Stories

🏆 7 Freelance Success Stories*

Here are some inspiring freelance success stories to help you move forward in this industry!

1. Chiara Ferragni, Blogger

An exciting freelance writing success story is that of Chiara Ferragni. She owns a travel blog known as "The Blond Salad." She started small but now owns one of the most famous travel blogs. She travels the world and shares her stories with an audience that adores her.

Over time, "The Blond Salad" has grown into an online store, has sixteen million followers on Instagram, and is recognized internationally. In 2018 Chiara was listed as one of the most influential people in Italy alongside Giorgio Armani and Mario Draghi.

2. Andrea Reggio, Freelance Writer

Andrea Reggio comes from a finance background and has experience working in finance; however, she was looking for more flexible work with a more relaxed lifestyle, which is when she discovered the freelance world.

Andrea also started slowly as a freelancer, but she managed to turn freelancing into a full-time job with some patience and commitment. She learned an invaluable lesson that made her a freelance success – even though you start slow, it gets easier and is a good source of income with some hard work.

Freelance writers can start with options like an essay paper writing service, which offers writing or editing opportunities. You can begin by writing academic papers and move on to serious work for bigger companies. You can also work as a magazine editor or journalist. You can also look for freelance platforms such as Freelancer, Upwork, or Fiverr. Once you get a few reviews and build a reputation, there is an ample amount of work out there just waiting for you to start.

3. David Nuff, Artist and Web Developer

Another freelance success story is that of David Nuff. David Nuff traveled a lot and was adept at computer science as a child. However, his heart was set on arts, and as he grew up, he found a way to combine the two. He made his way through web design and then applied for the Montreal Biking project. In 2008, he finished the bike system of easily accessible solar-powered bike rental stations. He then developed a software that made the bicycles easy to track, and it turned out to be a technical breakthrough! Eventually, David worked for multinational companies like Google and was a huge success.

4. Hilary Umeoka, Writer

We have another fantastic freelance writing success story for you; Hilary Umeoka is a Nigerian priest who became a successful freelancer and is the founder of an international charitable movement. Now he is a multi-millionaire and lends others a helping hand whenever possible. Hilary says that knowledge and open-mindedness opened up these fantastic opportunities for him. He graduated with an honors degree and was also awarded the title of the best student of the year at his seminary.

After studying to become a priest, he moved to the IT industry and started freelancing at an international platform. Today, he has written thousands of articles and wiki pages for his clients and has also published a best-selling book about the emerging world of the Internet.

He now manages his own team of writers and helps others build their portfolios.

5. AbdulGaniy Shehu, Freelance Writer

AbdulGaniy Shehu started as a freelancer right after his university. He contemplated starting at a traditional job or starting his own business. Eventually, he began writing for famous publications. His story taught us that having a freelance writing success story comes through hard work, dedication, and a strong level of commitment to your work. Starting, most freelancers work for longer hours than they would've at a traditional job. For example, building yourself in the essay service industry sometimes requires submitting work within three hours. Hence, if a freelancer is not committed enough, it can get tricky to earn a living through freelancing

6. Alex Chia, Day Trader

Another freelance success story is that of Alex Chia. he is a successful trader that managed to turn his dreams into reality. He started by working at Starbucks, in the same rut of waiting for his monthly salary, waiting for a promotion, and working for long hours. However, the only difference between him and other employees is that he'd come home after work and spend sleepless nights researching the stock market. He eventually made a brokerage account and invested the money he saved into different stocks. Over the years, he faced losses, lost some accounts, but he never gave up and faced all challenges that came his way head-on. Now he shares his knowledge with the trading community, helps others become successful, and is a source of inspiration for many people across the globe.

7. Kelly Vaughn, Web Developer

Before becoming a freelancer, Kelly Vaughn worked at a government job with the basic benefits. But, soon, she mustered the courage to take a step towards the freelance industry and wade the waters. Now she travels the world, tells people about her adventures, and is also a web developer. She gets the freedom to work from any location on her own time and has complete control over how much work she would like to take on.

* https://www.peppercontent.io/blog/freelance-success-stories/

🏢 Meet Betsy, a Brand Strategy Expert With a Diverse Client Base*

*https://www.upwork.com/success-stories

Betsy Grote has more than a decade of experience in brand strategy, naming, and copywriting. She's an expert at helping business leaders uncover and define their authentic brand identity to move from one stage of growth to the next.

Grote started her career working on in-house marketing and branding teams for businesses ranging from startups to enterprises. At the time however, she dreamed of working in an agency environment.

But soon after Grote achieved her dream of working at an agency, she realized that she could have more flexibility by running her own business.

"My last full-time job was leading a strategy team at a Cincinnati-based brand agency," said Grote. "The experience was great and I learned a lot. But at the end of the day, I realized that what would make me happiest and most fulfilled was doing this kind of work, but having the freedom to design my life the way I wanted."

In 2019, Grote made the switch to freelancing and initially relied on professional connections in her network to begin building her client base. By 2020, she started exploring additional ways to grow her business.

Growing a business on Upwork

When Grote was looking for new opportunities to expand her client base, she spoke with a friend who'd built a thriving business on Upwork. Her friend recommended a course from a successful freelancer about how to build a copywriting business on the platform.

Grote completed the course and her first project on Upwork helped her cover the cost. By the second month on Upwork, Grote quickly experienced noticeable business growth.

Grote has worked with a variety of clients, from U.S.-based independent business owners to international enterprise businesses. "Upwork opened a global marketplace to me," said Grote. "I've worked with clients in Dubai, Hong Kong, and all over Europe. I wouldn't have been able to get this kind of exposure on my own. Along the way, you learn how to identify top clients who value your work and are great to collaborate with, of which there are many on Upwork."

Collaborating with diverse clients and brands

Grote's primary focus area is brand strategy and naming. Through this type of work, she has the opportunity to think strategically and analytically, as well as creatively.

"My work tends to vary and includes a really cool balance of right brain and left brain, or art and science as I sometimes like to say," shared Grote. "My projects involve a lot of analysis but at the end of that analysis, there's always some creative leap that takes place."

With access to a global client base through Upwork, Grote also has the flexibility to partner with brands and clients across a diverse range of business sizes and industries.

"Upwork is awesome because it has connected me with enterprise-level clients, which is really cool." explained Grote. "But I also love working with startups or medium-sized businesses whose leadership have a real stake in the business and really deeply care.

"They've been a hands-on part of building the business, which is exciting to me because the work I do can make that much more of an impact," continued Grote. "I would say, startups and medium-sized businesses are my specialty."

Brand strategy and naming project examples

Here are a few examples of brand strategy and naming projects that Grote has completed:

Life coach. Grote worked on a branding project with a life coach who was in the early stages of building her business. She got to know the client on a personal level and the two collaborated to define and clarify the client's brand strategy. "I really love working with people like her who are so passionate," shared Grote. "With smaller clients, it's less of, 'Here's the work, run with it,' which I'm happy to do as well. But we really got to work together to create this strategy for the client that has clarified the way forward for her brand. With this type of project, you really feel like you're giving the client a gift."

Pickleball racket manufacturer. Pickleball has grown in popularity in recent years and new brands continue to emerge in the space. Grote partnered with a brand that makes high-end, professional-grade pickleball rackets. The company is small and needed a strong brand strategy to stay competitive with larger, more well-known pickleball brands. Grote worked with the team to hone in on their brand voice and identify key differentiators.

Pharmaceutical company. Grote partnered with a pharmaceutical company that previously went through multiple name changes and brand evolutions. The team wanted a name that represented a shift away from their old brand and also differentiated themselves from traditional pharmaceutical companies. They wanted to show that they have a soul and truly care about not only treating people, but curing them on a deep level with their medications. Grote's job was to identify name options that aligned with the pharma-with-a-soul element.

Looking ahead: Balancing personal and professional priorities

Over the next few years, Grote plans to focus on growing her business while also spending time with her family. She recently married and had her first child. Running her own business gives Grote the flexibility to dedicate time to both her personal and professional lives.

"A beautiful part about freelancing is that I don't feel like I have to choose between being a mom or working," said Grote. "I can create a life that's integrated and includes spending time with my family and continuing to work on exciting, challenging projects."

As Grote continues to build her business, she also plans to partner with other independent professionals on Upwork to work on more in-depth branding projects. Thinking about her future goals, she explained, "I'd like to build out a roster of designers whom I can turn to and work with to build out branding projects that are larger in scope."

❗From Freelancing to Founding*

*https://blog.fiverr.com/post/from-freelancing-to-founding

It all began in 2005, when 8th grade classmates Darshak and Abhi realized they were neighbors. They were friends after just one day.

After graduating in 2014, they headed to Melbourne, Australia to pursue their tertiary education together. But before they left, Darshak decided to try out new freelancing platforms. When Fiverr began to feel like his miracle, he recommended that Abhi try the same.

Today, they are 6-figure top sellers in Fiverr's busiest category: Logo Design. Even though they work with different agencies, they're always ready to help and support each other.

1) Would you mind sharing your experience of how you hired your first employee?

Darshak: Initially in 2016, just after I made a decision to try Fiverr full time, I started getting more orders that I alone couldn't manage. An idea was triggered in my mind that an extra pair of hands could process more orders and assist me in the designing areas. With that in mind, I hired my first employee from my city and he is now the Head of the Graphic Design department in my agency.

Abhi: After completing several orders and gathering a few pools of buyers, I wasn't able to manage the work alone. At that time, I thought about hiring an employee.

2) What was the trigger that helped you make such a decision?

Darshak: As I shared earlier and to convert my part-time freelancing to a full-time agency, I knew I'll need a bigger workforce beside me. It was simple math: the bigger the team, the better the results!

Abhi: Instead of working alone and increasing delivery time, it seemed better to get a helping hand to decrease the delivery time and increase the revenue as well as the order flow. Also, the extra oomph that another person gives in brainpower, creativity, and sheer legwork is totally worth it. Things that would otherwise take you weeks will be doable in days. Entire work streams will disappear from your to-do list.

3) How do you find the right person?

Darshak: I wanted to work with an employee with whom I could talk to and guide in person! So I asked a local job/recruitment agency to find a designer who already has a bit of experience in the designing field. Within a few days, after sorting out a few resumes and interviews, I got a perfect match!

Abhi: If you have a budget and social media then the right person isn't far away. When I thought to hire my first employee, I posted ads on LinkedIn, Facebook, and Instagram. After going through the round of discussions with 5-6 candidates, I got my first employee.

4) How long does it take to return the investment?

Darshak: It wasn't so hard to find my first employee after I paid the recruitment agency and within a couple of months, I earned more than I invested. For some sellers in a different category, it will take more time but believe me, try and hire employees even if you have to pay more so that you can focus more on growing your business.

Abhi: Well, that actually depends upon many factors like your Gig pricing, your local currency, the service you sell, etc. For me, it just took a week to return the investment (employee salary + ad expense) at that time.

5) What is your recommendation to other sellers?

Darshak: Personally, I would recommend other sellers to focus more on developing and expanding your Fiverr account/Gigs into different categories and hire talented people around you. Simply focus on growing your Fiverr Gigs and let other people work with you.

Abhi: I would recommend other sellers to identify the right time to hire and train an employee, develop a team, and get your online business rolling on Fiverr just like me.

weperfectionist

Darshak (from India), enthusiastic and creative graphic artist who is passionate about Logo and Banner Design.

Joined Fiverr on Dec 2015 , and enrolled in Seller Plus on Feb 2021

Mrtranscendence

Abhi (from India), passionate graphic designer with over 7 years of experience.

Joined Fiverr on Nov 2016, and enrolled in Seller Plus on Feb 2021

Chapter 16: When Bids Don't Attract A Response

☹ How To Manage Disappointment?

When your bids on freelancing platforms don't attract a response, it can be disheartening, but there are several strategies you can employ to manage disappointment and improve your chances of getting noticed:

Evaluate Your Profile:

Review your freelancer profile critically. Ensure it is complete, professional, and highlights your skills and experience effectively. Make any necessary updates to improve its appeal.

Optimize Your Proposal:

Tailor each proposal to the specific project requirements. Clearly demonstrate how your skills and experience align with the client's needs. Craft compelling and personalized proposals that stand out from the competition.

Research Client and Project:

Before submitting a bid, thoroughly research the client and project. Understand their needs, challenges, and preferences. Reference specific details in your proposal to show that you've done your homework.

Showcase Relevant Work:

Include relevant samples of your past work in your proposals. This provides clients with tangible examples of your capabilities and helps them visualize how you can contribute to their project.

Set a Competitive Rate:

Price your services competitively based on industry standards and your skill level. If your rates are too high, you may be pricing yourself out of consideration. Conversely, be cautious of undervaluing your skills.

Build a Strong Portfolio:

Regularly update your portfolio with high-quality work. A strong portfolio can grab the attention of potential clients and give them confidence in your abilities.

Improve Your Skillset:

Identify in-demand skills within your niche and invest time in upgrading your skillset. Demonstrating expertise in sought-after areas can make you more attractive to clients.

Seek Feedback:

If possible, request feedback from clients or peers. Constructive feedback can provide valuable insights into areas for improvement and help you refine your approach.

Diversify Your Platforms:

Explore additional freelancing platforms to expand your opportunities. Different platforms may attract different types of clients, and diversification increases your visibility.

Network and Engage:

Actively participate in freelancing community forums, groups, and discussions. Networking can lead to valuable connections, and engaging with others can enhance your visibility.

Patience and Persistence:

Building a successful freelancing career takes time. Be patient and persistent. Keep refining your approach, learning from experiences, and adapting to the evolving freelance landscape.

Take Breaks When Needed:

If disappointment becomes overwhelming, take short breaks to recharge. Burnout can impact the quality of your proposals, so it's essential to maintain a healthy work-life balance.

Remember that the freelancing market can be competitive, and success often comes with perseverance and continuous improvement. Use each experience as an opportunity to learn and enhance your freelancing strategy.

⊙ Think Un-Orthodox

When traditional bidding approaches don't yield responses, thinking unorthodox or outside the box can help you stand out and increase your chances of attracting attention:

Creative Proposals:

Consider incorporating creative elements into your proposals. This could be a short video introducing yourself, a visually appealing infographic showcasing your skills, or any other unique format that sets you apart.

Interactive Demonstrations:

Instead of just describing your skills, offer to provide a small interactive demonstration. This could be a brief consultation, a sample piece of work, or a personalized solution to a part of the client's problem.

Unique Value Proposition:

Clearly communicate a unique value proposition. Highlight what makes you different from other freelancers and how your approach can bring additional value to the client.

Challenge-Based Responses:

If appropriate, propose a solution to a specific challenge mentioned in the project description. Showcasing your problem-solving skills can capture the client's attention and demonstrate your understanding of their needs.

Engage on Social Media:

Connect with potential clients on social media platforms. Engage with their content, comment on their posts, and build a subtle online presence. This can create familiarity and increase the likelihood of your bids being noticed.

Pitching via Alternative Channels:

If the platform allows, explore alternative channels for pitching. This could include sending a creative email or even reaching out through social media with a brief pitch.

Offering Limited-Time Benefits:

Create a sense of urgency by offering limited-time benefits, such as a discount for the first project or additional services at no extra cost. This can incentivize clients to respond sooner.

Humor and Personality:

Injecting a bit of humor or showcasing your personality in your proposals can make you more memorable. Just ensure it aligns with the professional tone expected in your industry.

Strategic Follow-Ups:

Instead of traditional follow-up messages, send a follow-up that adds value. Share an interesting article related to the client's industry, offer a new insight, or provide a quick update on relevant industry trends.

Collaborative Suggestions:

Propose collaboration ideas that go beyond the immediate project. Suggest ways you can work together on a longer-term basis or contribute to the client's broader business goals.

Online Presence Enhancement:

Work on enhancing your online presence. This could include publishing insightful content on platforms like LinkedIn, starting a blog, or creating engaging social media posts. A strong online presence can make clients more receptive to your proposals.

Remember, the key is to be professional while incorporating elements that capture attention. Unorthodox approaches should align with the nature of the project and the expectations of your target clients. Always prioritize building a positive and lasting professional relationship.

↻ Go Back To Previous Clients

If your bids on freelancing platforms aren't generating responses, revisiting previous clients can be a valuable strategy. Past clients already know your work, and re-establishing a connection with them may lead to new opportunities. Here's how you can go back to previous clients:

Review Past Projects:

Reflect on the projects you completed for previous clients. Identify successful collaborations, positive feedback, and projects where you delivered exceptional results.

Update Your Portfolio:

Ensure that your portfolio showcases your best work, especially projects you completed for previous clients. Highlight the impact of your contributions and any positive feedback received.

Craft a Personalized Message:

Send a personalized message to your previous clients. Express appreciation for the past collaboration, briefly mention the positive outcomes of the project, and inquire about their current needs.

Mention Relevant Skills:

Remind clients of your relevant skills and expertise. If you've acquired new skills or certifications since your last collaboration, share this information to demonstrate your continuous improvement.

Offer Special Deals:

Consider offering special deals or discounts for repeat clients. This can be an incentive for them to consider hiring you again, especially if they have new projects in the pipeline.

Share Updates:

Update clients on any significant developments in your freelancing career. If you've worked on high-profile projects, received awards, or achieved milestones, share this information to showcase your professional growth.

Ask for Feedback:

Politely ask for feedback on the previous projects. This not only shows that you value their opinions but also opens a channel for communication, making it easier to discuss potential new collaborations.

Propose New Ideas:

Propose new ideas or improvements based on their current business needs. Demonstrate that you've thought about how your skills can contribute to their ongoing success.

Be Timely and Professional:

Timing is crucial. Reach out when there's a natural opportunity, such as the anniversary of your past collaboration or when you see they have posted a new project. Maintain a professional tone in your messages.

Offer a Catch-Up Call:

Suggest a brief catch-up call to discuss their current projects and explore ways you can contribute. This personal touch can strengthen the connection and make it easier to discuss potential collaborations.

Stay Persistent but Respectful:

If you don't receive a response initially, follow up respectfully. Acknowledge that they may be busy and express your continued interest in collaborating. Persistence should be balanced with respect for their time.

Reconnecting with previous clients not only increases your chances of securing new projects but also reinforces positive relationships. Building a network of satisfied clients who are willing to rehire you is a valuable asset in your freelancing career.

📣 Give An Amazing Offer

When your bids on freelancing platforms are not getting the desired responses, offering an amazing deal or incentive can grab the attention of potential clients. Here are some strategies to give an amazing offer:

1. Limited-Time Discounts:

Create a sense of urgency by offering a limited-time discount on your services. Clearly communicate the discounted rate and specify the timeframe during which the client can avail themselves of the special pricing.

2. Bundle Services:

Bundle your services together and offer a package deal at a discounted rate. This provides clients with added value and makes your proposal more enticing.

3. Bonus Deliverables:

Include bonus deliverables or additional services at no extra cost. Highlight these bonuses in your proposal to showcase the extra value the client will receive.

4. Extended Support or Revisions:

Offer extended support or additional revisions beyond the standard terms. This can be particularly appealing for clients who value ongoing assistance or meticulous attention to detail.

5. Free Consultation:

Include a free consultation as part of your offer. This gives clients the opportunity to discuss their project in detail with you before committing, building trust and showcasing your expertise.

6. Money-Back Guarantee:

Provide a money-back guarantee to alleviate any concerns the client might have. This demonstrates your confidence in delivering quality work and reassures the client about the value they will receive.

7. Flexible Payment Terms:

Offer flexible payment terms, such as installment payments or deferred payments. This can make your services more accessible to clients with budget constraints.

8. Refer-a-Friend Discount:

Introduce a refer-a-friend discount where the client receives a further discount or bonus for referring others to your services. This can help expand your client base through word of mouth.

9. Complimentary Add-Ons:

Include complimentary add-ons or premium features with your proposal. This could be additional features, resources, or tools that enhance the overall value of your services.

10. Customized Packages:

Tailor your offer to the specific needs of the client. Create customized packages that address their unique requirements, demonstrating that you've taken the time to understand their project.

11. Early Bird Specials:

Introduce an early bird special for clients who commit to your services within a specified timeframe. This encourages prompt decision-making and can lead to quicker responses.

12. Exclusive Access or Discounts:

Offer exclusive access to certain resources or exclusive discounts for being a preferred client. This creates a sense of exclusivity and appreciation for their business.

When presenting your amazing offer, clearly communicate the added value the client will receive and how it aligns with their project goals. Be genuine and transparent in your approach to build trust and increase the likelihood of a positive response.

🗪 Check Your Bid Time, PMB Response

When your bids on freelancing platforms aren't getting responses, it's essential to analyze and optimize various aspects, including bid timing and Project Message Board (PMB) responses. Here's what you can do:

1. Optimize Bid Timing:

Consider the timing of your bids. Clients may receive numerous proposals, and the timing of yours can impact visibility. Experiment with submitting bids during peak times when clients are likely to review proposals, such as during business hours or early in the week.

2. Monitor Project Message Board (PMB):

Regularly check the Project Message Board for updates from clients. Some clients may prefer direct communication through the PMB rather than relying solely on bid responses. Respond promptly and professionally to any messages or inquiries posted on the PMB.

3. Craft Compelling PMB Responses:

When responding on the PMB, craft compelling and personalized messages. Address the client by name, reiterate your understanding of their project, and showcase your enthusiasm for the opportunity. Use this as an additional chance to stand out.

4. Clarify Doubts or Seek Clarification:

If there are any uncertainties about the project details, use the PMB to seek clarification. Clear and detailed communication can demonstrate your professionalism and commitment to delivering the best results.

5. Avoid Generic Responses:

Steer clear of generic responses. Tailor your PMB responses to the specific project requirements and client's needs. Show that you've carefully read the project description and are genuinely interested in providing a solution.

6. Highlight Relevant Experience:

Emphasize your relevant experience and skills in your PMB responses. Clearly articulate how your expertise aligns with the client's needs and why you are the best fit for the project.

7. Express Availability:

Communicate your availability and willingness to discuss the project further. Offer to schedule a call or video meeting to address any questions the client may have and to provide additional insights into your approach.

8. Professional Tone:

Maintain a professional and courteous tone in your PMB responses. Use proper grammar and punctuation to convey a sense of professionalism. A well-written response can leave a positive impression.

9. Follow Up:

If you haven't received a response after a reasonable period, consider sending a polite follow-up message on the PMB. Express your continued interest in the project and reiterate your availability for further discussions.

10. Request Feedback:

If the client has reviewed your proposal but hasn't responded, politely ask for feedback. Understanding the reasons behind their decision can provide valuable insights for improving future bids.

By optimizing your bid timing and actively engaging on the Project Message Board, you enhance your chances of capturing the client's attention and initiating meaningful conversations that can lead to successful collaborations.

Chapter 17: Winning Your First Client as A Freelancer

⚜ How To Win Your First Client as A Freelancer

1. Self confidence

Winning your first client as a freelancer requires a combination of skills, strategies, and self-confidence. Here's how self-confidence plays a crucial role in this process:

2. Believe in Your Skills:

Confidence starts with a belief in your own abilities. Recognize and acknowledge the skills you possess that make you a valuable freelancer. This belief will be evident in your communications with potential clients.

3. Craft a Strong Profile:

Develop a comprehensive and compelling freelancer profile. Highlight your skills, experience, and achievements. A well-crafted profile exudes confidence and attracts clients who are looking for competent professionals.

4. Create a Professional Portfolio:

Showcase your work in a professional portfolio. Include examples that demonstrate your capabilities and the quality of your work. A visually appealing and well-organized portfolio reinforces your confidence in your skills.

5. Set Clear Goals:

Establish clear goals for your freelancing career. Knowing what you want to achieve and having a plan to get there can boost your confidence and provide a sense of direction.

6. Research Your Niche:

Deepen your knowledge in your specific niche. Being well-informed about industry trends, best practices, and client needs builds your expertise and, consequently, your confidence when discussing potential projects.

7. Perfect Your Pitch:

Craft a compelling pitch that effectively communicates your value proposition. Clearly articulate how your skills and expertise can address the client's needs. A confident and convincing pitch sets a positive tone for client interactions.

8. Network and Build Relationships:

Engage in networking to build relationships with potential clients and fellow freelancers. Genuine connections can boost your confidence, provide insights, and even lead to referrals or direct opportunities.

9. Practice Effective Communication:

Practice effective communication skills. Be concise, articulate, and responsive in your messages. Clear and confident communication instills trust in clients and sets the foundation for successful collaborations.

10. Offer a Competitive Rate:

Determine a competitive yet fair rate for your services. Knowing your worth and pricing yourself accordingly demonstrates confidence in the value you bring to the table.

11. Handle Rejections Positively:

Rejections are part of the freelancing journey. Approach them with a positive mindset. Learn from the feedback, if available, and use it to refine your approach. Confidence is about resilience and learning from experiences.

12. Showcase Testimonials:

If you have received positive feedback from previous clients or employers, showcase these testimonials. They serve as social proof of your capabilities and can boost the confidence of potential clients in hiring you.

13. Continuous Learning:

Stay committed to continuous learning and improvement. The more you invest in enhancing your skills and staying updated, the more confident you'll feel in tackling diverse projects.

Remember, building confidence is an ongoing process. Celebrate your achievements, learn from challenges, and approach each opportunity with the belief that you have the skills and qualities that make you a successful freelancer.

Mastering A Skill and Knowledge

Mastering a skill and acquiring knowledge are critical components in winning your first client as a freelancer. Here's how you can leverage these aspects effectively:

1. Identify a Niche Skill:

Specialize in a niche skill that aligns with your interests and has demand in the market. Focusing on a specific area allows you to become an expert, making you more appealing to clients seeking specialized services.

2. Continuous Learning:

Stay committed to continuous learning. Industry trends and technologies evolve, so staying updated enhances your skill set. Online courses, workshops, and certifications can contribute to your knowledge base and make you more competitive.

3. Build a Strong Portfolio:

Showcase your mastery of the skill through a well-curated portfolio. Include examples of completed projects or work samples that highlight your proficiency. A strong portfolio serves as tangible evidence of your capabilities.

4. Offer Value in Your Proposal:

Craft proposals that emphasize the value you bring to the client. Clearly articulate how your skill set can address their specific needs or challenges. Use real-world examples from your experience or projects to demonstrate your expertise.

5. Network in Your Industry:

Engage with professionals in your industry through networking events, forums, and social media. Building relationships with peers and potential clients can lead to opportunities, referrals, and insights into the needs of your target audience.

6. Participate in Freelancing Platforms:

Join freelancing platforms that match your skill set. Create a compelling profile that highlights your expertise and experience. Actively bid on relevant projects, and tailor your proposals to showcase how your skill meets the client's requirements.

7. Seek Feedback and Testimonials:

Request feedback from previous employers or clients. Positive testimonials can validate your skills and build trust with potential clients. Display these testimonials prominently in your profile or portfolio.

8. Demonstrate Problem-Solving Abilities:

Showcase not only your technical skills but also your problem-solving abilities. Clients often appreciate freelancers who can offer innovative solutions to their challenges. Use case studies or examples to illustrate your problem-solving approach.

9. Attend Industry Events and Webinars:

Attend industry events, webinars, and conferences to stay informed about the latest developments in your field. Networking at such events can expose you to potential clients and collaborators.

10. Collaborate on Personal Projects:

Undertake personal projects to apply and showcase your skills. These projects can be added to your portfolio and serve as practical demonstrations of your mastery.

11. Participate in Open Source Communities:

If applicable to your skill set, contribute to open-source projects or communities. This not only demonstrates your expertise but also allows you to collaborate with others in your field.

12. Offer Free Resources:

Provide valuable resources related to your skill through blog posts, tutorials, or webinars. This not only establishes you as an authority in your field but also attracts potential clients looking for expertise.

Remember, mastering a skill is an ongoing process, and the dedication to continuous improvement will set you apart in the competitive freelancing landscape. As you showcase your expertise and knowledge, clients will be more inclined to trust your abilities and hire you for their projects.

Amazing Formula of Landing Your First Project

Winning your first client as a freelancer involves a combination of strategies, skills, and a proactive approach. Here's an amazing formula to help you land your first project:

Define Your Niche:

Clearly define your niche and target market. Specializing in a specific area makes it easier for clients to identify your expertise and understand how you can fulfill their needs.

Create a Professional Profile:

Build a professional and compelling freelancer profile. Highlight your skills, experience, and achievements. Use a clear and friendly profile picture to make a positive first impression.

Craft an Irresistible Elevator Pitch:

Develop a concise and compelling elevator pitch that introduces you and your services. Clearly articulate the value you bring to clients and why they should choose you over other freelancers.

Build an Outstanding Portfolio:

Create a portfolio that showcases your best work. Include a variety of projects that demonstrate your skills and versatility. Attach case studies or descriptions to provide context and highlight your problem-solving abilities.

Set a Competitive Rate:

Research market rates for your skills and set a competitive but realistic rate. Consider offering introductory pricing for your first few projects to attract clients and build your portfolio.

Optimize Your Freelance Platform Profile:

If using freelancing platforms, optimize your profile with relevant keywords. Ensure that your profile is complete, including skills, certifications, and a captivating bio. Platforms often use algorithms, so a well-optimized profile increases visibility.

Create a Targeted Proposal:

Craft personalized and targeted proposals for each project you bid on. Address the client's specific needs, showcase your understanding of the project, and explain how your skills make you the ideal candidate.

Highlight Your Unique Selling Points:

Identify and emphasize your unique selling points. Whether it's a rare skill, a specific approach, or a quick turnaround time, make sure clients know what sets you apart from other freelancers.

Network and Connect:

Actively network with other freelancers and potential clients. Engage in discussions on social media platforms, attend virtual events, and join relevant forums. Building connections can lead to referrals and project opportunities.

Offer Limited-Time Promotions:

Create a sense of urgency by offering limited-time promotions for your services. This can incentivize clients to hire you, especially if they feel they are getting a great deal.

Ask for Recommendations:

If you have worked with clients or employers in the past, ask for recommendations or testimonials. Positive reviews add credibility and trust, making it more likely for new clients to hire you.

Be Proactive and Responsive:

Actively monitor job postings and be quick to respond. Proactivity and responsiveness show clients that you are serious and eager to work on their projects.

Continuous Improvement:

Commit to continuous improvement. Stay updated on industry trends, expand your skill set, and seek feedback from clients. The more you evolve, the more valuable you become to potential clients.

Remember, landing your first project may take time, but by consistently applying these strategies, showcasing your skills, and maintaining a proactive attitude, you increase your chances of securing that crucial first client.

Chapter 18: Freelancing As a Business

✍️Business Side of Freelancing: How Much Money Can You Make?

The amount of money you can make as a freelancer varies widely and depends on several factors. These factors include your skillset, experience, the demand for your services, the industry you're working in, your marketing efforts, and the rates you set. Here are some key considerations:

Skillset and Expertise:

Highly specialized and in-demand skills often command higher rates. If you possess unique or sought-after skills, you may be able to charge premium prices for your services.

Experience and Reputation:

As you gain experience and build a positive reputation through client reviews and testimonials, you can justify charging higher rates. Clients are often willing to pay more for seasoned freelancers with a proven track record.

Industry Demand:

The demand for your particular skills in the market influences your earning potential. Some industries have higher demand for freelancers, leading to increased opportunities and potentially higher rates.

Market Rates:

Research market rates for freelancers in your industry and location. Understanding the average rates helps you set competitive prices while considering your experience and expertise.

Efficiency and Productivity:

Your efficiency and productivity play a role in your earnings. If
you can complete projects quickly without compromising
quality, you may be able to take on more work and increase
your overall income.

Diversification of Services:

Offering a variety of services within your skillset can attract a
broader range of clients. Diversifying your services may open
up additional income streams and opportunities.

Negotiation Skills:

Strong negotiation skills are valuable in freelancing. Being able
to negotiate fair rates that reflect the value of your work
contributes to maximizing your income.

Marketing and Branding:

Effective marketing and branding efforts can increase your visibility and attract more clients. A well-branded freelancer with a strong online presence is likely to receive more inquiries and projects.

Networking:

Building a strong professional network can lead to referrals and repeat business. Networking with other freelancers and professionals in your industry can open doors to lucrative projects.

Efficient Financial Management:

Efficient financial management is crucial. Keep track of your expenses, taxes, and other financial considerations to ensure that you're maximizing your earnings.

It's important to note that freelancing income can be variable, with some months being more lucrative than others. Additionally, freelancers need to factor in expenses such as taxes, software/tools, and healthcare. Success in freelancing often involves a combination of skills, business acumen, and adaptability to market changes. As you gain experience and build your freelancing career, your earning potential is likely to increase.

⊞ Importance Of Creating A Brand

Importance Of Creating Your Business Logo (Your Brand)

Creating a brand and having a business logo are crucial components of establishing a professional and memorable identity for your freelancing business. Here's why creating a brand, including a business logo, is important:

Professionalism:

A well-designed logo and a cohesive brand image convey professionalism. Clients are more likely to trust and hire freelancers who present themselves as serious and committed professionals.

Memorability:

A distinctive logo makes your business more memorable. Clients who remember your brand are more likely to return for future projects or refer you to others. A memorable brand sets you apart in a competitive market.

Credibility:

A strong brand builds credibility. When clients see a consistent and professional brand across various platforms, it instills confidence in your abilities. Credibility is essential for attracting high-value projects.

Differentiation:

A unique logo and brand help you stand out from the crowd. In a competitive freelancing landscape, differentiation is key. Your brand should communicate what makes you unique and why clients should choose you over others.

Brand Recognition:

Consistent branding, including a recognizable logo, contributes to brand recognition. Over time, clients will associate your logo with your skills and the quality of your work, leading to increased trust and loyalty.

Marketing Tool:

Your logo becomes a powerful marketing tool. It can be used on your website, business cards, social media profiles, and other promotional materials. A visually appealing logo attracts attention and reinforces your brand identity.

Professional Online Presence:

A well-designed logo is an integral part of your online presence. It enhances the visual appeal of your website and social media profiles, making your brand more appealing to potential clients who visit your online platforms.

Consistency Across Platforms:

A cohesive brand, including a consistent logo, ensures that your presence is uniform across various platforms. This consistency reinforces your brand and makes it easier for clients to recognize and remember you.

Brand Trust:

A thoughtfully designed logo contributes to building trust with your audience. Trust is a crucial factor in freelancing, as clients want to work with professionals they can rely on to deliver quality work.

Brand Storytelling:

Your brand, including your logo, can tell a story about your values, style, and the type of work you do. Clients are drawn to brands that resonate with them on a personal or professional level.

Repeat Business and Referrals:

A strong brand encourages repeat business and referrals. Satisfied clients are more likely to remember and recommend a freelancer with a memorable and trustworthy brand.

In short, creating a brand, along with a distinctive business logo, is an investment in the long-term success of your freelancing business. It establishes credibility, builds trust, and sets the foundation for a positive and memorable client experience.

Importance Of Creating Your Website

Creating a website is a fundamental aspect of building a strong brand presence for your freelancing business. Here's why having a website is crucial for freelancers:

Professionalism:

A website adds a level of professionalism to your freelancing business. It serves as a central hub where clients can learn about your services, view your portfolio, and contact you. A professionally designed website enhances your credibility.

Brand Visibility:

Your website acts as a 24/7 online presence, increasing your brand visibility. Clients can find you at any time, regardless of their time zone, which expands your reach and potential client base.

Brand Control:

With your website, you have control over your brand's presentation. You can showcase your work, highlight your skills, and convey your brand message exactly as you want it to be perceived.

Portfolio Showcase:

A website provides an ideal platform to showcase your portfolio. Displaying your best work with detailed descriptions allows potential clients to assess your skills and expertise, making it easier for them to decide to hire you.

Contact Hub:

Having a designated contact page on your website streamlines communication. Clients can easily find your contact information, making it convenient for them to reach out for inquiries, project discussions, or collaborations.

Brand Consistency:

Your website ensures consistency in your brand presentation. It allows you to use consistent branding elements, such as colors, fonts, and logo placement, across all pages, reinforcing your brand identity.

Information Hub:

Your website serves as an information hub where clients can learn about your background, experience, and the services you offer. Including an "About Me" section adds a personal touch, helping clients connect with you on a more human level.

SEO Benefits:

A well-optimized website can improve your visibility on search engines. By incorporating relevant keywords and creating quality content, you increase the likelihood of being found by clients searching for freelancers with your skill set.

Showcasing Testimonials:

Testimonials from satisfied clients contribute to your credibility. Your website is an excellent platform to display client testimonials, adding social proof to your skills and reliability.

Blog and Content Sharing:

Having a blog on your website allows you to share industry insights, tips, and relevant content. Regularly updating your blog not only positions you as an authority in your field but also improves your website's search engine ranking.

Online Portfolio Link:

A website provides you with a professional domain to link to in your profiles on freelancing platforms and social media. This directs potential clients to a comprehensive showcase of your work and services.

Control Over Brand Narrative:

Your website gives you control over the narrative of your brand. You can share your story, values, and mission, helping clients understand what sets you apart and why they should choose your services.

In conclusion, a website is a powerful tool for freelancers to establish and reinforce their brand. It enhances professionalism, provides a centralized platform for client interaction, and allows for greater control over brand messaging and presentation.

How To Create a Free Website

Creating a free website is a viable option for freelancers looking to establish an online presence without incurring additional costs. Here's a step-by-step guide on how to create a free website:

Choose a Website Builder:

Select a user-friendly website builder that offers free plans. Popular options include Wix, Weebly, WordPress.com, and Google Sites. These platforms provide templates and tools to simplify the website creation process.

Sign Up for an Account:

Register for an account on the chosen website builder platform. Provide the required information, such as your email address and password, to create your account.

Select a Template:

Choose a template that aligns with your freelancing business and personal style. Most website builders offer a variety of templates that you can customize to suit your preferences.

Customize Your Website:

Customize the template by adding your brand colors, logo, and relevant images. Modify the layout and structure to create a website that reflects your freelancing services. Ensure that the design is visually appealing and easy to navigate.

Add Content:

Populate your website with essential content. Create pages that cover key information such as:

Home: Introduction to your freelancing services.

About Me: Personal and professional background.

Services: Detailed information about the services you offer.

Portfolio: Showcase your work with images, descriptions, and case studies.

Contact: Provide contact details or a contact form for inquiries.

Optimize for SEO: Implement basic search engine optimization (SEO) practices.

Use relevant keywords in your content, headings, and meta descriptions. This helps improve the visibility of your website on search engines.

Integrate Social Media:

Connect your social media accounts to your website. Add links to your profiles so visitors can easily follow you on platforms like LinkedIn, Twitter, or Instagram.

Preview and Test:

Before publishing, preview your website to ensure everything looks and functions as intended. Test navigation, forms, and links to guarantee a seamless user experience.

Publish Your Website:

Once you're satisfied with the design and content, publish your website. The URL provided by the website builder will be in the format of yourusername.buildername.com. While this is free, it may be worth considering a custom domain for a more professional appearance.

Promote Your Website:

Share your website on social media, freelancing platforms, and in your email signature. Actively promote it to increase visibility and attract potential clients.

Remember that while creating a free website is a cost-effective way to establish your online presence, upgrading to a paid plan or purchasing a custom domain may offer additional features, branding options, and a more professional image for your freelancing business.

Getting Hosting and A Domain Name for Very Low Cost

Getting hosting and a domain name for a low cost is possible through various budget-friendly hosting providers and domain registration services. Here's a step-by-step guide on how to obtain hosting and a domain name at an affordable price:

1. Research Budget-Friendly Hosting Providers:

Look for hosting providers that offer low-cost plans without compromising on essential features. Some popular budget-friendly hosting providers include GoDaddy, Bluehost, HostGator, SiteGround, and A2 Hosting.

2. Compare Hosting Plans:

Compare the hosting plans offered by different providers. Look for plans that meet your specific needs, such as sufficient storage, bandwidth, and support for your chosen website platform (e.g., WordPress).

3. Utilize Promotions and Discounts:

Many hosting providers offer promotions, discounts, or introductory pricing for new customers. Take advantage of these offers to reduce your initial costs. Be aware of the renewal prices after the initial term.

4. Opt for Shared Hosting:

Shared hosting is generally more affordable than other hosting options like dedicated or VPS hosting. Shared hosting is suitable for most freelancers and small businesses with moderate website traffic.

5. Consider Long-Term Plans:

Some hosting providers offer additional discounts if you choose a longer billing cycle (e.g., 12 months, 24 months, or 36 months). While this requires a larger upfront payment, it can save you money in the long run.

6. Register a Domain Name:

Many hosting providers offer a free domain name registration with their hosting plans for the first year. Choose a memorable and relevant domain name for your freelancing business.

7. Check for Additional Costs:

Be aware of any additional costs associated with domain registration or hosting, such as domain privacy protection or SSL certificates. Some providers may include these features for free, while others charge extra.

8. Use Domain Registration Discounts:

If you prefer to register your domain separately, look for domain registration services that offer discounts or promotions. Popular domain registrars include Namecheap, GoDaddy, and Google Domains.

9. Consider Free Website Builders:

Some hosting providers offer free website builders as part of their hosting packages. These tools can simplify the website creation process, making it more cost-effective for those on a tight budget.

10. Explore Alternative Extensions:

If your preferred domain name with a popular extension (.com, .net, .org) is already taken, consider using alternative extensions like .co, .io, or .tech. These extensions may be more affordable and offer creative options.

11. Seek Community Recommendations:

Ask for recommendations from online communities or forums for budget-friendly hosting providers. Personal experiences from other freelancers can help you make an informed decision.

By carefully researching hosting providers, taking advantage of discounts, and considering your long-term needs, you can secure hosting and a domain name for your freelancing business at a reasonable cost.

Importance of Creating a PDF Profile

Creating a PDF profile is an effective way for freelancers to showcase their skills, experience, and portfolio in a professional and easily shareable format. Here are some key reasons why creating a PDF profile is important for building your brand as a freelancer:

Professional Presentation:

A PDF profile allows you to present your information in a polished and professional manner. It gives you control over the layout, design, and overall aesthetics, ensuring a cohesive and visually appealing representation of your brand.

Customization:

Unlike some online platforms that have limitations on customization, a PDF profile gives you the flexibility to tailor the content and design according to your brand identity. You can highlight specific projects, skills, and achievements that align with your target clients.

Versatility:

A PDF profile is versatile and can be easily shared through various channels, including email attachments, messaging apps, and social media. This makes it convenient for you to distribute your profile to potential clients, collaborators, or employers.

Offline Accessibility:

PDF profiles can be downloaded and accessed offline, making them accessible to individuals who may not have constant internet connectivity. This is especially valuable if you're networking at events, conferences, or meetings where internet access may be limited.

Brand Consistency:

Maintaining consistency in your brand presentation is essential. A PDF profile allows you to incorporate consistent branding elements, such as colors, fonts, and logos, reinforcing your professional identity.

Comprehensive Information:

You can include comprehensive information in your PDF profile, covering your professional background, skills, services, and a detailed portfolio. This depth of information helps potential clients gain a thorough understanding of your capabilities.

Showcasing Work Samples:

Including visuals of your work samples within the PDF allows you to showcase the quality and diversity of your projects. Visual elements make a strong impact and can help potential clients assess the suitability of your skills for their needs.

Ease of Printing:

Some clients may prefer to have a physical copy of your profile. A PDF is easily printable, enabling you to provide a hard copy when needed, especially in situations where a tangible document is preferred.

Document Security:

PDFs offer options for securing your document with password protection or restrictions on editing and copying. This can be useful when sharing sensitive information or proprietary work.

Call-to-Action:

Include a call-to-action within your PDF, guiding potential clients on the next steps, such as contacting you for a consultation or viewing your full online portfolio. This helps in directing interested parties toward meaningful engagement.

Time Efficiency:

Clients often appreciate concise and well-organized information. A PDF profile allows you to present your key details efficiently, saving clients time in reviewing your qualifications and work.

In summary, creating a PDF profile is a strategic component of your freelancing brand. It enhances your professionalism, provides customization options, and offers a versatile and offline-accessible tool for showcasing your skills and portfolio to potential clients.

Importance Of Creating Facebook Page

Creating a Facebook page for your freelancing business is a valuable strategy for building and promoting your brand. Here are several reasons highlighting the importance of having a Facebook page:

Online Visibility:

A Facebook page increases your online visibility by providing a dedicated space for your freelancing business on a widely used social media platform. This visibility is crucial for attracting potential clients and networking within your industry.

Professionalism:

Having a Facebook page adds a professional touch to your freelancing brand. It serves as a centralized, branded space where clients and collaborators can learn more about your services, view your work, and engage with your content.

Brand Consistency:

Your Facebook page allows you to maintain consistency in your brand presentation. You can incorporate your logo, brand colors, and a cohesive design that aligns with your overall branding strategy.

Engagement and Interaction:

The interactive nature of Facebook enables you to engage with your audience directly. Clients and followers can leave comments, ask questions, and share their thoughts, fostering a sense of community around your brand.

Showcasing Work:

Use your Facebook page to showcase your portfolio, highlighting completed projects, testimonials, and success stories. Visual content can have a strong impact and help potential clients understand the quality of your work.

Announcements and Updates:

Keep your audience informed about your latest projects, achievements, and announcements. Whether you're launching a new service, celebrating milestones, or sharing industry insights, your Facebook page is an ideal platform for these updates.

Networking Opportunities:

Facebook is a powerful networking tool. Join relevant groups, participate in discussions, and connect with other freelancers, clients, or businesses in your niche. Networking can lead to collaboration opportunities and referrals.

Advertising and Promotions:

Utilize Facebook's advertising features to promote your freelancing services to a targeted audience. Boosting posts or creating targeted ads can increase your visibility and reach potential clients who may be interested in your offerings.

Client Testimonials:

Encourage satisfied clients to leave testimonials on your Facebook page. Positive reviews build trust and credibility, influencing potential clients who may be considering your services.

Accessibility:

Facebook is easily accessible from various devices, including smartphones and tablets. This accessibility ensures that clients can connect with you and view your content regardless of their location or device preference.

Insights and Analytics:

Facebook provides insights and analytics tools that allow you to track the performance of your page. Monitor metrics such as engagement, reach, and page views to assess the effectiveness of your content and adjust your strategy accordingly.

SEO Benefits:

Facebook pages are indexed by search engines, contributing to your online presence. When someone searches for your freelancing services, having an active Facebook page can increase the likelihood of appearing in search results.

In conclusion, creating a Facebook page for your freelancing business is a multifaceted strategy that enhances your online presence, professionalism, and engagement with your audience. It serves as a dynamic platform to promote your brand, showcase your work, and connect with potential clients and collaborators.

✦ Use Of social media To Promote Your Freelance Profile

The importance of LinkedIn

LinkedIn is a powerful tool for freelancers to promote their profiles and build a professional online presence. Here are several reasons highlighting the importance of LinkedIn for freelancers:

Professional Networking:

LinkedIn is designed for professional networking. It allows freelancers to connect with other professionals, potential clients, and collaborators within their industry. Building a robust network opens up opportunities for collaboration and referrals.

Online Resume:

LinkedIn serves as an online resume, providing a comprehensive overview of your skills, experience, and achievements. Freelancers can showcase their expertise, education, and professional background, making it easy for potential clients to assess their qualifications.

Showcasing Portfolio:

Freelancers can use the "Featured" section on LinkedIn to showcase their work, including articles, projects, and multimedia content. This feature allows clients to see real examples of your capabilities and the quality of your work.

Endorsements and Recommendations:

LinkedIn allows colleagues and clients to endorse your skills and provide recommendations. Positive endorsements and recommendations enhance your credibility and build trust with potential clients who are considering your services.

Industry Insights and Thought Leadership:

Share industry insights, articles, and thought leadership on your LinkedIn profile. Positioning yourself as an authority in your field can attract clients who are looking for knowledgeable and experienced freelancers.

Job Opportunities:

LinkedIn is a platform where businesses and recruiters actively seek freelancers for various projects. Having a well-optimized profile increases your visibility, making it more likely for potential clients to discover your services and reach out with job opportunities.

Engagement and Interaction:

Engage with your network by participating in discussions, sharing relevant content, and commenting on posts. Active engagement helps you stay top-of-mind with your connections and fosters a sense of community around your freelancing brand.

Search Engine Visibility:

LinkedIn profiles often rank high in search engine results. When potential clients search for freelancers with specific skills, having an optimized LinkedIn profile increases the chances of being discovered through search engines.

Freelance Services Marketplace:

LinkedIn has a dedicated Freelance Services Marketplace that allows freelancers to showcase their services, connect with clients, and find project opportunities. This feature provides an additional avenue for freelancers to promote their offerings.

Event Participation:

LinkedIn allows you to join and participate in industry-related events and groups. Engaging in discussions and events relevant to your freelancing niche can expand your network and connect you with potential clients and collaborators.

Brand Consistency:

Ensure that your LinkedIn profile aligns with your freelancing brand. Consistent branding, including profile pictures, headlines, and summaries, reinforces your professional identity across different platforms.

Analytics and Insights:

LinkedIn provides analytics and insights about profile views, engagement, and the performance of your posts. Monitoring these metrics helps you understand the effectiveness of your LinkedIn strategy and make adjustments to optimize your profile.

LinkedIn is a valuable platform for freelancers to promote their profiles, connect with industry professionals, and showcase their expertise. It serves as a dynamic tool for building a professional online presence and opening doors to new opportunities within the freelancing landscape.

Paid vs Free promotion

Promoting your freelance profile on social media can be done through both paid and free methods. Each approach has its own advantages and considerations. Here's a comparison of paid and free promotion on social media for freelancers:

Paid Promotion

Targeted Reach:

Paid promotion allows you to target specific demographics, interests, and locations. This targeted approach ensures that your content reaches the most relevant audience for your freelancing services.

Faster Results:

Paid advertising can generate quicker results in terms of visibility and engagement. Boosting posts or running ads can rapidly increase the reach of your content, potentially attracting more clients in a shorter time frame.

Ad Formats:

Paid promotion offers various ad formats, including sponsored posts, display ads, and video ads. These formats can be optimized for specific business goals, such as brand awareness, lead generation, or website traffic.

Analytics and Insights:

Paid promotions come with detailed analytics and insights. You can track metrics such as impressions, clicks, and conversions, allowing you to measure the effectiveness of your advertising campaign and make data-driven decisions.

Ad Retargeting:

Retargeting is a powerful feature in paid advertising. It allows you to re-engage users who have previously interacted with your content or visited your website. This can enhance your chances of converting potential clients.

Flexible Budgeting:

Paid promotion allows you to set a flexible budget based on your advertising goals. Whether you have a small budget or a larger one, you can adjust your spending to align with your business objectives.

Free Promotion

Cost-Effective:

Free promotion, such as organic social media posts, is cost-effective. You don't need to allocate a budget for boosting posts or running ads. This makes it an ideal option for freelancers with limited financial resources.

Authentic Engagement:

Organic promotion often leads to more authentic engagement. Users are more likely to interact with content that doesn't feel overly promotional. Building genuine connections can contribute to long-term relationships with clients.

Community Building:

Free promotion allows you to focus on building a community around your freelancing brand. Engaging with your audience through comments, discussions, and shared content can foster a sense of community and loyalty.

Content Quality:

With free promotion, the emphasis is on creating high-quality, valuable content. Consistently sharing valuable content can establish you as an authority in your field and attract clients who appreciate your expertise.

SEO Benefits:

Organic social media activity contributes to your online presence and can have indirect benefits for search engine optimization (SEO). Regularly updating your profiles and sharing relevant content can improve your overall online visibility.

Long-Term Results:

While free promotion may take longer to generate results, the relationships and reputation you build can lead to sustained success. Over time, a strong organic presence can contribute to a steady stream of clients.

Conclusion:

The choice between paid and free promotion depends on your specific goals, budget, and timeline. A combination of both approaches can be effective, allowing you to leverage the benefits of targeted advertising while also building a genuine, engaged audience through organic methods.

Chapter 19: Outsourcing

🌐 Outsourcing: Introduction

Outsourcing in freelancing refers to the practice of hiring external individuals or agencies to handle specific tasks or aspects of a project that a freelancer cannot or chooses not to perform themselves. It involves delegating certain responsibilities to other freelancers or service providers, often with the goal of enhancing efficiency, accessing specialized skills, or managing a workload that exceeds the individual freelancer's capacity.

Key Points About Outsourcing in Freelancing

Task Delegation:

Freelancers may outsource tasks that are outside their expertise or time constraints. This could include activities such as graphic design, content writing, programming, or administrative tasks.

Specialized Skills:

Outsourcing allows freelancers to tap into the expertise of individuals or agencies with specialized skills. For example, a freelance web developer might outsource graphic design tasks to a specialist in that field.

Global Talent Pool:

Freelancers can leverage a global talent pool by outsourcing tasks to individuals or teams located in different geographic regions. This provides access to diverse skills and perspectives.

Time Management:

Outsourcing helps freelancers manage their time more effectively. By delegating certain tasks, freelancers can focus on core activities that align with their skills and contribute to the overall success of the project.

Project Scaling:

When freelancers have a high volume of work or large-scale projects, outsourcing allows them to scale their operations without taking on the full burden of the workload. This is particularly beneficial for handling peaks in demand.

Collaboration:

Outsourcing fosters collaboration within the freelance community. Freelancers can build relationships with other professionals and create a network of trusted collaborators for future projects.

Cost Efficiency:

Outsourcing can be a cost-effective solution, especially when hiring freelancers from regions with lower labor costs. This can result in savings compared to hiring local resources for certain tasks.

Flexibility:

Freelancers can adapt their team composition based on the requirements of each project. Outsourcing provides flexibility to work with different individuals or agencies depending on the specific skills needed.

Risk Mitigation:

Freelancers can mitigate risks associated with unfamiliar tasks by outsourcing to experts. This helps ensure the quality and timely completion of tasks that may fall outside the freelancer's core competency.

It's important for freelancers to carefully manage and communicate with the individuals or agencies they outsource to, ensuring that expectations, timelines, and quality standards are clearly defined. Successful outsourcing can contribute to the overall success and growth of a freelancer's business.

☑ Right Time for Outsourcing

Freelancers should consider outsourcing when they encounter specific situations or challenges that could be effectively addressed by delegating tasks to external individuals or agencies. Here are some scenarios that indicate it may be time to think about outsourcing:

Overwhelming Workload:

When the volume of work becomes too high for a freelancer to handle on their own, outsourcing can be a solution. This is especially relevant during periods of increased demand or when facing multiple large projects simultaneously.

Lack of Expertise:

If a freelancer encounters tasks that require specialized skills or knowledge that they don't possess, outsourcing to experts in those areas can ensure the quality and efficiency of the work.

Time Constraints:

When time constraints prevent a freelancer from meeting project deadlines or dedicating sufficient time to core activities, outsourcing less critical tasks can help manage time more effectively.

Scaling Business Operations:

As freelancers experience growth in their business, they may need to scale their operations. Outsourcing allows freelancers to expand their capabilities without overburdening themselves.

Focus on Core Competencies:

If a freelancer wants to concentrate on tasks that align with their core competencies and bring the most value to their clients, outsourcing peripheral tasks can help maintain focus on strategic and high-impact activities.

Globalization and Diverse Skill Sets:

Outsourcing becomes beneficial when freelancers want to tap into a global talent pool with diverse skill sets. This allows them to access a broader range of expertise and perspectives.

Project Complexity:

Complex projects that involve various components, such as design, development, and content creation, may benefit from outsourcing specific elements to specialists who can contribute to the project's overall success.

Cost-Efficiency:

If a freelancer is looking to reduce costs without compromising on quality, outsourcing tasks to freelancers or agencies in regions with lower labor costs can be a cost-effective strategy.

Client Expectations:

If client expectations exceed the freelancer's current capabilities, outsourcing certain tasks can help meet or exceed those expectations, enhancing client satisfaction.

Networking and Collaboration:

Freelancers who want to build a network of collaborators and establish relationships with other professionals in their industry can use outsourcing as a means of fostering collaboration.

Seasonal or Cyclical Work:

During periods of seasonal or cyclical demand, freelancers may face fluctuations in workload. Outsourcing allows them to handle peak times more efficiently without the need for permanent hires.

It's important for freelancers to assess their specific needs, project requirements, and business goals before deciding to outsource. Effective communication, clear expectations, and collaboration with trusted individuals or agencies are crucial for successful outsourcing experiences.

💻 Using Software to Keep The Check On Progress

Using software to monitor and track the progress of outsourced tasks is a smart and efficient approach for freelancers. Here are some ways in which software can be utilized to keep a check on the progress of outsourced work:

Project Management Tools:

Implement project management tools such as Trello, Asana, or Jira to create tasks, set deadlines, and track the progress of each task. These tools provide a centralized platform where both freelancers and outsourced team members can collaborate, update task statuses, and share files.

Communication Platforms:

Utilize communication tools like Slack or Microsoft Teams to maintain real-time communication with outsourced team members. These platforms facilitate quick updates, file sharing, and discussions, ensuring that everyone involved in the project stays informed about progress.

Time Tracking Software:

Implement time tracking software such as Toggl or Harvest to monitor the amount of time spent on specific tasks. This helps in understanding the efficiency of outsourced work and provides insights into how time is allocated across different aspects of the project.

Cloud-Based Document Collaboration:

Use cloud-based document collaboration tools like Google Workspace or Microsoft 365 to create, share, and edit documents in real-time. This ensures that all team members, including outsourced contributors, have access to the most up-to-date information.

Version Control Systems:

For projects involving software development or design, version control systems like Git can be employed. These systems help track changes made to code or design files, allowing for collaboration without the risk of conflicting modifications.

Task Tracking Software:

Task tracking tools like ClickUp or Monday.com enable freelancers to create and assign tasks, set priorities, and monitor the status of each task. This provides a visual representation of the project's progress.

Screen Sharing and Recording:

Platforms that allow for screen sharing and recording, such as Loom or Zoom, can be valuable. Freelancers can use these tools to provide detailed instructions, share feedback, or visually demonstrate specific aspects of the project.

Collaborative Whiteboarding:

Collaborative whiteboarding tools like Miro or InVision Freehand can enhance visual communication. They allow team members, including those outsourced, to collaborate on visual elements, such as design mockups or process flows.

Automated Reporting:

Implement tools that offer automated reporting features, summarizing key metrics and progress updates. This can save time and provide a quick overview of how different aspects of the project are progressing.

Feedback and Annotation Tools:

Use feedback and annotation tools like Markup Hero or Frame.io to provide specific feedback on documents, designs, or other project elements. This streamlines the feedback process and ensures clarity in communication.

Kanban Boards:

Kanban board tools like KanbanFlow or Trello provide a visual representation of tasks, allowing freelancers to quickly see the status of each task and identify any bottlenecks in the workflow.

By integrating these software tools into the outsourcing process, freelancers can effectively monitor progress, foster collaboration, and ensure that outsourced tasks align with project timelines and expectations.

Outsourcing: Payment milestones

Implementing payment milestones is a crucial aspect of outsourcing to ensure that both freelancers and outsourced team members are compensated fairly for completed work. Payment milestones help break down the project into manageable parts, aligning payments with the achievement of specific goals.

Here's how to establish and manage payment milestones when outsourcing:

Define Project Scope:

Clearly define the scope of the project before establishing payment milestones. Identify the major tasks, deliverables, and goals that need to be achieved for the successful completion of the project.

Break Down Tasks:

Break down the project into smaller, manageable tasks. Each task should represent a significant step toward the overall completion of the project. This division makes it easier to set realistic milestones and track progress.

Assign Milestone Values:

Assign a monetary value to each milestone based on the effort, complexity, and importance of the associated task. The values should reflect fair compensation for the completion of that specific milestone.

Set Clear Deadlines:

Establish clear deadlines for each milestone to ensure a structured timeline for project completion. This helps in managing expectations and provides a sense of accountability for both freelancers and outsourced team members.

Communicate Expectations:

Clearly communicate the expectations associated with each milestone, including the specific deliverables, quality standards, and any other relevant details. This ensures that everyone involved is on the same page regarding project requirements.

Use a Contract or Agreement:

Formalize the arrangement by using a contract or agreement that outlines the payment milestones, deadlines, and terms of collaboration. This legal document serves as a reference point and provides protection for both parties.

Verify Milestone Completion:

Before making payments, verify that the milestones have been completed according to the agreed-upon standards. This may involve reviewing deliverables, conducting tests, or ensuring that specific criteria have been met.

Flexible Milestone Adjustments:

Be open to adjusting milestones if needed during the course of the project. Changes in project scope, unexpected challenges, or additional requirements may necessitate modifications to the initially defined milestones.

Partial Payments:

Break down payments for each milestone into partial payments to further incentivize progress. For example, rather than paying the full amount upon completion, consider dividing payments into installments based on different stages of task completion.

Automated Payment Systems:

Use automated payment systems or freelancing platforms that facilitate milestone-based payments. These platforms often have built-in features for creating, tracking, and releasing payments for specific project milestones.

Regular Communication:

Maintain regular communication with the outsourced team to address any challenges, provide feedback, and ensure that everyone is aligned with the project's progress. This helps in preventing misunderstandings and resolving issues promptly.

Completion Sign-Off:

Obtain formal sign-off or approval from the outsourced team upon the successful completion of each milestone. This provides a clear record of acknowledgment and acceptance of the delivered work.

Implementing payment milestones fosters a transparent and collaborative outsourcing process, encouraging accountability and ensuring that compensation is tied to tangible progress in the project.

📇 Importance Of Networking with Your Outsourced Team

Networking with your outsourced team is crucial for fostering collaboration, building relationships, and ensuring the success of your outsourcing endeavors. Here are key reasons highlighting the importance of networking with your outsourced team:

Effective Communication:

Networking enables effective communication between you and your outsourced team members. Establishing open lines of communication helps in conveying expectations, providing feedback, and addressing any concerns promptly.

Building Trust and Rapport:

Networking builds trust and rapport among team members. Developing personal connections through regular communication creates a positive working environment, leading to increased trust and cooperation.

Understanding Cultural Differences:

Outsourcing often involves working with individuals from different cultural backgrounds. Networking provides an opportunity to understand and appreciate cultural differences, promoting a more inclusive and collaborative working environment.

Enhanced Collaboration:

Networking fosters a collaborative spirit within the team. Team members who feel connected are more likely to share ideas, collaborate on solutions, and contribute to the overall success of the project.

Problem-Solving and Conflict Resolution:

In the course of a project, challenges may arise. A strong network allows for effective problem-solving and conflict resolution. Team members who feel connected are more likely to work together to address issues constructively.

Sharing Expertise and Insights:

Networking provides a platform for sharing expertise and insights among team members. This collaborative knowledge-sharing contributes to the overall improvement of skills and the quality of work.

Facilitating Team Building:

Networking activities, such as virtual meetings, team-building exercises, or informal chats, contribute to a sense of team unity. Team building is essential for fostering a positive and productive working relationship.

Quick Adaptation to Changes:

In dynamic projects, changes may occur, and the ability to adapt swiftly is crucial. A well-connected team is more adaptable, as members can quickly communicate and adjust to changes in project requirements.

Promoting a Positive Work Environment:

Networking helps create a positive work environment, even in a virtual setting. A positive atmosphere encourages team members to be more engaged, motivated, and committed to the success of the project.

Opportunities for Future Collaboration:

Building a network with your outsourced team opens doors for future collaboration. If you work well together on one project, there may be opportunities for continued collaboration on subsequent projects.

Recognizing Individual Contributions:

Networking allows you to recognize and appreciate the individual contributions of each team member. Acknowledging their efforts boosts morale and motivates team members to continue delivering high-quality work.

Mitigating Misunderstandings:

Regular communication through networking helps prevent misunderstandings. Miscommunications can be addressed promptly, ensuring that everyone is on the same page and aligned with project goals.

In conclusion, networking is a key component of successful outsourcing, contributing to effective communication, collaboration, and the overall success of the project. Building strong connections with your outsourced team enhances the working relationship and creates a positive and productive collaborative environment.

Chapter 20: Hiring An In-House Team Member

☐ The Right Time to Hire A Resource

Deciding when to hire an in-house team member depends on various factors, and the timing is critical for the success of your business. Here are some indicators that suggest the right time to hire an in-house team member:

Increased Workload:

When the workload consistently exceeds the capacity of your current team or freelance collaborators, it may be time to hire an in-house team member. This is particularly true if the workload is expected to continue growing.

Consistent Revenue and Stability:

If your business has achieved consistent revenue and financial stability, it may be an opportune time to hire in-house. This financial stability ensures that you can afford to bring on a new team member without jeopardizing the financial health of your business.

Recurring Tasks and Responsibilities:

If there are recurring tasks or responsibilities that require ongoing attention and specialization, hiring an in-house team member can provide dedicated support and expertise for these specific areas.

Strategic Growth Plans:

If your business has strategic growth plans and you foresee the need for additional skills or manpower to achieve those goals, hiring an in-house team member becomes a strategic move to support expansion.

Customer Demand:

An increase in customer demand for your products or services may necessitate additional resources. Hiring in-house allows you to better manage customer expectations and maintain or improve service quality.

Time-Consuming Administrative Tasks:

If you find yourself spending a significant amount of time on administrative tasks that could be delegated, hiring an in-house team member to handle these responsibilities can free up your time for more strategic and revenue-generating activities.

Skill Gap in Current Team:

If there's a noticeable skill gap in your current team, and this gap is impeding the efficiency or quality of your work, hiring an in-house team member with the required skills can fill this void.

Consistent Freelance Dependency:

If your business heavily relies on freelancers for essential tasks and you find this arrangement becoming challenging to manage or costly in the long term, hiring an in-house team member could provide more stability and control.

Specialized Expertise Needed:

When your business requires specialized expertise that is not readily available through freelancers or current team members, hiring in-house allows you to bring in the specific skills needed for your unique challenges.

Increased Complexity of Projects:

If the projects your business undertakes are becoming more complex and demanding, an in-house team member can contribute to better project management, coordination, and the overall success of intricate tasks.

Market Expansion:

If your business is expanding into new markets or territories, hiring an in-house team member with local expertise can be beneficial for navigating and succeeding in these new environments.

Quality Control and Brand Consistency:

If maintaining quality control and brand consistency is becoming challenging with a decentralized or outsourced team, bringing tasks in-house can provide better control over these aspects.

Ultimately, the decision to hire an in-house team member should align with your business goals, financial capabilities, and the need for specialized skills or additional capacity to meet demand. Careful consideration of these factors will help you determine the right time to expand your team in-house.

☛ The Appropriate Talent Hunt

Hiring an in-house team member involves a strategic talent hunt to ensure you find the right fit for your business needs. Here are key considerations for an appropriate talent hunt when hiring an in-house team member:

Define Clear Roles and Responsibilities:

Clearly define the roles and responsibilities of the in-house team member before starting the talent hunt. This includes outlining specific tasks, required skills, and expectations for the position.

Create a Detailed Job Description:

Develop a detailed and comprehensive job description that highlights the key responsibilities, qualifications, and desired skills for the role. This document will serve as a guide for potential candidates and help set clear expectations.

Identify Necessary Skills and Qualifications:

Clearly identify the skills and qualifications required for the position. This includes technical skills, soft skills, and any industry-specific knowledge that is essential for success in the role.

Consider Cultural Fit:

Assess the cultural fit of potential candidates with your company's values, work culture, and mission. A candidate who aligns with your company culture is more likely to integrate seamlessly into the team.

Utilize Multiple Recruitment Channels:

Cast a wide net by using multiple recruitment channels. This may include job boards, professional networking platforms, social media, and industry-specific forums. Diversifying your approach increases the chances of finding qualified candidates.

Leverage Employee Referrals:

Encourage and leverage employee referrals. Current employees often have a good understanding of your company culture and can refer candidates who may be a good fit for the team.

Engage in Networking Events:

Attend industry-related events, conferences, and networking functions to connect with potential candidates. Networking events provide an opportunity to meet professionals in person and gauge their suitability for the role.

Use Recruitment Agencies:

Consider partnering with recruitment agencies that specialize in your industry. These agencies often have access to a pool of qualified candidates and can streamline the hiring process.

Conduct Thorough Interviews:

Conduct thorough interviews to assess a candidate's skills, experience, and cultural fit. Use a combination of behavioral and situational questions to gain insights into how candidates approach challenges and tasks.

Assess Problem-Solving Skills:

Incorporate tasks or scenarios that assess a candidate's problem-solving skills. This could include case studies, practical assignments, or discussions around how they would handle specific challenges related to the role.

Evaluate Communication Skills:

Communication skills are crucial for effective collaboration. Assess a candidate's communication skills through interviews, written communication samples, and, if relevant, presentations.

Check References:

Verify a candidate's work history and performance by checking references. Contact previous employers or colleagues to gain insights into the candidate's work ethic, collaboration skills, and overall performance.

Consider Remote Work Skills (if applicable):

If the role involves remote work, assess a candidate's ability to work independently, manage time effectively, and communicate virtually. Remote work skills are increasingly important in today's flexible work environment.

Competitive Compensation Package:

Offer a competitive compensation package that aligns with industry standards. This includes salary, benefits, and any additional perks that make your offer attractive to potential candidates.

Transparent and Efficient Hiring Process:

Maintain transparency throughout the hiring process, providing clear information about timelines, expectations, and the stages of the recruitment process. An efficient and transparent process reflects positively on your company.

By carefully planning and executing a talent hunt based on these considerations, you increase the likelihood of finding a qualified and well-suited in-house team member for your business.

☐ **Websites To Hire Talent for Your Work**

When looking to hire in-house team members, there are several websites and platforms that cater specifically to talent recruitment. Here are some popular websites where you can find and hire talent for your work:

LinkedIn

LinkedIn is a professional networking platform where you can find a wide range of professionals. You can use LinkedIn to post job openings, search for candidates, and connect with potential hires based on their professional profiles.

Indeed

Indeed is a widely used job search engine that allows employers to post job listings. It has a broad reach and attracts candidates from various industries and skill levels.

Glassdoor

Glassdoor not only allows you to post job listings but also provides insights into company reviews and salaries. This can be helpful for attracting candidates who are not only looking for a job but also a positive work environment.

Monster

Monster is a global employment website that connects employers with potential candidates. It provides a platform for posting jobs, searching resumes, and finding qualified individuals.

CareerBuilder

CareerBuilder is an online job board that covers a wide range of industries. It allows employers to post job listings and search for candidates based on various criteria.

ZipRecruiter

ZipRecruiter is a platform that simplifies the hiring process by allowing employers to post jobs to multiple job boards with a single submission. It also offers features like candidate screening.

AngelList

AngelList is a platform focused on connecting startups with talent. If your business is in the startup space, AngelList can be a valuable resource for finding skilled professionals.

Dice

Dice is a specialized platform for tech and IT professionals. If you're specifically looking for candidates in the technology industry, Dice can be a targeted option.

Upwork

While Upwork is traditionally known as a freelancing platform, it also offers a feature called Upwork Pro that connects businesses with highly skilled freelancers or potential in-house team members.

SimplyHired

SimplyHired is a job search engine that aggregates job listings from various sources. It provides a platform for employers to post jobs and reach a broad audience of job seekers.

Freelancer Platforms like Freelancer.com, Fiverr

Platforms like Freelancer.com and Fiverr, though primarily focused on freelancing, also have sections for hiring full-time or part-time employees. You can find a diverse range of talents on these platforms.

Company Careers Page

Don't forget to utilize your own company's careers page on your website. Make sure it's well-maintained and optimized for search engines so that potential candidates can easily find and apply for positions within your organization.

When using these platforms, it's essential to create compelling job listings that clearly outline the job requirements, responsibilities, and the benefits of working for your company. Additionally, actively engage with candidates through the recruitment process to ensure a positive experience.

⊞ Growing Your Work And Team

Growing your work and team involves strategic planning and execution. Here are steps to consider when expanding your work and building a larger in-house team:

Evaluate Workload and Demand:

Assess your current workload and analyze the demand for your products or services. If there's a consistent and increasing demand, it may be time to consider expanding your team.

Set Clear Business Goals:

Define clear business goals for growth. Whether it's increasing revenue, expanding into new markets, or launching new products/services, having specific goals will guide your expansion strategy.

Financial Planning:

Conduct a thorough financial analysis to ensure your business is financially ready for expansion. Consider the costs associated with hiring new team members, training, infrastructure, and any additional resources required.

Identify Key Roles:

Determine the key roles needed to support your business growth. Identify positions that will contribute directly to achieving your business goals.

Skill Gap Analysis:

Conduct a skill gap analysis to understand the expertise required for new roles. Identify the skills your current team possesses and pinpoint areas where additional skills are needed.

Recruitment Strategy:

Develop a comprehensive recruitment strategy to attract top talent. This may include leveraging online job platforms, networking events, employee referrals, and partnerships with educational institutions.

Effective Onboarding:

Plan an effective onboarding process to integrate new team members seamlessly. A well-structured onboarding program ensures that new hires quickly adapt to the company culture and understand their roles.

Employee Development:

Invest in the development of your existing team members. Provide training programs and opportunities for skill enhancement. This not only benefits your current team but also helps in promoting from within as your business grows.

Promote a Positive Work Culture:

Foster a positive work culture that attracts and retains talent. A supportive and inclusive environment encourages team members to stay committed to the company.

Implement Scalable Systems:

Ensure that your business systems and processes are scalable. Implementing scalable technologies and workflows will support the increased workload and the addition of new team members.

Diversify Roles and Responsibilities:

Diversify roles and responsibilities among team members to ensure efficiency. Clearly define job roles and encourage collaboration among team members to achieve collective goals.

Continuous Performance Monitoring:

Implement a system for continuous performance monitoring. Regularly assess individual and team performance to identify areas for improvement and recognize achievements.

Client and Customer Management:

If applicable, strengthen client and customer management processes. As your team grows, maintaining strong relationships with clients and customers is crucial for sustaining business growth.

Adaptability and Flexibility:

Foster an environment of adaptability and flexibility. The ability to pivot and adjust to changing circumstances is essential for sustained growth.

Monitor Market Trends:

Stay informed about market trends and changes in your industry. Being proactive in adapting to market shifts will position your business for continued success.

Strategic Partnerships:

Explore strategic partnerships that can contribute to your growth. Collaborating with other businesses or professionals can open new opportunities and expand your reach.

Customer Feedback:

Collect and analyze customer feedback. Understanding customer needs and preferences is essential for tailoring your products or services to meet market demands.

Legal and Regulatory Compliance:

Ensure that your expansion plans comply with legal and regulatory requirements. This includes employment laws, industry regulations, and any other legal considerations.

By following these steps, you can strategically grow your work and build a team that contributes to the long-term success of your business.

Chapter 21: Importance Of Using Software for Project Management

⌨ Why software?

The use of project management software is crucial for several reasons, as it offers numerous advantages that contribute to efficient, organized, and successful project execution. Here are key reasons highlighting the importance of using software for project management:

Centralized Information Hub:

Project management software serves as a centralized repository for all project-related information. This includes project plans, timelines, tasks, documents, communication, and other essential data. Having a single, accessible hub ensures that everyone involved in the project is on the same page.

Improved Collaboration and Communication:

Project management software facilitates seamless collaboration and communication among team members, regardless of their physical location. Features such as real-time messaging, discussion boards, and file sharing enhance team communication and foster a collaborative work environment.

Task and Time Management:

Software allows for efficient task and time management. Teams can create and assign tasks, set deadlines, and track progress in real-time. This helps in prioritizing work, ensuring that deadlines are met, and providing a clear overview of project timelines.

Resource Allocation and Optimization:

Project management software enables effective resource allocation by providing insights into team members' workloads and availability. This helps in optimizing resources, preventing overloading of team members, and ensuring that each resource is utilized efficiently.

Real-Time Progress Tracking:

Tracking project progress in real-time is a key benefit of project management software. Project managers and team members can monitor tasks, milestones, and overall progress instantly, allowing for timely interventions if issues arise or adjustments are needed.

Risk Management:

Project management software often includes features for identifying, assessing, and managing risks. This proactive approach allows teams to anticipate potential issues, develop mitigation strategies, and respond promptly to unforeseen challenges.

Document Management and Version Control:

Centralized document management within the software ensures that all team members have access to the latest versions of project documents. This helps in avoiding confusion, maintaining consistency, and preventing errors that can arise from using outdated information.

Enhanced Reporting and Analytics:

Software provides robust reporting and analytics capabilities, allowing project managers to generate detailed reports on various aspects of the project. This data-driven approach facilitates informed decision-making, identifies trends, and provides insights for continuous improvement.

Client and Stakeholder Collaboration:

Project management software often includes features for client and stakeholder collaboration. This enables transparent communication, sharing of project updates, and obtaining feedback, fostering stronger relationships with clients and stakeholders.

Scalability and Flexibility:

Project management software is designed to be scalable and adaptable to the needs of different projects and teams. Whether you're managing a small team or a large enterprise-level project, the software can be customized to suit the scale and requirements of the project.

Increased Accountability:

Assigning tasks and responsibilities within the software enhances individual and team accountability. Team members are aware of their roles, deadlines, and expectations, reducing the likelihood of missed deliverables.

Audit Trail and Documentation:

Many project management tools maintain an audit trail, documenting changes, updates, and user actions. This feature enhances transparency, provides a history of project activities, and serves as a valuable reference for future projects or audits.

In summary, the use of project management software is essential for streamlining workflows, improving collaboration, and ensuring the overall success of projects by providing a structured and organized approach to project planning and execution.

👍 Best Software for Project Management

There are various project management software options available, each catering to different needs and preferences. The best software for project management depends on factors such as the size of the team, the complexity of the projects, collaboration requirements, and budget considerations. Here are some popular and widely-used project management tools:

Asana

Asana is a versatile project management tool that allows teams to organize tasks, set due dates, and track project progress. It offers a user-friendly interface and is suitable for both small and large teams.

Trello

Trello is known for its visual board layout, making it easy for teams to manage tasks and workflows. It's particularly effective for teams that prefer a simple and visual project management approach.

Jira

Jira, developed by Atlassian, is widely used for agile project management. It's especially popular among software development teams. Jira offers robust features for tracking issues, managing sprints, and maintaining a backlog.

Monday.com

Monday.com is a work operating system that allows teams to plan, track, and manage projects in a visually appealing and customizable interface. It supports a wide range of project management methodologies.

Microsoft Project

Microsoft Project is a comprehensive project management tool that provides in-depth planning, scheduling, and reporting features. It's suitable for larger enterprises and organizations with complex project requirements.

Basecamp

Basecamp is a user-friendly project management tool that emphasizes communication and collaboration. It offers features such as to-do lists, file sharing, and message boards, making it suitable for smaller teams and projects.

Wrike

Wrike is a robust project management and collaboration platform suitable for teams of various sizes. It offers features such as task management, Gantt charts, and real-time collaboration.

Smartsheet

Smartsheet combines spreadsheet functionality with project management features. It's a versatile tool for tracking and managing tasks, projects, and workflows. It's suitable for teams with a preference for spreadsheet-style interfaces.

ClickUp

ClickUp is an all-in-one project management platform that offers features for task management, document collaboration, and goal tracking. It's known for its flexibility and customizable interface.

Airtable

Airtable is a hybrid between a spreadsheet and a database, offering a unique way to organize and track work. It's suitable for teams that require flexibility in structuring their project data.

Notion

Notion is an all-in-one workspace that combines note-taking, project management, and collaboration features. It allows teams to create databases, wikis, and task boards within a single platform.

Teamwork

Teamwork is a comprehensive project management and collaboration tool that offers features such as task tracking, document sharing, and time tracking. It's suitable for teams of various sizes.

When selecting project management software, it's important to consider factors such as user interface preferences, integration capabilities, scalability, and the specific needs of your team or organization. Additionally, many of these tools offer free trials, allowing you to explore their features before making a commitment.

Chapter 22: Freelancer Vs Home-Based Service Business

⊙ The Balanced, Logical Differentiation

Let's explore into a balanced and logical differentiation between a freelancer and a home-based service business:

1. Nature of Work

Freelancer:

Freelancers are typically individual professionals who offer specialized services on a project-by-project basis. They often work independently and may provide skills like writing, graphic design, programming, or marketing.

Freelancers are hired for specific tasks or short-term projects and may work with multiple clients simultaneously.

Home-Based Service Business:

A home-based service business may involve a broader range of services and may have a more comprehensive business structure. This could include ongoing services such as consulting, virtual assistance, or tutoring.

Home-based service businesses may offer a suite of services rather than focusing solely on individual projects.

2. Business Structure

Freelancer:

Freelancers often operate as sole proprietors or independent contractors. Their business structure is typically straightforward, and they may use their personal name or a brand name for their services.

Freelancers may not have a formalized business structure beyond being self-employed.

Home-Based Service Business:

Home-based service businesses may have a more formal business structure, such as a sole proprietorship, LLC, or corporation. They may have multiple employees or collaborators.

The business may operate under a distinct brand name and may have a more complex organizational hierarchy.

3. Client Interaction

Freelancer:

Freelancers often have direct and personal interactions with clients. They handle negotiations, project details, and communication on an individual basis.

The freelancer-client relationship is often more one-on-one.

Home-Based Service Business:

Home-based service businesses may have a more structured process for client interactions. They may use contracts, service agreements, and have a designated point of contact for client communication.

The business-client relationship may be more formalized.

4. Scale and Growth

Freelancer:

Freelancers may choose to keep their operations small and specialized, focusing on refining their skills. Growth for a freelancer might involve expanding their expertise or acquiring more clients.

The emphasis is often on individual expertise rather than building a larger business entity.

Home-Based Service Business:

Home-based service businesses have the potential for broader scalability and growth. They may hire additional staff, expand their service offerings, and take on a larger volume of clients.

The business may have a strategic growth plan and could evolve into a more extensive operation.

5. Branding and Marketing

Freelancer:

Freelancers often market their personal brand, emphasizing their skills and expertise. Marketing efforts may revolve around the freelancer's portfolio and reputation.

Personal networking and word-of-mouth referrals are common methods of attracting clients.

Home-Based Service Business:

Home-based service businesses may invest in branding efforts beyond the individual. They create a business website, develop a brand identity, and implement marketing strategies to attract a wider client base.

The marketing focus extends beyond individual expertise to the overall value proposition of the business.

In short, while both freelancers and home-based service businesses operate from a home setting, the distinction lies in the nature of work, business structure, client interactions, scalability, and branding approach. Freelancers often emphasize individual expertise on a project basis, while home-based service businesses may have a more comprehensive structure with the potential for broader growth and scalability.

🔊 Decide What You Want to Offer

"Decide what you want to offer" is a crucial step in establishing either a freelance career or a home-based service business. Let's explore how this decision-making process differs for freelancers and home-based service businesses:

Freelancer:

- Freelancers typically offer specialized skills or services in a specific niche. The decision-making process for freelancers involves identifying their core strengths and expertise.

- Freelancers may choose to offer services such as writing, graphic design, web development, marketing, or any other skill they excel in.

- The focus is on honing a specific skill set that can be marketed to potential clients on a project-by-project basis.
- Freelancers may diversify their offerings over time as they acquire new skills or choose to specialize further in a particular area.

Home-Based Service Business:

- For a home-based service business, the decision-making process is broader and may involve offering a range of services rather than a single skill.
- The business owner needs to define the scope of services the business will provide. This could include consulting, virtual assistance, tutoring, or other professional services.
- The decision-making process may also involve identifying target markets and understanding the needs of a broader client base.
- Home-based service businesses often create a portfolio of services that can be packaged and marketed as comprehensive solutions.

Common Considerations for Both:

Market Research: Both freelancers and home-based service businesses need to conduct market research to identify demand, competition, and potential opportunities in their chosen field.

Target Audience: Understanding the target audience is crucial. Freelancers and businesses alike need to define their ideal clients and tailor their offerings to meet their needs.

Differentiation: Both freelancers and businesses must identify what sets them apart in the market. Whether it's unique skills, a distinctive approach, or specialized services, differentiation is key.

In conclusion, while both freelancers and home-based service businesses start by deciding what they want to offer, the decision-making process differs in scope. Freelancers focus on their individual skills and expertise, offering specialized services, while home-based service businesses have a broader decision-making process, defining a range of services to meet the needs of a more diverse client base.

◎ The Target Market

let's explore the difference in target markets between freelancers and home-based service businesses:

Target Market for Freelancer

- Freelancers typically target a niche market that aligns with their specialized skills and expertise. Their target audience is often specific to the services they offer.
- The target market for a freelancer is often individuals, small businesses, or specific industries that require their particular skill set.
- Freelancers may focus on building a personal brand, and their marketing efforts are directed towards showcasing their individual expertise to attract clients seeking their specific skills.

Target Market for Home-Based Service Business

- A home-based service business may have a broader target market, as it can offer a range of services that appeal to different client needs.
- The target market for a home-based service business may include individuals, small businesses, and larger enterprises, depending on the scope and variety of services offered.

- Marketing efforts for a home-based service business may focus on the overall value proposition of the business, including a range of services and solutions to meet diverse client requirements.

Common Considerations for Both

Market Segmentation: Both freelancers and home-based service businesses need to identify and segment their target markets based on factors such as industry, demographics, and needs.

Client Persona: Creating a client persona helps in understanding the characteristics, preferences, and pain points of the target audience, enabling more effective marketing and service delivery.

Networking: Building relationships and networking within the chosen target market is essential for both freelancers and home-based service businesses. This can lead to referrals and repeat business.

In summary, while freelancers have a more focused target market aligned with their specific skills, home-based service businesses may have a broader target market, offering a variety of services to cater to different client needs. Both must understand their audience, tailor their marketing strategies accordingly, and establish a strong presence within their chosen target market.

✈ Reach Out to Your Target Market

let's discuss now how reaching out to the target market differs for freelancers and home-based service businesses:

Freelancer:

Freelancers often reach out to their target market through personalized efforts that showcase their individual expertise. This may include:

- **Personal Branding:** Building a strong personal brand is crucial. Freelancers often use their name or a unique brand identity to represent their skills.

- **Portfolio:** A well-curated portfolio showcasing past projects and skills is a key tool for freelancers to demonstrate their capabilities.

- **Networking:** Freelancers often rely on personal networking, both online and offline, to connect with potential clients and colleagues in their industry.

Home-Based Service Business:

Home-based service businesses take a more comprehensive approach to reaching their target market, considering the broader range of services they offer. Strategies may include:

- **Business Branding:** Creating a brand identity for the business as a whole. This may involve designing a professional logo, establishing a business name, and developing a consistent brand image.
- **Service Packages:** Offering packaged services that cater to different client needs. This allows the business to appeal to a broader audience with varied requirements.
- **Online Presence:** Maintaining a robust online presence through a business website, social media, and other platforms. This ensures visibility for the entire business, not just an individual.

Common Considerations for Both:

- **Online Platforms:** Utilizing online platforms such as freelance marketplaces, social media, and professional networks to connect with potential clients.
- **Content Marketing:** Creating and sharing valuable content related to their industry. This positions both

freelancers and home-based service businesses as experts in their field.

- **Client Testimonials:** Showcasing positive client testimonials and reviews to build credibility and trust with potential clients.

While freelancers focus on personal branding and showcasing individual skills, home-based service businesses take a more holistic approach, emphasizing the overall brand identity and a diverse range of services. Both can benefit from online platforms, content marketing, and client testimonials to effectively reach and connect with their target markets.

Chapter 23: The Pros of Being A Freelancer

The freelance lifestyle brings with it a myriad of advantages that cater to the desires of those seeking autonomy and flexibility in their professional journey. One of the most appealing aspects is the potential for higher compensation, as freelancers often have the freedom to set their own rates and take on multiple projects simultaneously. Work-life balance takes center stage, allowing freelancers to design their schedules around personal commitments and preferences. Location independence is another significant perk, enabling freelancers to work from virtually anywhere, breaking free from the constraints of a traditional office space.

Embracing the role of an entrepreneur of one's craft, freelancers also have the opportunity to explore diverse projects, continuously honing their skills and building a dynamic portfolio. The prospect of weathering economic fluctuations with resilience and adapting to evolving industries positions freelancers as versatile contributors in the ever-changing landscape of work.

💰 Compensation

The compensation aspect is indeed a significant pro for many freelancers. Here's a breakdown of the compensation-related advantages of being a freelancer:

1. Flexibility in Rates:

Freelancers have the freedom to set their own rates based on their skills, experience, and the value they provide. This flexibility allows them to adjust prices as they gain expertise or take on more complex projects.

2. Direct Earning Potential:

Freelancers receive direct compensation for their work. There's no intermediary between the freelancer and the client, meaning they retain a larger portion of the project fee compared to traditional employment models.

3. Opportunity for Multiple Income Streams:

Freelancers can take on multiple projects simultaneously, diversifying their income streams. This ability to work with different clients on various projects can lead to a more stable and potentially higher overall income.

4. Performance-Based Rewards:

The potential for performance-based rewards is higher for freelancers. Successful project completion, client satisfaction, and the quality of work can lead to positive reviews, referrals, and repeat business, ultimately impacting their earning potential.

5. Negotiation Power:

Freelancers can negotiate contract terms, including payment schedules and methods. This negotiation power allows them to secure favorable arrangements and tailor agreements to meet their financial needs.

6. Profit Retention:

Unlike traditional employees, freelancers don't have deductions for taxes, benefits, or other employer-related expenses. They retain more control over their earnings and can manage their finances more independently.

7. Global Market Access:

Freelancers can tap into a global market, offering their services to clients around the world. This expanded reach increases the potential for higher-paying opportunities as they may be able to charge rates that align with the economic conditions of clients' locations.

8. Capacity for Scaling Income:

As freelancers gain experience, build a strong portfolio, and establish a positive reputation, they have the potential to increase their rates and attract higher-paying clients. This scalability allows for continuous growth in income over time.

It's important to note that while the compensation benefits of freelancing are significant, freelancers also need to consider factors such as irregular income, self-employment taxes, and the need for financial planning to manage their earnings effectively.

🏃 Work Life Balance

Achieving a better work-life balance is a notable advantage for many freelancers. Here's a breakdown of the work-life balance-related pros of being a freelancer:

Flexible Schedule:

Freelancers have the freedom to set their own work hours. This flexibility allows them to align their work with their natural productivity rhythms, family commitments, or personal preferences, resulting in a more balanced daily schedule.

Control Over Work Environment:

Freelancers can choose their work environment, whether it's a home office, a co-working space, or a favorite cafe. This level of control contributes to increased comfort and a more pleasant work atmosphere, promoting overall well-being.

Reduced Commute Stress:

Working remotely eliminates the need for a daily commute. Freelancers save time and energy that would otherwise be spent on commuting, contributing to a less stressful daily routine and allowing for a smoother transition between work and personal life.

Ability to Prioritize Personal Time:

Freelancers can allocate time for personal activities, hobbies, or family commitments without the constraints of a traditional 9-to-5 schedule. This flexibility promotes a healthier work-life integration and the ability to prioritize personal well-being.

Customizable Breaks:

Freelancers can take breaks when needed, whether for short walks, exercise, or relaxation. This adaptability contributes to improved mental health and increased productivity during work hours.

Reduced Office Politics:

Freelancers often work independently or in smaller teams, minimizing office politics and distractions. This allows them to focus more on their work tasks and maintain a positive mindset.

Personalized Time Management:

Freelancers have the autonomy to manage their time according to their peak productivity periods. This personalized approach to time management can result in more efficient and effective work.

Increased Autonomy:

Freelancers have a higher degree of control over their projects, deadlines, and work methods. This autonomy fosters a sense of ownership and responsibility, contributing to a healthier work-life balance.

Improved Stress Management:

The ability to structure work in a way that suits individual preferences and circumstances can lead to reduced stress levels. Freelancers often have the freedom to adapt their workload to avoid burnout and maintain mental well-being.

It's important to note that while freelancing offers the potential for an improved work-life balance, freelancers need to establish effective self-discipline and boundaries to prevent work from encroaching too heavily on personal time. Additionally, the level of control over work hours may vary depending on the nature of the freelance work and client requirements.

🌍 Location

The aspect of location is a significant advantage for freelancers. Here's a breakdown of the location-related pros of being a freelancer:

1. **Remote Work Opportunities:**

Freelancers can work from anywhere with an internet connection. This flexibility allows them to choose their work environment, whether it's from home, a co-working space, a cafe, or even while traveling.

2. Geographical Independence:

Freelancers are not bound by a specific location or office. They have the freedom to live in different cities, countries, or time zones, providing a level of geographical independence that traditional office jobs may not offer.

3. Access to a Global Client Base:

Freelancers can tap into a global market, offering their services to clients around the world. This expanded reach increases the potential for diverse and international work opportunities, contributing to a broader professional experience.

4. Cost Savings:

Working remotely eliminates the need for commuting and the associated costs. Freelancers can choose to live in areas with a lower cost of living, allowing them to optimize their expenses and potentially increase their overall quality of life.

5. Cultural Exposure:

Freelancers who work with clients from different regions gain exposure to diverse cultures and working styles. This cultural enrichment can broaden their perspectives and enhance their adaptability in a globalized work environment.

6. Family and Lifestyle Choices:

Freelancers have the flexibility to choose a living situation that aligns with their personal preferences and family needs. Whether it's living close to family, in a specific community, or in a preferred climate, freelancers can make lifestyle choices that suit them.

7. Escape from Commute Stress:

The ability to work remotely eliminates the need for a daily commute, saving time and reducing stress associated with transportation. Freelancers can design their workspaces to promote productivity and well-being.

8. Work-Life Integration:

Location independence enables freelancers to seamlessly integrate work into their lives. They can blend professional responsibilities with personal activities and achieve a balance that suits their individual preferences.

9. Adaptability to Changing Circumstances:

Freelancers can easily adapt to changing circumstances, such as moving for personal reasons, without the constraints of a fixed office location. This adaptability contributes to a more resilient and sustainable work lifestyle.

It's important to note that while location independence is a significant advantage, freelancers need to consider factors such as time zone differences, communication challenges, and the importance of maintaining effective virtual collaboration with clients and colleagues.

💡 Optimism

Optimism is a valuable mindset that can benefit freelancers in various ways. Here's a breakdown of the optimism-related pros of being a freelancer:

1. Entrepreneurial Spirit:

Freelancers often approach their work with an entrepreneurial mindset. Optimism plays a crucial role in navigating the uncertainties of freelancing, fostering creativity, and embracing a can-do attitude towards challenges.

2. Positive Client Interactions:

Maintaining an optimistic and positive outlook enhances client interactions. Optimistic freelancers are more likely to build strong relationships with clients, leading to positive feedback, referrals, and repeat business.

3. Resilience in Face of Setbacks:

Optimistic freelancers are more resilient in the face of setbacks or project challenges. They view difficulties as opportunities for growth, learning, and improvement, allowing them to bounce back from setbacks with a positive attitude.

4. Adaptability to Change:

Freelancers often operate in dynamic environments with evolving client needs and industry trends. Optimism fosters adaptability, enabling freelancers to embrace change, stay updated on industry shifts, and proactively adjust their strategies.

5. Motivation and Productivity:

Optimistic freelancers are generally more motivated and productive. A positive mindset can drive a strong work ethic, creativity, and a commitment to delivering high-quality work, ultimately contributing to professional success.

6. Risk-Taking and Innovation:

Optimistic freelancers are more willing to take calculated risks and explore innovative solutions. This mindset can lead to the development of unique service offerings, the pursuit of new opportunities, and the ability to stand out in a competitive market.

7. Effective Problem Solving:

Optimistic freelancers approach problems with a solution-oriented mindset. They are more likely to find constructive and creative solutions to challenges, enhancing their problem-solving skills and overall effectiveness in delivering client satisfaction.

8. Personal Well-Being:

Maintaining optimism contributes to positive mental and emotional well-being. Optimistic freelancers experience lower levels of stress and burnout, allowing them to enjoy their work and personal lives more fully.

9. Building a Strong Personal Brand:

An optimistic and positive demeanor contributes to building a strong personal brand. Clients are often drawn to freelancers who exude confidence, enthusiasm, and a positive attitude, fostering trust and credibility.

Optimism, when balanced with realistic expectations, can be a powerful asset for freelancers, influencing their professional success, client relationships, and overall satisfaction in the freelancing journey.

◪ Recession Proof

The recession-proof nature of freelancing is a notable advantage. Here's a breakdown of the recession-proof pros of being a freelancer:

1. Diverse Client Base:

Freelancers often work with a diverse range of clients across industries. This diversity provides a level of insulation during economic downturns, as freelancers can tap into different sectors that may be more resilient to recessionary pressures.

2. Agility and Adaptability:

Freelancers, by nature, are adaptable and agile. During economic challenges, companies may opt for freelancers to fulfill specific needs without committing to long-term employment. This flexibility positions freelancers as valuable resources in times of economic uncertainty.

3. Reduced Overheads:

Freelancers typically have lower overhead costs compared to businesses with physical offices and employees. This cost efficiency allows freelancers to offer competitive rates and remain attractive to clients even when budgets are constrained.

4. Diversified Income Streams:

Freelancers often have the ability to diversify their income streams by taking on multiple projects or working with clients from different industries. This diversification helps mitigate the impact of a recession in any single sector.

5. Global Opportunities:

Freelancers can access a global market, allowing them to find work across different regions. This global reach provides opportunities to secure projects from areas where economic conditions might be more stable during a recession.

6. Remote Work Trends:

The trend towards remote work, accelerated by technological advancements, has made freelancers well-positioned to adapt to changing work dynamics. Remote work is often more feasible and cost-effective for businesses facing economic challenges.

7. Increased Demand for Specialized Skills:

During economic downturns, companies may prioritize specialized skills over hiring full-time employees. Freelancers, with their niche expertise, become valuable assets as businesses seek specific talents for project-based work.

8. Entrepreneurial Mindset:

Freelancers operate with an entrepreneurial mindset, actively seeking opportunities and adapting to market conditions. This mindset aligns with the resilience required to navigate and thrive in the changing economic landscape.

9. Resource Efficiency:

Freelancers can operate efficiently with minimal resources. This adaptability allows them to weather economic uncertainties without the burden of excess costs, making them a cost-effective choice for businesses.

While freelancing offers resilience in the face of economic challenges, it's essential for freelancers to maintain financial discipline, build a robust client base, and continuously enhance their skills to remain competitive in a fluctuating market.

🚗 Entrepreneurs Of the Future

Being considered as entrepreneurs of the future is a significant advantage for freelancers. Here's a breakdown of the pros associated with freelancers being seen as entrepreneurs of the future:

1. Innovative Problem Solvers:

Freelancers often approach challenges with an entrepreneurial spirit, seeking innovative solutions and creative approaches to problem-solving. This mindset positions them as adaptable and forward-thinking contributors in the evolving business landscape.

2. Continuous Learning and Adaptation:

Entrepreneurs of the future need to be adaptable and committed to continuous learning. Freelancers naturally embrace these qualities, staying ahead of industry trends, acquiring new skills, and adapting to the changing demands of the market.

3. Ownership and Accountability:

Freelancers take ownership of their work, projects, and professional development. This sense of accountability aligns with the entrepreneurial mindset, where individuals are responsible for the success of their ventures and the quality of their output.

4. Brand Building and Marketing Savvy:

Entrepreneurs must excel in brand building and marketing, and freelancers often build personal brands to showcase their skills. Freelancers understand the importance of marketing themselves effectively, differentiating their services, and building a strong online presence.

5. Client Relationship Management:

Freelancers, as entrepreneurs of their own services, excel in managing client relationships. Building trust, delivering exceptional service, and cultivating long-term partnerships are essential skills that align with the entrepreneurial journey.

6. Business Development Skills:

Freelancers engage in business development to secure projects and clients. This proactive approach to seeking opportunities mirrors the entrepreneurial spirit, where individuals actively identify and pursue avenues for growth.

7. Risk-Taking and Initiative:

Entrepreneurs are known for taking calculated risks and seizing opportunities. Freelancers, too, exhibit a willingness to take risks, whether in pursuing new projects, entering different markets, or embracing emerging technologies to enhance their services.

8. Financial Management:

Freelancers manage their finances independently, a crucial aspect of entrepreneurship. This includes budgeting, setting rates, invoicing, and financial planning. These skills are transferable to entrepreneurial ventures in various fields.

9. Global Perspective:

The ability to work with clients from around the world gives freelancers a global perspective. Entrepreneurs of the future need to understand diverse markets and cultural nuances, and freelancers, through their international experiences, are well-prepared for this.

10. Ecosystem Participation:

Freelancers often participate in professional ecosystems, collaborating with other freelancers, agencies, and businesses. This collaborative spirit aligns with the evolving nature of entrepreneurial ecosystems, where partnerships and networking are vital.

By embodying these entrepreneurial qualities, freelancers position themselves as valuable contributors to the future of work, showcasing the skills and mindset needed to thrive in an ever-changing business landscape.

Chapter 24: Cons of Freelancing

☹ Pessimism

Pessimism, when prevalent, can pose challenges for freelancers. Here's a breakdown of the cons associated with pessimism in freelancing:

1. Negative Client Interactions:

Pessimism can impact client interactions, leading to a negative perception of your work and services. Clients may be deterred by a consistently pessimistic attitude, affecting your professional relationships and reputation.

2. Impact on Work Quality:

A pessimistic mindset can influence the quality of your work. Lack of enthusiasm and a negative outlook may result in reduced creativity, productivity, and attention to detail, ultimately affecting the value you deliver to clients.

3. Strained Professional Relationships:

Building and maintaining positive professional relationships is crucial in freelancing. Pessimism can strain relationships with clients, collaborators, and peers, making it challenging to secure repeat business or referrals.

4. Limited Adaptability:

Freelancers often face changing client needs, industry trends, and technological advancements. Pessimism can hinder your ability to adapt to these changes, making it difficult to stay relevant and competitive in a dynamic work environment.

5. Difficulty in Handling Setbacks:

Freelancing involves dealing with uncertainties and occasional setbacks. Pessimism can amplify the impact of setbacks, making it challenging to bounce back, learn from experiences, and move forward with a positive and constructive mindset.

6. Impact on Well-Being:

Pessimism can take a toll on your mental and emotional well-being. Constant negative thoughts and attitudes may contribute to stress, anxiety, and burnout, affecting both your personal and professional life.

7. Limited Client Attraction:

Clients are often drawn to freelancers who exude confidence, positivity, and a can-do attitude. Pessimism may limit your ability to attract new clients, as they may prefer freelancers who convey optimism and enthusiasm for their projects.

8. Undermined Professional Development:

Embracing a pessimistic outlook can hinder your commitment to ongoing professional development. This reluctance to invest in acquiring new skills or staying updated on industry trends may limit your competitiveness in the freelancing market.

9. Reduced Motivation:

Pessimism can lead to a lack of motivation and engagement in your work. The absence of a positive mindset may result in procrastination, missed deadlines, and a diminished sense of accomplishment in your freelancing endeavors.

10. Impact on Networking:

Networking is vital in freelancing, and a pessimistic attitude may hinder your ability to connect with peers, mentors, and potential clients. Positive interactions and collaboration opportunities may be limited by a consistently negative demeanor.

To mitigate the cons associated with pessimism, freelancers can proactively work on developing a positive mindset, seeking support when needed, and focusing on the aspects of their work that bring satisfaction and fulfillment. Cultivating optimism can contribute to a more resilient and successful freelancing journey.

☂ Profession Of Freelancing Is Difficult

The assertion that the profession of freelancing may not prove to be a veritable paradise is grounded in certain drawbacks and challenges associated with freelancing. Here's a breakdown of the cons:

Income Inconsistency:

Freelancers often face income variability due to the nature of project-based work. Fluctuations in the volume of projects and the time between securing contracts can lead to inconsistent income, making financial planning challenging.

Lack of Job Security:

Freelancers lack the traditional job security associated with full-time employment. The absence of a guaranteed monthly salary and benefits can create uncertainty, especially during periods of economic downturn or reduced client demand.

Isolation and Loneliness:

Freelancers typically work independently, which can lead to feelings of isolation and loneliness. The absence of daily interactions with colleagues in a traditional office setting may impact social well-being and contribute to a sense of professional detachment.

Self-Employment Challenges:

Freelancers are essentially self-employed entrepreneurs, which entails managing aspects like taxes, insurance, and business development. Navigating these responsibilities can be time-consuming and complex, requiring additional effort beyond the core service offerings.

Client Dependence:

Relying on a limited number of clients for a significant portion of income can be risky. If a major client decides to discontinue or reduce their engagement, freelancers may face financial challenges and need to quickly find alternative opportunities.

Unpredictable Workload:

Workloads in freelancing can be unpredictable. There may be periods of high demand with multiple projects overlapping, followed by quieter times where securing new contracts becomes a priority. Balancing these fluctuations requires effective time management and planning.

No Employer Benefits:

Freelancers do not receive traditional employment benefits such as health insurance, retirement plans, or paid time off. Managing personal benefits becomes the freelancer's responsibility, potentially leading to higher out-of-pocket expenses.

Overemphasis on Administrative Tasks:

Freelancers spend a significant amount of time on administrative tasks, including invoicing, marketing, and client communication. This focus on non-billable activities can reduce the time available for actual project work.

Marketplace Competition:

Freelancing platforms have a large pool of talented individuals competing for projects. Standing out in a crowded marketplace can be challenging, and pricing pressures may arise as freelancers vie for clients.

Limited Career Growth Opportunities:

Freelancers may face limitations in terms of traditional career growth. Advancement opportunities, promotions, or hierarchical career paths found in traditional employment may not be readily available in freelancing.

While freelancing offers flexibility and independence, acknowledging and addressing these challenges can help freelancers navigate the profession more effectively. Proactive measures, such as building a diverse client base, investing in skill development, and establishing a strong professional network, can contribute to a more sustainable freelancing career.

Low productivity

Low productivity can be a significant drawback for freelancers. Here's a breakdown of the cons associated with low productivity in freelancing:

Self-Discipline Challenges:

Freelancers often work independently, requiring a high level of self-discipline to manage their time effectively. Without a structured office environment, some freelancers may struggle to establish and maintain a productive work routine.

Procrastination:

The absence of immediate supervision can lead to procrastination. Freelancers may postpone tasks or struggle to initiate work, impacting project timelines and overall productivity.

Distractions at Home:

Working from home can present numerous distractions, ranging from household chores to personal responsibilities. It's essential for freelancers to create a dedicated workspace and establish boundaries to minimize disruptions.

Lack of Accountability:

Without a direct supervisor or team to provide accountability, freelancers may find it challenging to stay focused and meet deadlines. The absence of external pressure can contribute to a lax approach to project delivery.

Difficulty in Time Management:

Effective time management is crucial for freelancers, but some may struggle to allocate time efficiently across different tasks. Juggling multiple projects, administrative duties, and personal commitments requires strong time management skills.

Burnout Risk:

Freelancers who overcommit themselves or struggle with time management may face a higher risk of burnout. Constantly working long hours to catch up on delayed tasks can negatively impact both mental and physical well-being.

Inability to Disconnect:

The boundary between work and personal life can blur for freelancers, leading to an inability to disconnect from work. This constant connectivity may contribute to fatigue and reduce overall job satisfaction.

Lack of Collaborative Environment:

Freelancers may miss out on the collaborative and motivational aspects of working in a team. The absence of colleagues can result in a lack of shared goals and mutual support, potentially impacting creativity and motivation.

Limited Professional Development Opportunities:

Productivity challenges may hinder freelancers from actively pursuing professional development opportunities. Continuous learning and skill enhancement may take a back seat when struggling with daily productivity.

Difficulty in Setting Boundaries:

Establishing clear boundaries between work and personal life can be challenging for freelancers. This difficulty may lead to working extended hours or experiencing interruptions during leisure time.

To address low productivity, freelancers can implement strategies such as creating a structured daily schedule, setting realistic goals, minimizing distractions, and periodically reassessing their workload. Additionally, adopting productivity tools and techniques can help freelancers optimize their work habits and enhance overall efficiency.

$$ Constantly Seeking Better Reward

If the idea is that freelancers are constantly seeking better rewards, it can indeed introduce challenges. Here's a breakdown of the potential cons associated with the constant pursuit of better rewards in freelancing:

Continuous Striving:

The quest for better rewards may lead to a continuous cycle of striving for higher-paying projects. While ambition is positive, an excessive focus on financial gains might contribute to stress and a sense of never being satisfied.

Potential Burnout:

Frequent efforts to secure higher-paying opportunities can lead to burnout if freelancers consistently push themselves beyond sustainable limits. Balancing financial goals with personal well-being is crucial to avoid exhaustion.

Comparison and Discontent:

Constantly comparing one's earnings with others in the freelancing community or industry benchmarks can breed discontent. This comparison mindset may overshadow personal achievements and contribute to dissatisfaction.

Risk of Overcommitting:

The desire for better rewards may prompt freelancers to take on more projects than they can handle. Overcommitting can compromise the quality of work, jeopardizing client relationships and professional reputation.

Impact on Work-Life Balance:

The pursuit of better rewards may lead to extended working hours and challenges in maintaining a healthy work-life balance. This imbalance can affect personal relationships, overall well-being, and job satisfaction.

Unrealistic Expectations:

Freelancers may set high financial expectations, and when these expectations are not met consistently, it can lead to disappointment. Unrealistic financial goals may not align with market realities or the availability of high-paying projects.

Client Relationship Focus:

Placing too much emphasis on financial gains may shift the focus away from building strong and sustainable client relationships.

Client satisfaction and repeat business are vital for long-term success in freelancing.

Influence on Project Selection:

The pursuit of better rewards may influence freelancers to prioritize projects solely based on financial gains rather than aligning with their skills, interests, or long-term career goals.

Financial Insecurity:

Constantly seeking better rewards may create a sense of financial insecurity, especially during periods of lower project availability or economic uncertainties. Freelancers may experience stress when faced with fluctuations in income.

Diminished Passion:

Overemphasis on monetary rewards may diminish the passion and enjoyment freelancers initially found in their work. The intrinsic satisfaction of delivering quality work may take a back seat to the pursuit of financial gains.

Balancing the pursuit of better rewards with a realistic assessment of personal and professional priorities is essential. Freelancers can benefit from setting clear financial goals, maintaining a healthy work-life balance, and finding satisfaction in both the monetary and intrinsic rewards of their work.

⊗ No Health Security

The absence of health security is indeed a notable drawback of freelancing. Here's a breakdown of the cons associated with the lack of health security in freelancing:

Lack of Employer-Sponsored Health Benefits:

Freelancers are responsible for securing their health insurance, as they do not receive employer-sponsored benefits such as medical, dental, or vision coverage. This can result in higher out-of-pocket expenses for healthcare.

Financial Burden of Health Insurance:

Purchasing individual health insurance plans can be expensive for freelancers, especially when compared to group plans offered by traditional employers.

The financial burden of premiums and deductibles may impact the overall budget.

Limited Access to Employee Assistance Programs (EAPs):

EAPs, which provide mental health and wellness support, are often available to traditional employees. Freelancers may miss out on these programs, making it challenging to access resources for mental health and well-being.

No Paid Sick Leave:

Freelancers typically do not receive paid sick leave. In the event of illness or medical emergencies, taking time off may result in a loss of income, adding financial stress during health-related challenges.

Vulnerability to Income Disruption:

Health issues that hinder a freelancer's ability to work can lead to income disruption. Unlike traditional employees who may receive paid sick leave, freelancers may face financial consequences during periods of illness or recovery.

Pre-existing Conditions Impacting Coverage:

Health insurance for freelancers may be impacted by pre-existing conditions, potentially resulting in higher premiums or limited coverage. This can create additional challenges in obtaining comprehensive health security.

Retirement and Long-Term Care Considerations:

Freelancers must also consider long-term health security, including retirement and potential long-term care needs. Planning for these aspects requires careful financial management and saving.

Difficulty in Budgeting for Health Expenses:

Health expenses can be unpredictable, making it challenging for freelancers to budget effectively. Emergencies or unexpected medical costs may strain financial resources.

Dependency on Affordable Care Act (ACA) Marketplace:

In many countries, freelancers may rely on government-sponsored healthcare marketplaces, such as the Affordable Care Act (ACA) Marketplace in the United States.

Changes to healthcare policies and market dynamics can impact the availability and affordability of plans.

Influence on Career Choices:

Health security considerations may influence freelancers' career choices, as they may need to factor in the availability and cost of health insurance when deciding on the types of projects to pursue.

To mitigate these challenges, freelancers should carefully research and choose health insurance plans that align with their needs, explore professional associations that offer group plans, and incorporate healthcare expenses into their overall financial planning. Additionally, building an emergency fund can provide a financial buffer during periods of health-related disruptions.

⚡ Stability

The lack of stability is a significant drawback associated with freelancing. Here's a breakdown of the cons related to the absence of stability in freelancing:

Income Inconsistency:

Freelancers often experience fluctuations in income due to the nature of project-based work. The inconsistency in the volume and timing of projects can lead to unpredictable financial outcomes.

Uncertain Workload:

The availability of projects is not guaranteed, leading to uncertainty in the freelancer's workload. There may be periods of high demand followed by quieter times, making it challenging to maintain a steady flow of work.

No Guaranteed Contracts:

Freelancers lack the security of guaranteed long-term contracts that traditional employees may enjoy. The absence of contractual stability can contribute to a sense of professional insecurity.

Client Dependence:

Relying on a limited number of clients for a significant portion of income can be risky. If a major client decides to discontinue or reduce their engagement, freelancers may face financial challenges and need to quickly find alternative opportunities.

Marketplace Competition:

Freelancing platforms have a large pool of talented individuals competing for projects. Standing out in a crowded marketplace can be challenging, and pricing pressures may arise as freelancers vie for clients.

Economic Downturn Impact:

Freelancers may be more susceptible to the impact of economic downturns or recessions. During challenging economic periods, businesses may reduce spending on freelance services, affecting the availability of projects.

Limited Job Security:

Freelancers do not enjoy the job security associated with traditional employment. The lack of a stable position within a company or organization can create feelings of professional instability.

Varied Project Durations:

Projects in freelancing can vary in duration, from short-term gigs to longer-term contracts. The inconsistency in project durations makes it challenging for freelancers to plan for the future.

No Benefits Package:

Freelancers do not receive traditional employee benefits such as health insurance, retirement plans, or paid time off. The absence of these benefits adds to the overall lack of stability in a freelancer's professional life.

Difficulty in Planning:

Without a stable and predictable stream of income, freelancers may find it difficult to plan for major life events, such as buying a home, starting a family, or saving for long-term goals.

To navigate the lack of stability, freelancers can adopt proactive strategies such as building a diverse client base, maintaining a financial buffer for lean periods, and continuously updating their skills to stay competitive in the evolving market. Establishing a strong professional network can also provide support during challenging times.

◌ Effected By Economic Ups and Downs

Being influenced by economic ups and downs is indeed a significant challenge in freelancing. Here's a breakdown of the cons associated with the impact of economic fluctuations on freelancing:

Sensitivity to Economic Trends:

Freelancers are often more susceptible to changes in the broader economy. Economic downturns can result in reduced demand for freelance services as businesses cut back on spending, affecting the availability of projects.

Reduced Client Budgets:

During economic downturns, clients may have tighter budgets, leading to a decrease in the rates they are willing to pay for freelance services. This can directly impact the income potential for freelancers.

Industry-Specific Challenges:

Certain industries may experience more significant downturns during economic contractions. Freelancers specializing in sectors heavily affected by economic challenges may find it harder to secure projects.

Increased Competition:

Economic downturns often lead to an influx of freelancers into the market as individuals seek alternative sources of income. The resulting increase in competition can make it harder for freelancers to secure projects and maintain their usual rates.

Delayed Payments and Cash Flow Issues:

Economic uncertainties may lead to clients delaying payments or facing financial difficulties, impacting the cash flow of freelancers. Late or sporadic payments can create financial stress during already challenging times.

Limited Financial Safety Nets:

Freelancers may lack the financial safety nets provided by traditional employment, such as unemployment benefits. Economic downturns can exacerbate financial vulnerabilities for freelancers.

Client Closures and Business Failures:

Economic downturns can lead to business closures and a reduction in the number of potential clients. Freelancers heavily reliant on specific industries or clients may face challenges when those businesses cease operations.

Impact on Project Diversity:

Economic downturns can result in a reduction of diverse project opportunities as businesses focus on essential services or cost-cutting measures. This can limit the variety of projects available to freelancers.

Difficulty in Navigating Economic Uncertainty:

Freelancers must navigate economic uncertainties independently. The lack of a stable employer or company structure makes it challenging to receive guidance or support during challenging economic times.

Longer Sales Cycles:

Economic downturns may lengthen the sales cycles for freelancers, as clients become more cautious and deliberate in their decision-making processes. Securing new projects may require additional time and effort.

To address these challenges, freelancers can adopt proactive measures such as diversifying their skills, maintaining strong client relationships, and creating financial buffers during periods of economic stability. Staying informed about industry trends and economic indicators can also help freelancers anticipate potential challenges and adapt their strategies accordingly.

Chapter 25: Lesser Known but Powerful Freelance Websites

▣ 99designs

99designs is a notable freelance platform, especially for those involved in graphic design and creative services. Here's a brief overview that you can include in your book:

99designs: Unlocking Creative Potential

While many freelancers gravitate towards mainstream platforms, a hidden gem in the freelance landscape is 99designs. This platform is a haven for creative professionals, particularly in the field of graphic design. What sets 99designs apart is its unique approach to project initiation. Clients submit a design brief, and multiple designers compete to provide the best solution. The client then selects the design they prefer, and the winning designer receives compensation. This model fosters creativity, encourages collaboration, and offers a chance for designers to showcase their skills in a competitive environment. For freelancers with a passion for visual arts, 99designs provides an exciting platform to unleash their creative prowess and connect with clients seeking standout designs.

▣ Freelance Writing Gigs: Nurturing Wordsmiths

For wordsmiths seeking freelance opportunities beyond the mainstream platforms, Freelance Writing Gigs stands as a testament to the expansive world of online writing. This platform caters specifically to freelance writers, offering a curated list of writing opportunities from around the web. What sets Freelance Writing Gigs apart is its commitment to providing a consolidated space for writers to discover diverse projects. From content creation and blogging to technical writing and journalism, the platform covers a broad spectrum of writing genres. Freelancers can explore daily listings of writing gigs, ensuring a steady stream of potential projects. For writers keen on honing their craft and expanding their portfolio, Freelance Writing Gigs serves as a valuable portal into the vast and varied landscape of freelance writing opportunities.

▣ Toptal: Elevating Freelance Talent to the Top

In the realm of freelancing, Toptal stands out as a premium platform that caters to the elite echelon of freelance talent. What distinguishes Toptal is its rigorous screening process, ensuring that only the top 3% of applicants are accepted. This meticulous vetting results in a curated pool of high-caliber freelancers across various domains, including software development, design, and finance. For businesses seeking top-tier expertise, Toptal offers a refined selection of freelancers who have demonstrated exceptional skills and professionalism. Likewise, freelancers benefit from access to exclusive opportunities and a network of like-minded, accomplished professionals. Toptal's commitment to excellence positions it as a beacon for those who aspire to achieve and engage with the pinnacle of freelance talent in the digital landscape.

▣ Simply Hired: A Gateway to Diverse Freelance Opportunities

For freelancers seeking a comprehensive platform that spans a wide array of industries, Simply Hired emerges as a versatile option. This platform transcends the boundaries of conventional freelancing platforms, offering a diverse range of job listings that encompass both freelance and traditional employment opportunities. What sets Simply Hired apart is its commitment to simplifying the job search process, providing freelancers with a user-friendly interface to explore a multitude of projects. From short-term gigs to long-term contracts, Simply Hired caters to freelancers across various skill sets and professions. Its extensive job database and intuitive search features make it a valuable resource for those navigating the dynamic landscape of freelance opportunities. Freelancers and employers alike can connect seamlessly through Simply Hired, creating a bridge between talent and projects in the ever-evolving freelance ecosystem.

Chapter 26: Conclusion

⚡ Empowering Your Freelance Journey

As we conclude this exploration into the realm of freelancing, it becomes evident that freelancing is more than just a career choice; it's a dynamic and liberating way of working that has reshaped the landscape of professional engagement.

Throughout this guide, we've navigated the intricacies of freelancing, from its foundational principles to the nuances of various freelance marketplaces.

Freelancing, with its flexibility and autonomy, offers a pathway to professional fulfillment that transcends traditional employment models. It empowers individuals to take control of their careers, providing the freedom to choose projects aligned with their passions and skills. The diverse range of freelance opportunities, spanning from creative endeavors to technical projects, underscores the breadth of possibilities within this expansive ecosystem.

Whether you're a seasoned freelancer looking to refine your approach or someone contemplating the leap into freelancing, this guide has provided insights into the strategies, platforms, and essential skills that can elevate your freelancing journey. From the meticulous art of crafting a winning proposal to the nuances of client communication, each facet contributes to the mosaic of success in freelancing.

As you embark on your freelance odyssey, remember that continuous learning, adaptability, and a proactive mindset are your allies. Embrace the challenges as opportunities for growth, and leverage the plethora of online resources and lesser-known platforms to expand your horizons.

Freelancing is not just about securing projects; it's about building a brand, fostering client relationships, and crafting a career that aligns with your vision. Your journey in freelancing is a dynamic narrative waiting to unfold, filled with chapters of creativity, independence, and professional accomplishment.

So, whether you're a designer refining the visual landscape, a writer shaping narratives, a developer crafting digital solutions, or a professional offering specialized expertise, the world of freelancing beckons you. It's a journey where your skills, passion, and commitment converge to create a tapestry of success uniquely yours.

Here's to the art of freelancing — where autonomy meets ambition, and every project is a canvas for your skills to shine. May your freelance endeavors be both rewarding and transformative.

⊞A Freelancer's Role in Elevating Both Career and Country

As we conclude this journey into the world of freelancing, it's essential to recognize the profound impact that individuals can have, not only on their personal careers but also on the broader economic landscape of their country. Freelancing is not just a solitary pursuit; it's a force that can contribute to national progress and economic development.

By choosing the path of freelancing, you are not only shaping your professional destiny but also playing a crucial role in improving your country's ranking in the global workforce. The freelance ecosystem, with its ability to transcend geographical boundaries, allows individuals to showcase their skills on an international stage.

As a freelancer, you become an ambassador of your country's talent, offering unique perspectives and expertise to a global clientele. Your success in freelancing not only enhances your personal brand but also contributes to building a positive reputation for your country in the international business community.

In an era where remote work and digital collaboration are reshaping traditional work models, freelancers hold the power to influence economic indicators and rankings. As you embark on your freelancing journey, consider the ripple effect that your success can have on the collective progress of your country.

Embrace the role of a freelance trailblazer — someone who not only excels in their craft but also contributes to the growth and recognition of their homeland. Leverage your skills to attract international clients, foster collaborations, and, in doing so, become a catalyst for positive change.

Remember that every project you undertake, every client relationship you build, and every successful delivery is a testament to the capabilities of freelancers from your country. Your dedication to excellence not only elevates your personal standing but also adds a valuable brick to the foundation of your nation's economic success.

So, as you navigate the dynamic landscape of freelancing, envision your role not just as an individual contributor but as a key player in a global orchestra, each note harmonizing to create a melody of progress. Your journey as a freelancer is not just about personal achievements; it's about contributing to a larger narrative of innovation, collaboration, and economic advancement.

Here's to the freelancers who are not just shaping their own destinies but are also leaving an indelible mark on the global map. May your freelancing endeavors be a source of pride for both yourself and your country.

⇧ Empowering Freelancers, Boosting Foreign Remittance

As we draw the curtains on this exploration of the freelancing landscape, it's crucial to recognize the ripple effect that freelancers can have on the economic well-being of their home countries. One of the compelling avenues through which freelancing can make a substantial impact is the increase in foreign remittance.

Freelancers, by nature of their work, engage with clients from diverse corners of the globe. This geographical flexibility not only broadens their professional horizons but also presents a unique opportunity for contributing to the economic prosperity of their countries of origin.

The rise in freelancing has become a driving force behind the surge in foreign remittance. As freelancers secure projects and deliver high-quality services to international clients, they bring home income in the form of foreign currency. This influx of foreign remittance serves as a lifeline for many economies, contributing to increased currency reserves and bolstering the financial stability of nations.

For freelancers, this isn't merely about securing projects; it's about playing a pivotal role in their country's economic landscape. By actively participating in the global marketplace, freelancers become ambassadors of their nations, showcasing the talent and expertise that resides within their borders.

As a freelancer, every successfully completed project becomes a testament to the capabilities of professionals from your country. The financial rewards earned from international clients translate into increased foreign remittance, providing tangible benefits to both freelancers and their home countries.

In this era of digital connectivity and global collaboration, freelancers wield the power to transcend borders and contribute significantly to the economic growth of their nations. By embracing freelancing, individuals not only carve out successful careers for themselves but also become catalysts for positive economic change at a macro level.

So, as you navigate the dynamic world of freelancing, consider the profound impact your work can have on the foreign remittance landscape. Your success isn't just a personal triumph; it's a contribution to the economic vitality of your homeland. May your freelancing endeavors continue to empower not only yourself but also play a part in the economic resurgence of your country.

■ Passive Ways of Income Besides Freelancing

Diversifying Your Revenue Streams

While freelancing offers a dynamic way to earn income, exploring passive income avenues adds another layer to your financial strategy. Passive income involves earning money with minimal effort or direct involvement.

Here are some passive income options to consider:

Investing in Stocks and Dividends:

Putting your money to work in the stock market can generate dividends and capital gains. By investing in dividend-paying stocks, you earn a share of the company's profits, providing a steady income stream.

Real Estate Investments:

Owning rental properties or investing in real estate crowdfunding platforms can generate passive income through rental payments or returns on real estate projects.

Creating and Selling Digital Products:

Develop and sell digital products like e-books, online courses, or stock photography. Once created, these products can generate income without ongoing effort.

Affiliate Marketing:

Promote products or services through affiliate marketing. Earn commissions for every sale or lead generated through your referral links.

Royalties from Intellectual Property:

If you have created intellectual property like books, music, or art, you can earn royalties from sales or licensing agreements.

Automated Online Businesses:

Build and automate online businesses such as dropshipping or print-on-demand stores. Once set up, these businesses can operate with minimal day-to-day involvement.

Peer-to-Peer Lending:

Participate in peer-to-peer lending platforms where you can earn interest by lending money directly to individuals or small businesses.

Create a Mobile App or Software:

Develop and monetize a mobile app or software. Revenue can come from app sales, in-app purchases, or subscription models.

Dividend-Paying Investments:

Invest in dividend-paying mutual funds or exchange-traded funds (ETFs). These funds distribute a portion of their earnings to investors regularly.

Automated Dropshipping:

Set up a dropshipping business where products are shipped directly from suppliers to customers, minimizing the need for inventory management.

Exploring these passive income streams alongside freelancing can provide financial stability and build a diversified portfolio. Keep in mind that while passive income requires less day-to-day involvement, initial effort and strategic planning are crucial for success.

🗣 The Last Advice: Navigating Your Freelance Odyssey

As you embark on your freelance journey, let the spirit of curiosity guide you. Freelancing is not just a career choice; it's an odyssey filled with challenges, triumphs, and continuous learning. Embrace the unknown, for it is within the realms of uncertainty that creativity flourishes and new opportunities unfold.

Stay adaptable, for the freelance landscape is ever-evolving. Technologies change, market demands shift, and trends come and go. Your ability to adapt, learn new skills, and pivot when necessary will be your compass through uncharted territories.

Build a network of fellow freelancers and mentors. The freelancing community is a rich tapestry of experiences and insights. Connect with others who share your journey, exchange ideas, and seek guidance from those who have treaded similar paths. Their wisdom can illuminate your way and offer perspectives you might not have considered.

Value your time and set boundaries. While the allure of flexibility is a hallmark of freelancing, maintaining a balance is essential. Establish clear boundaries between work and personal life to prevent burnout. Respect your time as a valuable asset, and others will follow suit.

Invest in your skills continually. The freelance landscape rewards those who stay ahead of the curve. Dedicate time to upgrade your skills, explore emerging trends, and deepen your expertise. This commitment to self-improvement will not only make you a sought-after freelancer but also open doors to exciting opportunities.

Finally, find joy in the process. Freelancing is not just about the end goal; it's about the daily journey, the projects you undertake, and the clients you collaborate with. Cultivate a passion for your craft, and let that passion be the guiding force that propels you forward.

As you navigate the highs and lows of freelancing, remember that each challenge is an opportunity to grow, and each success is a stepping stone to greater achievements. Your freelance odyssey is a narrative waiting to be written, filled with chapters of resilience, creativity, and professional fulfillment.

May your freelancing adventure be both rewarding and transformative. Here's to the exciting road ahead — happy freelancing!

THE END